Data as a Service

Data as a Service
A Framework for
Providing Reusable
Enterprise Data Services

Pushpak Sarkar

IEEE PRESS

WILEY

Published by John Wiley & Sons, Inc., Hoboken, New Jersey.
Published simultaneously in Canada.

For general information on our other products and services or for technical support, please contact our Customer Care Department within the United States at (800) 762-2974, outside the United States at (317) 572-3993 or fax (317) 572-4002.

Wiley also publishes its books in a variety of electronic formats. Some content that appears in print may not be available in electronic formats. For more information about Wiley products, visit our web site at www.wiley.com.

Library of Congress Cataloging-in-Publication Data is available.

ISBN: 978-1-119-04658-5

Dedicated to my parents and family for making me believe that anything is possible if you dream big and work hard.

Contents

11. Big Data and Analytical Services   210

Part Four   Ensuring Organizational Success

12. DaaS Governance Framework   237

13. Securing the DaaS Environment   262

Guest Introduction

With the advent of social media and the Internet of Things (IoT), businesses are receiving a lot more data than they ever did in the past. The volume of data is increasing exponentially, the variety is increasing, and so is the velocity of its arrival. Companies who can analyze this data, derive insights and share their learnings across business lines within the company and with the ecosystem of partners externally in an effective manner to transform their businesses are invariably the ones who are going to win. This specific trend has been captured in Accenture's Technology Vision 2013 as "Data Velocity" and "Design for Analytics" and again in 2014 as "Data Supply Chain." Personally, as a Managing Director of Accenture, I have seen this trend resonate with our Fortune 500 clients across Accenture's five Operating Groups: Communications, Media & High Tech, Financial Services, Health and Public Services, Resources, and Products.

Given the need to consume data from heterogeneous sources, both internal and external to a company, hosted either in premises or in the cloud, and on the flip side, to make its own data available in exactly the same reuseable form for partners to consume, companies can no longer afford to keep data locked into silos of applications, nor can they treat it as a second class object when it comes to architecting its IT infrastructure. Data needs to be decoupled from applications so that the data generated by one application can be used effectively by a completely different set of applications, and the insights generated by analyzing the data within one business line of a company can be shared with other business lines in order to maximize the Return on Investment (RoI) on the data available to the company as a whole. I have seen this happen with a leading drugstore in the United States where sharing of data between the store's loyalty program and the sales department helped better targeting of products leading to significantly increased sales.

The most effective way of sharing the data and insights is to make data a first class object in the design of IT architecture and make it available as a service. Once exposed as a service, any application, whether internal or external to a company, can consume data in a seamless manner and use it creatively to make a tangible difference to business. In fact, there are several examples of completely new businesses created across industries from healthcare to insurance to automotive to real estate, fuelled by the sharing of data in the form of APIs by a company with its ecosystem of partners; and the huge impact created, in turn, by the ecosystem on the company's existing business due to the sharing of data, leading to mutual business benefits. For example, GM exposed their OnStar Application Programming Interface (API) to power a new business service via a start-up called RelayRides that enabled individuals to rent their personal cars, thereby disrupting the rental car business. We have seen the same trend with Walgreens who is offering access to its data through a variety of APIs and Software Development Kits (SDKs) to fuel new businesses with its ecosystem of partners.

Similarly, there is a plethora of examples of how companies have successfully exploited the synergy across their business lines by sharing data and insights within the company, leading to higher efficiency and creation of new revenue streams. The previously cited example of the leading drug store sharing data between the customer loyalty program and the sales department fits this category. Thus, data sharing internally as well as externally has proven to be transformational for businesses across industries.

With business transformations happening across the globe based on the availability of huge amount of data and its analysis, this book on Data as a Service, providing a comprehensive view into the world of Data Engineering and its implications on business, is a must read for every IT professional and business leader.

SANJOY PAUL, PhD
Managing Director – Accenture Technology Labs

Guest Introduction

When I wrote my first book, *Data Crush*, I attempted to capture the ways in which the technical innovations of mobility, Cloud computing, and big data were leading to entirely new social and business phenomena. Several of the impacts that these new technologies have had on our world are driving the demand for Data as a Service, hence I was elated when Pushpak asked me to introduce his work, that you now hold in your hands. There are three social forces that are making Data as a Service a new business imperative, and they are quantification, appification, and cloudification. Let us look at each in turn.

Quantification is the growing trend of measuring absolutely everything, across all aspects of business. I recently met the CIO of a commercial property management company that is spending over $1 billion to quantify his business. Over a two year period, his company will connect to the Internet every lightbulb in every one of their buildings. When I asked him what data he hoped to learn from these connected bulbs his response was, "I have no idea, but what I do know is that if I don't have the data there's nothing to analyze." You will likely see this sort of pervasive data collection occurring throughout every process in every organization over the coming decade.

Appification is our growing expectation of instant gratification, at little or no cost, regardless of how irrational this expectation may be. Indeed, we are becoming so appified that we expect our needs to be met predictively. Delivering on this expectation demands that organizations not only analyze data, they must do so perpetually and rapidly. The notion that business insights only come from a Research and Development department, or from IT is outdated, because there simply is not time to push analytics to a central organization. Rather, appification means that organizations must collect, digest, and act upon data as close to the customer as possible, in both time and space.

Finally, Cloudification is the notion that the paradigm of building and owning the assets of your business has become obsolete. Cloud initially entered the world of applications with Software as a Service, and is rapidly spreading to all other aspects of business operations. More and more, companies will simply aggregate third-party services in order to meet customer needs, rather than produce those outputs themselves. Data management and analysis will follow this trend, leading to Data as a Service being the standard mode of putting data to work in organizations.

Acting upon these societal forces is challenging. Much of this mode of operating runs counter to how we have run IT for half of a century. Nonetheless, it is imperative that organizations embrace Data as a Service if they hope to remain relevant in our accelerating world. This book provides a practical, implementable approach to reaching this goal. I trust that you will find Pushpak's guidance valuable as you work to meet the new expectations of an ever-more-competitive world.

CHRISTOPHER SURDAK
Engineer, ex-Rocket Scientist, Juris Doctor,
Technology Evangelist and author of "Data Crush,"
GetAbstract's International Book of the Year for 2014

Preface (Includes the Reader's Guide)

Typically, once every couple of decades a disruptive new technology emerges that fundamentally changes the business landscape. Innovative, high tech products that often start a trend come to the mainstream market with such rapidity that they transform the existing way of doing business. These trends also create a new market that eventually disrupts the existing market and related network, often displacing the earlier technology.

In most cases, organizations that understand underlying competitive dynamics of innovation and who adapt to these disruptive trends, win. Today such fundamental shifts take place in the world of data and analytics daily, and they are changing the global business landscape significantly.

If one closely observes the global marketplace, it is safe to say that many businesses are trying to harness an unprecedentedly large amount of data to derive new insights that support their competitive analyses. A huge amount of data that is gathered from diverse channels (e.g., social media, clickstream analysis) need to be translated by businesses to enable concrete actions. Organizations that understand the competitive dynamics at play and those that can then predictively analyze that data will win, whereas those that fail to recognize this challenge and respond to it will become extinct.

While data has always been considered an essential part of IT infrastructure across most organizations to support their business operations, today it is recognized as the key commodity upon which an enterprise runs its business and day-to-day operations. A complete paradigm shift has occurred in which data is increasingly recognized as an asset that can be commercially sold as a service, in and of itself.

Based on the author's first-hand experience and expertise, this book offers a proven framework for sharing core enterprise data using reusable data services. The book covers how organizations can generate business revenues by providing Data as a Service to their clients for fee-based subscriptions. The book goes on to explain in detail how to acquire and distribute data across heterogeneous platforms effectively using enterprise SOA principles, industry data standards, and leveraging new technologies such as data virtualization, cloud, and big data stream computing. The book also offers the following:

- Presents a comprehensive approach for introducing Data as a Service (DaaS) in any organization for the first time.
- Recommended best practices and industry standards for sharing master, reference, and big data with data consumers.

- Commercialization aspects of Data as a Service and its potential for generating revenues.

- Covers real-world applications of DaaS such as big Data as a Service.

- Real-life case studies on various innovative architecture blueprints and related patterns.

The topics covered in this book are wide ranging, starting with a presentation on the need for providing DaaS and the technical challenges involved in making that transformation. Some of the areas of the book that may particularly appeal to readers include:

- How DaaS can become a strategic enabler for sharing data with customers on company products they are interested in purchasing, browsing online, or viewing on social media.

- How the DaaS framework can help many organizations recognize monetizable intent and dependency of their customers on accessing their data while buying their company products.

- How enhanced on-demand data services can lead to potential clients by organizations that plan on mining customer, social media, and online conversations over a big data platform, using sophisticated predictive algorithms and data analytics tools.

- How to adopt best practices for successfully deploying reusable data services in your organization along with a reference architecture comprising common sets of data standards, guidelines, and processes.

Covering so much ground—from canonical modeling to data governance and XML based services—can be challenging for some readers, so the book offers a roadmap to help guide you through it.

The Reader's Guide

The Reader's Guide is provided to help readers determine who should read the book and why they need to read the book. A summary of each chapter to explain the step-by-step approach required for the successful introduction of DaaS in any organization is also provided.

The successful adoption of DaaS in any organization is based on three fundamental areas—architecture, adopting organizational processes, and ensuring the appropriate technology components are deployed. However, this should be based on real-world experiences and lessons learned from prior IT/DaaS implementations. This is one of the reasons this book includes case studies in several chapters.

The next section will guide readers on how best to use the book by sharing details of every chapter. It will also help guide readers to determine the best approach to use the DaaS framework in their current IT landscape within their organization. Figures 1 and 2 illustrate key topics in the book along with the suggested roadmap.

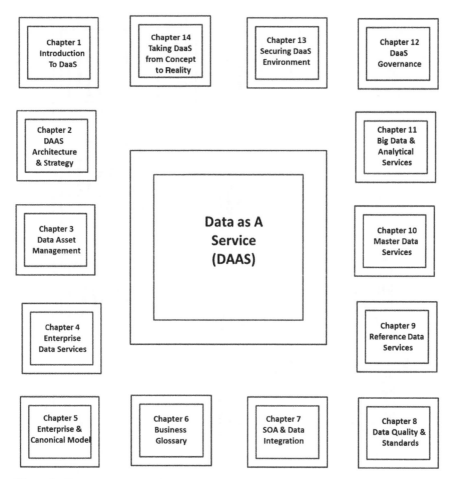

Figure 1   Key topics covered in the book by chapter

PART 1: Overview of Fundamental Concepts Includes Chapters 1 to 3

The introductory section of the book introduces you to Data as a Service (DaaS). It also provides readers with a clear overview on how an organization can deliver on the promise of providing DaaS to its business stakeholders and end customers.

Chapter 1: "Introduction to DaaS" provides a high-level overview on the core concepts of the DaaS framework. It also explores commercialization aspects of Data as a Service, its immense potential for generating revenues for most organizations, as well as some of its common limitations. It describes the details of service delivery management while suggesting necessary key steps for preparing the blueprint for enterprise data services in your organization.

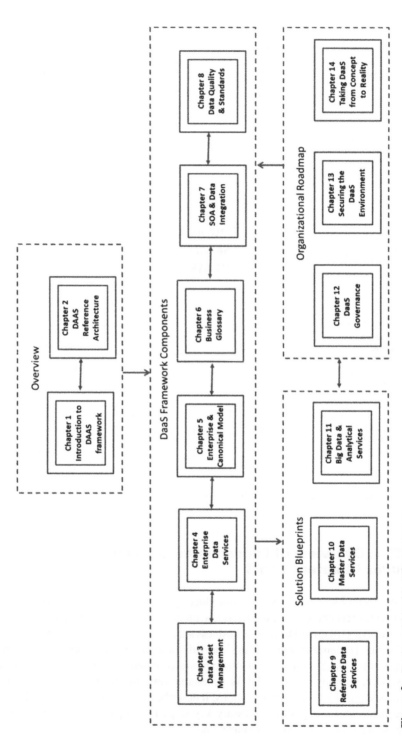

Figure 2 Roadmap the book's different chapters

Chapter 2: "DaaS Strategy and Reference Architecture" provides an overview of DaaS reference architecture along with the key components that make up the DaaS framework. It also explains the long-term significance of formally creating an enterprise data strategy in an organization that formulates a long-term roadmap to deliver Data as a Service (DaaS).

Chapter 3: "Data Asset Management" explores the significance of enterprise data and the foundational role it plays to make enterprise data services successful in any organization. It explains the underlying principles of data asset management and why companies need to treat data as a corporate asset. It also examines the various major types of enterprise data and contrasts their major features.

PART 2: DaaS Architecture Framework and Components Includes Chapters 4 to 8

This section of the book focuses on the architecture framework and components required to deploy DaaS in your organization. It also describes in detail common patterns, standards, and processes that can help shape the DaaS Reference Architecture. This section also provides readers with a high-level overview on best practices from a few related disciplines (e.g., EIM, EA, SOA, data services) to make DaaS a scalable data delivery mechanism for organizations.

Chapter 4: "Enterprise Data Services" describes the core concepts about enterprise data services as a fundamental component of the DaaS framework. It illustrates with examples how several organizations have successfully developed a set of standardized service interfaces (termed EDS) to enable data sharing with their various stakeholders (customers, vendors, regulatory agencies, government, etc.).

Chapter 5: "Enterprise and Canonical Modeling" explains the significance of enterprise and canonical modeling and its foundational role to promote consistent and reliable data exchange across disparate systems spread out over the organization. It also explains the significance of the enterprise data model (EDM) as the foundational component required for building a robust and mature set of data structures that can be reused across the entire organization.

Chapter 6: "Business Glossary for DaaS" environment provides a detailed overview of the underlying reasons why organizations need to develop a standardized business glossary for data services published for user consumption. Storing glossary terms in a shared metadata repository across the organization will improve the overall productivity of both the businesses and the external subscribers to enterprise data services (EDS).

Chapter 7: "SOA and Data Integration" provides a high-level overview on key data acquisition and integration patterns with service-oriented architecture (SOA) as the underlying foundation. It also covers a few technologies, e.g., data virtualization, stream computing for big data, data federation, which can be leveraged by the DaaS framework to publish data services with enhanced efficiency, performance, and a scalable architecture.

Chapter 8: "Data Quality and Standards" provides details on how to ensure that the quality of data published by enterprise data services is suitable and fit for public consumption. It explains the significance of data standards for the success of any DaaS program. The chapter also discusses the role of data profiling as a foundational process for the success of any DaaS quality program. Finally, it looks at some of the major data profiling and quality measures that are critical for implementing a DaaS project in real life.

PART 3: DaaS Solution Blueprints
Includes Chapters 9 to 11

This section of the book provides a number of important solution blueprints where the DaaS framework can benefit organizations across several industries. Solution blueprints of data services can be very useful for readers as they can help explain the relationship between the architecture patterns explained earlier to the specific business requirements of organizations to exchange various types of enterprise data. Solution blueprints are based on the DaaS reference architecture also explained in the earlier sections of the book. Finally, this section covers a variety of real-life case studies on how organizations have successfully utilized the DaaS framework and its architectural patterns to improve their business efficiency over the long term.

Chapter 9: "Reference Data Services" presents a detailed overview on how DaaS can be deployed successfully in organizations for disseminating shared reference data to downstream data subscribers and consumers. It also presents real-life case studies on reference data services from the financial and healthcare sectors.

Chapter 10: "Master Data Services" provides a detailed architectural pattern for designing and developing Master Data Services (MDS) that can be reused across an enterprise by using common design components and standards. It also evaluates how MDS can be utilized by organizations as an effective alternative to the existing styles of MDM implementation without physically consolidating master data in a single hub. A detailed case study on a MDS implementation at a large financial institution is presented.

Chapter 11: "Big Data and Analytical Services" explains how big data analytics users can leverage data services to access data they need for advanced analytics and take decisions in real time. This chapter includes several case studies presented from organizations that have successfully implemented big data and mobile-based analytics services, leveraging the DaaS framework. It provides a detailed solution blueprint for designing and developing big Data as a Service that can be reused across the enterprise by using the design components and standards proposed under the DaaS framework.

PART 4: Ensuring Organizational Success
Includes Chapters 12 to 14

Introducing DaaS is uncharted territory for many organizations. Not all businesses are likely to face the same urgency for providing Data as a Service to their consumer, nor will they encounter the same challenges. An organizational roadmap has been included containing several best practices with respect to DaaS program management and service delivery-related aspects. Adopting these best practices and guidelines will ensure that the DaaS program continues to be useful and provides business value to stakeholders over the long term.

Chapter 12: "DaaS Governance" explores the critical nature of data governance in DaaS and how people, process, and technology factors can be leveraged to successfully deploy data services within any organization. This chapter also suggests various governance policies and controls that an organization can utilize to track and monitor the overall user experience while using a reusable enterprise data service (EDS). It examines the emerging role of the chief data officer (CDO) across organizations, as a key change agent to align data initiatives with the business strategy of an organization.

Chapter 13: "Securing the DaaS Environment" explains why data security and privacy-related issues have become such a critical consideration for any organization interested in publishing data services. It also demonstrates the key features of a comprehensive information risk management program that can mitigate risks to the DaaS program. It provides a practical list of data security and privacy measures that can be deployed by any organization planning to set up DaaS operations.

Chapter 14: "Taking DaaS from Concept to Reality" discusses best practices with respect to DaaS project management and delivery. Adopting these best practices and guidelines will ensure that the DaaS program continues to be useful and relevant to stakeholders over the long term. It discusses the benefits of employing AGILE methodology for new data services development as an alternative to the traditional software development life cycle. The chapter also illustrates steps to build a DaaS performance scorecard monitoring overall service performance of a data provider organization.

Again, I strongly reiterate that adopting DaaS will decouple data from underlying business and application complexities, although technology constraints will not become entirely irrelevant. The flexibility gained from the de-coupling, should help IT organizations react more flexibly and quickly to technological changes. At the same time, business decision makers can focus on what they really need from their data organization and not how they circumvent their existing system or platform-related constraints. As is explained with numerous illustrative examples from the real-world, DaaS can potentially also offer a new monetization capability to some organizations by leveraging data as a revenue generating service. In short, reading this book will provide an excellent overview to the exciting possibilities of leveraging data assets in your organization as well as uncover its inherent commercial value in the business market.

Who Should Read this Book

This book should appeal to any practitioner interested in implementing or selling the value of the DaaS program to business stakeholders. It should be of value to a diverse business and technical audience, ranging from business executives to experienced IT architects to those new to the topic of DaaS. Given the wide range of readers, who may benefit from reading this book, there is no pre-determined order or sequence suggested on how to read it.

Some of the ways this book can be useful to specific reader communities are listed here.

- Business executives: If you are a stakeholder responsible for providing direction or governing data in your organization, then this book gives you an excellent overview of the exciting possibilities to leverage your organization's data so as to meet the needs of your consumers as well as formulate the economic value proposition of providing Data as a Service. If your organization has plans to become a DaaS service provider, this book will help you understand the requirements of your data customers and suggest service-based solutions that can help address the customer's data needs.
- Enterprise architects: If you are an enterprise architect, the book provides a good introduction to the key enterprise design considerations while developing a data services strategy. In addition to this benefit, you will learn how DaaS can add to your overall business strategy, by ensuring long-term improvements to the data infrastructure of an enterprise.
- Data architects: If you are a data architect, this book gives you valuable advice on the design of a valuable data foundation layer. You will learn how to ensure long-term improvements to the data infrastructure of an enterprise while leveraging the DaaS framework for fulfilling the master data, reference data, and analytical data needs of your consumers.
- SOA architects: If you are a SOA/data services architect, this book provides detailed guidelines on how to apply various technology and architecture patterns while deploying DaaS in your organization. It will also make you aware of the various data security standards and best practices to ensure integrity of published data services.
- IT applications designers or developers: If you are an experienced applications designer or developer, then you will find this book useful to understand the entire process of developing data services with an awareness on the specific benefits of data reuse and how reusing service patterns can help with quicker deployment of applications in your organization. The book also gives practical advice and detailed guidelines on how your business applications can save development time and costs by leveraging reusable data services.
- Systems management and IT/MIS students: If you are relatively unfamiliar with the role of data in IT Systems Management, this book provides you an excellent introduction to key data related disciplines like enterprise modeling, data governance, metadata, and SOA from a data practitioner's perspective.

What Is Not Covered in this Book

As mentioned earlier, this book should serve most readers as a comprehensive guide for setting up DaaS in their organizations. While the book attempts to cover all the key business and technical aspects of DaaS, one size rarely fits all. Subsequently, the book does not attempt to cover any physical implementation or related details such as those recommended by software products and vendor tools that are specific to your individual organization's needs. There are several organizational and IT aspects that are unique to every industry and country regarding implementation and deployment of DaaS solutions. Therefore, such detailed decision-making at the organizational level is best left to the people who know their organization needs closely. However, guidance has been provided throughout this book on how to address some of these implementation challenges from a larger perspective.

Acknowledgments

The creation of this book on such a complex and innovative area such as Data as a Service required the participation and support of a number of individuals. In fact, this book would not have been possible without their active support and encouragement.

I want to thank a number of thought leaders in data management, architecture, and analytics who have provided me their guidance and insights while writing the book: John Zachman, Prof. Peter Aiken, Dr. Sanjoy Paul, Aaron Zornes, Steve Hoberman, Krish Krishnan, and John Ladley.

I also want to thank Shiraz Kassam, Dr. Arka Mukherjee, and Dr. S. Kaisar Alam for helping me stay inspired while writing this book and sustain the effort. I want to acknowledge the contributions of Prithvijit Mazumder and Aditya Mehta in helping review and enhance various portions of the work. I want to thank Ms. Shreya Sarkar for her terrific edits to the initial manuscript and also the editorial team from Wiley, Mary Hatcher and Brady Chin, for their continued advice, help, and support during the authorship of this book.

Last but not least, I owe special gratitude to my family and friends for their time, patience, encouragement, and support in innumerable ways.

Part One

Overview of Fundamental Concepts

Chapter 1

Introduction to DaaS

TOPICS COVERED IN THIS CHAPTER

- This chapter introduces the Data as a Service (DaaS) framework and the approach taken by several organizations to introduce DaaS into their organization.

- It provides an introductory overview of the underlying drivers for transformation of data as a monetized asset and evaluates how commercial trends in the marketplace will further drive this service trend.

- It also suggests several key steps for preparing the blueprint for Enterprise Data Services in your organization. These steps include establishing a service delivery model (SDM) comprised of a service catalog, service governance, and a resourcing strategy.

- Finally, this chapter looks at commercialization aspects of data as a service, its potential for generating revenues as well as some of its common limitations.

The most profound technologies are those that disappear. They weave themselves into the fabric of our everyday life until they are indistinguishable from it.

—Late Prof. Mark Weiser (Father of Ubiquitous Computing)

This book offers a huge undertaking to its readers. It aims to offer a definitive roadmap on how to significantly transform your organization by providing Data as a Service (DaaS) to consumers of your data across the enterprise. It also suggests ways to explore the promise of data and its expanded role as a strategic business enabler.

Using DaaS as the unifying conceptual framework, the book shows readers how they can successfully integrate distributed systems across heterogeneous platforms virtually and publish data to subscribers securely using industry data standards and governance mechanisms.

This introductory chapter provides an overview of the exciting possibilities around leveraging reusable data services across any organization as well as the

Data as a Service: A Framework for Providing Reusable Enterprise Data Services,
First Edition. Pushpak Sarkar.
© 2015 the IEEE Computer Society. Published 2015 by John Wiley & Sons, Inc.

economic value proposition of providing DaaS to your customers. It also explains the overall approach and necessary steps for any data provider to establish a service delivery model (SDM) for offering DaaS to subscribers.

DATA-DRIVEN ENTERPRISE

In the words of Peter Drucker, a world-renowned management visionary, an information-based organization requires "clear, simple, and common objectives that translate into actions."

In this chapter, we examine what these guiding objectives are and how they define the new persona of a successful information-based organization.

The DaaS framework presented in this book entails a paradigm shift in a fundamental sense, a shift that can help any organization transform itself into a data services-driven organization. Indeed, the DaaS framework can offer end users the capability to have convenient and timely access to data from multiple, heterogeneous data sources within the company as reusable data services. These data services can be useful to external and internal data subscribers, business partners, regulatory agencies, etc., (Figure 1.1). Additionally, this capability can be leveraged by some organizations interested in becoming commercial data providers, by publishing data for their customers and subscribers as a marketable service.

For example, if we look at the high-tech sector, the underlying shift toward IT services is being driven by new advances in technology and its resulting societal consequences. In effect, many organizations need to change how they do business. They will need to respect demands from an increasingly tech-savvy generation of customers who now spend more time interacting with each other on mobile devices, through texting, and on social media sites.

All these factors have created a marketplace that will be dominated by organizations that understand new trends driving the global market. Organizations need to anticipate these changes before their competitors do and provide services rapidly whenever requested by their customers. Companies that undergo this business transformation are data-driven enterprises.

Concept of a Data Service Bus

To become more prompt and effective in responding to business or market demands, any service-based organization needs to place a larger emphasis on information sharing. The challenges faced while exchanging data usually result from a fragmented data environment made up of different platforms having no common standards. Consequently, the data entities and attributes of these systems often do not share the same syntax and semantics or even a common meaning, which is a necessary condition for systems to reliably share information. Currently, the majority of systems also have not been designed for data interoperability and sharing. This is where the DaaS framework can enhance the implementation of data services with the basic

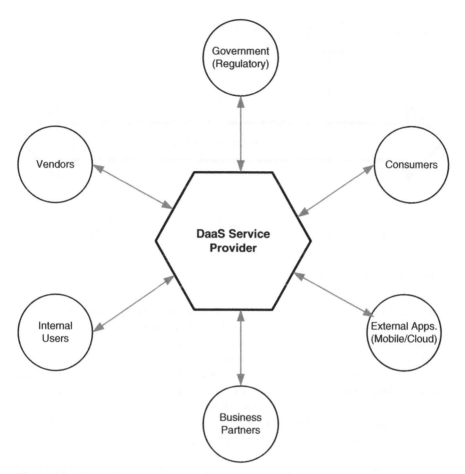

Figure 1.1   Daas in the business environment

concept of a real-world Data Service Bus. The Data Service Bus can act as a key foundation for data reuse in any DaaS deployment.

For effective sharing of enterprise data across divisions, it is essential for large organizations to build an underlying data foundation (similar to a bus architecture) that provides a consistent view of enterprise-level data in the organization. The concept of a data service bus, which is a logical data abstraction layer created at the enterprise level, can act as a foundation for virtually sharing and reusing information across IT applications. However, it should not be confused with the enterprise service bus (ESB). In some ways, the Data Service Bus can be compared to a data broker that facilitates exchange of enterprise data from a DaaS Provider, or Data Provider, to its subscribers.

In my view, the true potential of DaaS can be realized by an organization if it sets up a well-architected Data Service Bus, comprising common data modules for reuse by downstream applications and customers as well as using standardized

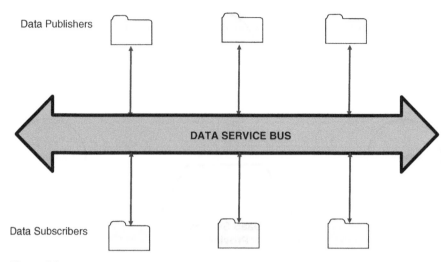

Figure 1.2 Data Service Bus

Enterprise Data Services. In addition to the data foundation layer, successful DaaS deployments also need to maintain standardized business logic and rules to process data that downstream systems can exploit (Figure 1.2).

To align the Data Service Bus with long-term business strategy, an organization interested in setting up DaaS should also establish an overall data strategy that integrates data from both internal and external data sources (social media, twitter feeds, etc.). Also recommended are the adoption of a few architectural principles and goals that will enable data sharing and interoperability across the enterprise as part of the DaaS architectural framework. This topic is explained in greater detail in Chapter 2 of this book.

Let us now try to understand the concept of a data-driven organization and what it means in the context of data-oriented services.

DEFINING A SERVICE

Over the last few years, businesses have increasingly felt pressure to transform into providers of value-added services. Often, these services become necessary for customers to fulfill some of their daily needs. This concept is not entirely new or radically different from the traditional definition of a service. As per the *Merriam-Webster's Collegiate* dictionary, service is defined as a "facility supplying some public demand." Consequently, in real life, we find the utility company providing households with water or electricity services. Similarly, a life insurance company exists in the service marketplace, primarily for fulfilling the need felt by most people for security and well-being (Figure 1.3).

Any type of service displays a few common characteristics:

- It provides the means of providing a clear **value** to customers.

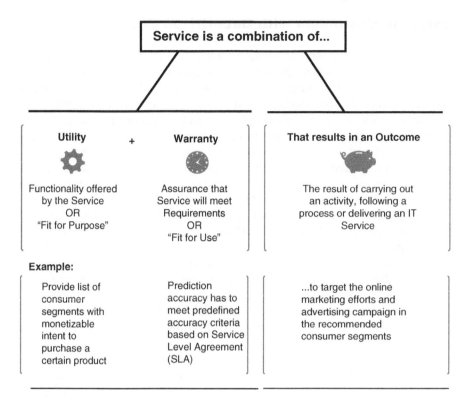

Figure 1.3   Key features of a service

- It facilitates **outcomes** that the customers want to achieve.
- It is delivered through a few **capabilities**, while managing associated **risks**.

Service Taxonomy and Decomposition

In the context of DaaS, a data service is referred to as a remotely accessible, self-contained module that provides data to authorized service consumers to help them carry out their business. Consumers can access the service in a standardized manner that is well documented and listed in a service catalog. The catalog can provide consumers with the ability to find whether a service exists and its functionality.

DRIVERS FOR PROVIDING DATA AS A SERVICE

The increasing pressure to provide data services to customers is being confronted by organizations around the world. Along with other business drivers, this pressure is often caused by several technology advances in the IT sector.

Engaging Customers with Data-Driven Choices

Over the last few years, we have witnessed a large trend toward "social shopping." Many online shoppers embrace the social-media ecosystem as their preferred channel. These shoppers usually conduct their own informal research by browsing products that they need or they find the latest products or services through what others find interesting on social media. For example, Facebook makes this process quite convenient by registering our likes and dislikes. Shoppers then compare online prices offered by different retailers, before committing to their actual purchase. Consequently, with this trend, a larger segment of customers have become dependent on the social network ecosystem and their online behavior will affect businesses on a significant scale in the future (Shih, 2009).

As an outcome of this new trend, customers are likely to feel encouraged by taking a more proactive role themselves, while deciding on their day-to-day purchases. Over the past few years, several online retailers (e.g., Amazon, Groupon, Alibaba) are seeing huge growth in their business globally, by providing customers with useful data that can help them decide on what products to purchase. In the face of new competition, many traditional retailers such as Walmart and Target have also followed suit. Similarly, supermarket chains such as UK-based Tesco have grown to be a market leader in recent years by transforming themselves to data-driven enterprises.

Leveraging data, predictive analytics, and customer insight have become part of retailers' competitive weaponry. In most of these cases, however, the customer has become the real beneficiary because they can now take fuller advantage of personalized discounts and reward coupons offered by web-based and traditional retailers.

Monetization

While the majority of business organizations offer DaaS to their customers as a complimentary service, some companies have been able to identify corporate data assets that they can rent to customers on a fee-based model also called monetization. Using monetization, several data providers within the DaaS market have generated revenues to seize initiative and grow their data services commercially. A good example of a business monetizing DaaS in the current market is Dun & Bradstreet (D&B), in particular, a subsidiary named Hoovers (Figure 1.4). This pioneer organization provides business data to their corporate clients and individual subscribers for a specific service fee. The D&B Hoovers website can stream data to its client organizations in the form of a list of specific leads, which go directly to sales teams who then contact people to make sales. There are several other firms in the market who have also been taking the lead as DaaS pioneers, providing various kinds of data services to interested subscribers. Some of these data services range from providing financial data to supplying data on a manufacturer's parts catalog for distributors as part of the supply-chain and logistics management (Soderling, 2010).

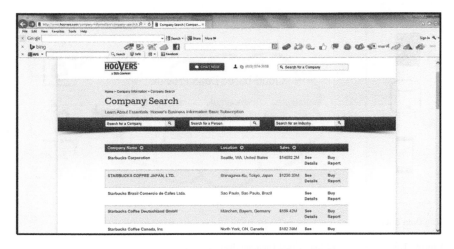

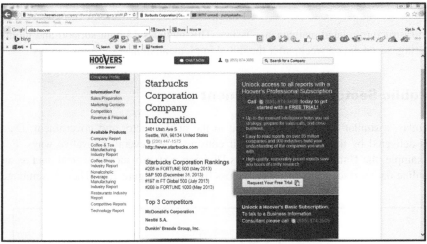

Figure 1.4   Real-life example of data services sold by D&B Hoovers (company search and results)

Another good example of an organization monetizing DaaS in the current market is cloud-based data services provider Treasure Data, a company recently named among the coolest big data vendors by Gartner. This company provides DaaS to several clients charging them a flat monthly rate for data offerings.

As part of their services, Treasure Data collects, manages, and analyzes massive volumes of big data for their clients (Figure 1.5). They can also store the client's data on the Cloud, based on a pre-built data model that supports easy data integration and export (storing different types of data formats).

The data provider can quickly set up the data requirements for their client in the cloud environment in a matter of weeks. The client can then focus on analyzing data without worrying about database administration or the other underlying DB

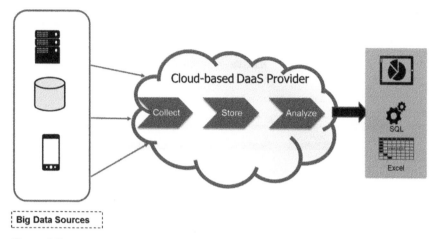

Big Data Sources

Figure 1.5   Overview of Cloud-based Data Services

infrastructure-related maintenance issues. This includes 24-hour support and monitoring, seven days a week, after the initial implementation.

Public Sector and Government

Today, a similar story is taking shape in the public sector and government. Data
is delivered by these agencies to their consumers in several innovative ways. For
example, the United Nations Statistics Division now provides statistical data as an
online data service to its members across the world (Figure 1.6). They disseminate

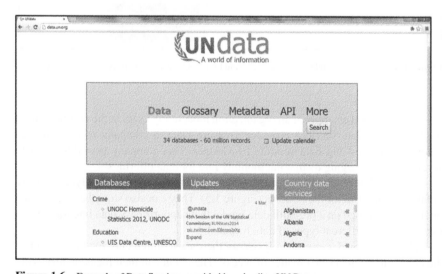

Figure 1.6   Example of Data Services provided by a leading UN Data agency

information on country-specific statistics such as country gross domestic product (GDP), population, education, life expectancy, crime, and so on.

Similarly, several community-based organizations in the healthcare sector are creating results from big-data analyses of patient data accessible to physicians and healthcare workers in real-time through data services to save innumerable lives. A prime example of this was witnessed recently when Harvard's HealthMap service (http://healthmap.org) spotted the Ebola outbreak and alerted the medical community before the World Health Organization formally announced the epidemic. HealthMap's role in tracking Ebola was heavily dependent on using big data analytics to harness public health information. HealthMap compiles, collates, and creates a visual report of global disease outbreaks, after sifting through millions of social media posts from health care workers in the affected African countries blogging about their work.

Technology Shift

Finally, the advent of new technology (e.g., mobile computing, big data) will expand exponentially as a higher number of customers in the world become more tech-savvy. For example, in the insurance sector, customers are finding it convenient to use automobile insurers such as geico.com or even to compare premium quotes from different insurers online using mobile or web-based applications rather than physically engaging with agents of traditional insurance companies. Some insurance companies have realized this change in customer behavior. They are actively addressing underlying technology enablers such as big data and analytics to better understand the customer and his or her preferences. Similarly, many customers prefer the convenience of hailing a taxi by using innovative software apps such as uber.com from their mobile devices.

The use of these newer mobile apps allows customers to share both huge amounts of data and their online shopping behavior on social media channels such as Facebook, Twitter, and Pinterest.

All of these new technology and socioeconomic trends will drive businesses toward sharing more of their corporate data with customers as on-demand service offerings.

In the electronics retail sector, customers often decide what electronic gadgets suit them best after they browse through different competitors' websites selling the products they are interested in buying (Figure 1.7). Similarly, while shopping around for holidays, customers may also prefer to visit travel websites that are easy to navigate or price friendly. Consequently, most, if not all, businesses now need to engage more directly and meaningfully with their online customers. They need to have meaningful customer interactions to retain their existing customers and attract prospective customers. On the flip side, mining vast amounts of customer data while customers are shopping online can be very profitable for any organization through pragmatic leveraging of big data and predictive analytics.

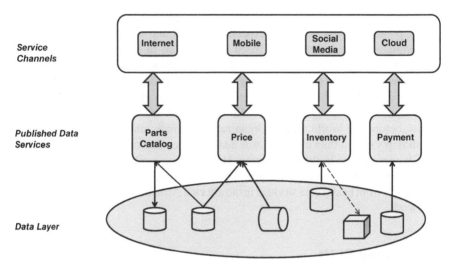

Service Channels

Published Data Services

Data Layer

Figure 1.7   Example of DaaS in the Retail Sector

Pioneering Organizations

Select groups of pioneering organizations have already started employing DaaS solutions for their customers. Bloomberg, Thomson Reuters, and S&P Capital IQ are several data providers in the current market who make financial data available to customers upon payment or who sell business data on various industries and organizations to their clients for a subscription-based fee (also see the earlier example of D&B Hoovers discussed in this chapter).

DATA AS A SERVICE FRAMEWORK: A PARADIGM SHIFT

The Cloud has created a paradigm shift, particularly among IT and business managers, away from the traditional view of data management as a support function. Just as with public utilities, banks, or insurance firms, most IT departments now need to view themselves as data service providers. They exist primarily as service providers that are responsible for providing high-quality information, accompanied by innovative analytics as services for their consumers, who are within their company, and who are also external customers and agencies. Just as new categories of products are being regularly created by manufacturers, IT service providers also have to provide innovative ways to analyze information gathered over various channels. The latest analytic models and technologies to help mine all of this underlying data could provide strategists with real-time intelligence to stay ahead of their market competitors.

Creating New Products

The downstream effect of creating these new products has consequences on numerous departments throughout an organization, but also impacts its external partners. As if this was not sufficient motivation, many organizations are also subject to increasing scrutiny by government agencies in areas of compliance and regulations, reporting, and risk assessment.

Successfully Delivering Value

To deliver value successfully to a business in a dynamic and fast-changing marketplace requires greater communication, collaboration, and social networking. Therefore, IT services provided by organizations also need to be flexible and responsive to changes in the marketplace. The means to access corporate data must be made highly efficient, consistent, and secure. The underlying data architecture adopted within the organization should also be flexible to adapt to business changes and to drive the underlying service processes and infrastructure. Without these changes at a fundamental level, organizations cannot be expected to provide consistent information to their global customers and partners.

IT Planners and Enterprise Architects

IT planners and architects within an organization also have to adapt their organization's outlook from a purely technology-driven mindset to a services-driven mindset. The recent emergence of on-demand software such as Software as a Service (SaaS) is proof of this change in direction. SaaS has become a common delivery model applied by a large number of businesses. Examples of SaaS applications include customer relationship management (CRM), master data management (MDM), and enterprise resource planning (ERP) modules to name a few. Similarly, some vendors now provide infrastructure as a service product (database platform) to help developers and users gain access to the relational and NoSQL DB hosted in the Cloud.

Exploding Data

For most customer- and client-oriented enterprises, providing DaaS to end customers has become difficult to ignore. This is often because large organizations are increasingly challenged by their business competitors and leadership to address demands for faster, more flexible data delivery to customers.

Clearly, this is not an ideal situation. DaaS can help address increased demands for data from customers by facilitating faster and more reliable ways of processing and distributing data to them over various channels such as the Internet, the Cloud, social media, etc. One of the underlying reasons for increased popularity of DaaS is new technology solutions in data integration. For instance, advances in data virtualization, analytics, data streaming, etc., can significantly enhance DaaS usage experience. Therefore, the virtual style of data access and integration discussed throughout this book can be viewed as a game changer in many respects.

As mentioned, Bloomberg, Thomson Reuters, and S&P Capital IQ are pioneering organizations that have already started employing DaaS solutions for their customers on a significant scale. For example, a supply chain and logistics management company employed a DaaS solution to deploy parts catalogs as a service for on-demand access and to aid in the purchase decisions of their customers. Several organizations have also started to make financial and market data available to customers as DaaS providers. These data providers sell business data on various industries and organizations to their clients upon payment.

DaaS Benefit Summary

Let us now cover the major benefits expected at data-driven organizations that either adopt the DaaS framework or become data service providers to their enterprise customers.

Benefit 1: Increased revenues

While the majority of business organizations offer DaaS to consumers as a complimentary service (such as in the earlier example of the UN Statistical Division), several companies determine which data assets they can rent to customers to gain a competitive advantage. Given recent opportunities, a few data providers such as those within the DaaS market can generate revenues using DaaS commercially.

For example, D&B Hoovers currently offers their corporate clients a variety of data-related services (Figure 1.5A and B). These data services include providing D&B clients with:

- Targeted lists of customer leads for salespersons worldwide
- Company-specific research details on the leads/suppliers/vendors
- Customer demographic data suitable for marketing companies
- Financial and analytical information
- Market analysis and leading competitors

Given the opportunities seen with DaaS pioneers such as D&B Hoovers, it is very likely that several data providers within the global DaaS market will be able to generate revenues if they seize the correct set of data initiatives to grow DaaS commercially (Williams, 2012).

Using DaaS can also help clients identify, access, manage, secure, and deliver information in real time, regardless of the type of information or the platform on which it is stored. Implementing this concept over a set of reusable EDS ensures consistent packaging of data, consistent application of rules for data, and centralized control and maintenance.

Usage of DaaS is not as uncommon in the financial industry. For example, financial software, data, and media company Bloomberg provides data services for their subscribers to access reference and market-related data, spanning millions of financial instruments across all asset classes. Similarly, the leading investment research firm Morningstar provides their clients with access to a wide range of its investment data from various equity exchanges and indexes worldwide. Its real-time data services also delivers data on its investment research products to individual investors, financial advisors, and financial institutions. The internationally-acclaimed credit rating agency, Standard & Poor's has set up DaaS through an online subsidiary of the ratings firm. The subsidiary is dedicated to provide real-time data, research, and analytics services to its subscribers, including S&P credit ratings, S&P Indices, as well as fundamental market data.

A lot of business value can also be realized by traditional corporations and public sector organizations (not just commercial DaaS service providers), by providing timely and easier customer access to their data, even if the data services do not directly generate any revenue stream. For some organizations, providing global accessibility to their published data with DaaS may even lead to market opportunities in other geographic regions.

Amidst increasing data volumes, diversity, and complexity of data sources, DaaS can facilitate faster and more reliable ways of distributing and processing data across any enterprise by providing data services. Several technology-related improvements have gradually reduced the impact from resistance bottlenecks. For instance, advances in data virtualization, real-time warehousing, etc., accompanied by better design adoption, have significantly enhanced the usage of service-oriented architecture (SOA). Therefore, EDS are employed as a virtual style of data access and integration.

For many years, companies such as Amazon have been leading the way in this area. For example, many of Amazon's products are sourced from suppliers in other countries and sold to online customers in western countries. So Amazon keeps its own product catalog updated on a real-time basis for the customer to access. All the suppliers' latest product offerings, changes in product lines, expired products, etc., are available to the customer via EDS. Additionally, internal projects can also save time, effort, and money by reusing the EDS across different departments in the organization. Thus, in terms of hard dollar benefits and savings, investments in EDS, and other common components can be justified both from the strategic and project-based perspectives.

Benefit 2: Efficiency gains through process simplification
DaaS is expected to facilitate a quicker and more consistent way of distributing and processing data, which leads to enhanced productivity across the organization. Significant process improvements are expected in the organization's workflow once the initial Data Service component has been deployed. Process simplification is expected to help in terms of faster information delivery to consumers across the globe (as in the UN Statistical Division example mentioned earlier). Having a foundational component such as data services will lead to better integration and alignment among different applications, largely due to the use of standardized tools, technology, and

standards (the use of common tools also leads to savings from reuse). Organizations need to be able to discover that data exists as well as have a good definition of the data types, structure, and semantics. Eliminating confusion and rework that can occur when multiple versions of the same data exist in different locations can also result in reduced administration costs. Ultimately, these factors are also likely to improve customer satisfaction and to improve satisfaction levels in other external parties who engage with the organization.

Benefit 3: Improved risk management and compliance

Across various industries, there has been steady increase in government regulations on data security and privacy issues. These new laws mean that organizations are now responsible for any breaches in data security or privacy related to their customer data. Service provider organizations (e.g., insurance companies, airlines, banks, or healthcare providers) can limit these compliance risks by ensuring their access/security-related policies, data interchange, and messaging standards (in terms of both format and structure) are embedded in the common Data Services modules. Moreover, monitoring compliance to risk regulations becomes much easier when using DaaS because of control provided by a single, managed interface to the data. It is also easier to review major components of an EDS both closely and regularly under the oversight of a central data governance council, instead of trying to oversee thousands of data services built by isolated application teams that have been released in a piecemeal manner.

Benefit 4: Facilitate data exchange and interoperability

For any large and complex environment, the need for interoperability is critical for data sharing and exchange across systems. Often organizations react to business needs tactically by building multiple applications that lack the ability to work in harmony or to exchange data with external systems and government agencies. The DaaS framework addresses this problem by providing clear and consistent data exchange standards along with a set of governance principles that can reduce inconsistent integration processes and redundant data stores spanning across the entire IT enterprise landscape.

A key benefits of following the DaaS approach is that it enables data-driven organizations to share data across multiple systems using standardized data formats. In the long term, usage of these standard formats makes data exchange feasible across different systems. Data can also be reused by different parts of the business over the long term, even if their data is hosted on disparate platforms.

Benefit 5: Separate technology from functionality

Any team that is invoking DaaS is not concerned with the internal technology or underlying architecture of the service. Consequently, as long as they input the correct parameters into the service, the service will return what was originally expected of it. This insulates enterprise services' user against any impacts or internal changes to the EDS that they are subscribing to. This decoupling also allows companies freedom to make faster changes and to adapt to market changes with more agility.

Benefit 6: Consistent standards
The DaaS framework is supported by industry-wide open standards that allow for data sharing across heterogeneous platforms and that make applications interoperable. By using consistent standards, the migration of existing applications across platforms is easier when large-scale changes become necessary. DaaS also supports organizations in enabling them to share master and reference data by ensuring consistent standards for data exchange are maintained. These standards also enable organizations to share results generated from big data and analytic platforms seamlessly with downstream applications.

DaaS Pricing Models

There has been a wide range of services offered to customers on the Cloud by service providers—ranging from applications to websites renting a shared infrastructure as a service (e.g., data centers). Whole classes of problems are being transitioned to the service provider, for a price, on the Cloud. A cloud-based data provider typically provides end-to-end technology and data capabilities, platform management, and support for one monthly or yearly subscription rate, which is similar to SaaS.

Based on research trends (Soderling, 2010), let us look at some of the leading DaaS pricing models that service providers can offer to their customers to use their data services. The preference for a specific DaaS pricing model may vary based on the nature of the industry sector as well as on the customer's individual preferences (based on their expected DaaS usage patterns and needs).

DaaS pricing models fall in to three major categories:

- *Request-based model*

The first option offered by data providers is more appropriate for customers with lower volume usage. The customer (or data service subscriber) is charged per transaction request, which involves charging a fixed amount, such as a few cents, every time a subscriber makes a request or call for data. A call is defined as a single request/response interaction made to the service provider's application-programming interface (API) for data.

- *Volume-based model*

This is a tier-based pricing approach based on the volume of services provided. The DaaS service provider charges the subscriber based on the volume of data accessed by them in a given period. The prices are capped at certain tier levels. For example, for a fixed monthly subscription fee, the customer (organization or individual subscriber) is allowed to make up to 500 calls to the DaaS service provider. However, if the subscriber ends up making more service calls, then they get charged at the next tier level. This is the easiest DaaS pricing model to implement, but it may not maximize revenue as it does not address overages across the quantity-based ties.

- *Data type-based model*

This pricing model separates the DaaS pricing tiers by data type or attribute. This is a fine-grained model under which data can be sliced or diced, depending on the complexity of the customer's data request. However, this is a complex model to administer, but may be ideal for certain sectors. An example is a mapping service that offers the geographic coordinates and zip codes of the neighborhoods in a city or town. However, if subscribers need additional details, then they can request more attributes such as school or post office locations, which are sold for an additional charge.

- *Corporate subscription model (company-wide or per user)*

This pricing model is probably the most prevalent subscription model in the market. Business organizations can choose to purchase a company-wide subscription or subscription per user from the DaaS vendor. For example, D&B Hoovers currently offers their clients a corporate subscription on a variety of data-related service offerings. These data services include providing D&B clients with customer leads, financial and analytical information, market analysis data, etc.

Data Services Enablement: Role of the Service Delivery Model

Every organization has a business strategy that is uniquely driven by the market and industry that it operates within. For any organization to transform itself into a DaaS data-driven organization, there must be a clear understanding of the overall strategy, vision, and goals. Thus, a formal roadmap and detailed blueprint for Data Services enablement has to be defined by the DaaS program team (Figure 1.8).

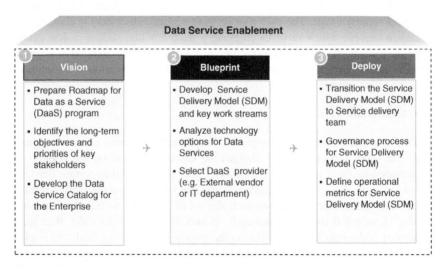

Figure 1.8   Key phases of enabling the DaaS vision phase

The finalized blueprint for enterprise-wide Data Services could impact critical areas of the organization's existing business processes. These impacts need to be communicated formally to top leadership and their support for these changes needs to be obtained.

After the vision and blueprint have been clearly defined and agreed upon by key stakeholders of the organization, we recommend a phased approach to the deployment of the Data Services Service Delivery Model.

During the vision phase, the organization plans out an overall roadmap for the DaaS program. The roadmap should be based on long-term objectives and priorities of key stakeholders. It should clearly articulate the catalog of services offered by the DaaS program.

The vision phase can include the following activities:

- Preparing a roadmap for the DaaS program
- Identifying long-term objectives and priorities of the key stakeholders
- Outlining the major business processes in the enterprise that can benefit by leveraging the DaaS framework

Blueprint Phase

The blueprint phase is the next part of the service-enablement process. In this phase, the organization develops the various Service Delivery Models and identifies the individual delivery workstreams along with the capabilities required for delivering different data services.

The team creating the blueprint should also refine the Data Service catalog by defining baseline data services required by the organization. It should also prioritize these services and define a phase-based approach to service deployment. This means some base data services can be implemented in the first phase due to their foundational nature. Then, other processes can be deployed in the next phases after considering the resource and budget constraints of the Data Services initiative (Figure 1.9).

The organizational structure for the Data Services deployment team also has to be proposed as part of the blueprint. This should clearly define resource requirements for every Data Services workstream. Stakeholders' roles and responsibilities in delivering data service also need to be clearly understood.

In addition to the organizational structure, a governance structure needs to be established with a formal governance council. The governance workstream ensures that the Data Services Service Delivery Model is implemented in accordance with the vision and the organization's larger data strategy.

Finally, the Service Delivery Model blueprint can provide technology recommendations for data services to be deployed. The tools and technology for data service fulfillment must be clearly identified during this exercise. The technology team should evaluate the options available to the organization for Data Services enablement and recommend what fits best with their organization. Technology recommendations would typically be driven by several underlying, organizational factors. For example,

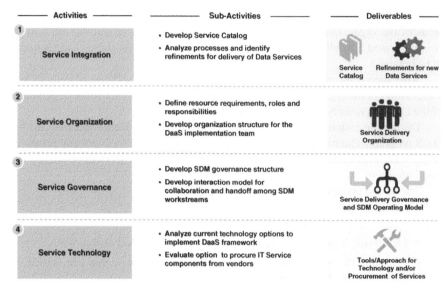

Figure 1.9   Data Services Blueprint: key activities and deliverables

does the organization have global customers or does it want to focus only on a particular region? Are the organization's customers primarily individual consumers or are they enterprise customers? The blueprint should also consider the existing level of in-house skills for a particular technology discipline. If in-house skills are not available, then the organizations needs to identify the service providers (e.g., enterprise IT or a Data Services vendor) best suited for helping individual service workstreams.

All of the preceding factors would help the Data Services team to finalize a blueprint that reflects the unique needs of the business organization and its daily challenges. The finalized blueprint for Data Services could impact certain critical areas of the organization's existing business processes. For example, while defining the Data Services blueprint, the organization would need to identify the right service provider to deliver the individual workstream deliverables. In some situations, the Data Services team may evaluate and recommend that the best option for an individual service workstream would be to use an external vendor. These impacts need to be formally communicated to top leadership and their support should be obtained before moving forward to the deployment phase.

After the blueprint has been clearly defined and agreed upon by key stakeholders in the organization, we recommend a phased approach to deploy data services.

Deployment Phase

After blueprinting activities are complete, the Data Services team has to review all of the proposed activities relating to the impacted Service Delivery workstreams. This should be followed by a well-planned transition of service delivery responsibilities to the teams responsible for individual workstreams. For example, responsibility

Key steps for implementing the service delivery model (SDM)
- Service catalog
  - Service description
  - Service exclusions
  - Service inputs (documentation), triggers, and invocation methods
  - SLAs
  - Prerequisites
  - Owners and users
  - Tools and technology for data service fulfillment

- Service delivery process
  - Define Service Delivery Model as well as individual service workstreams
  - Define processes for data service fulfillment
  - Dependencies and interactions with other processes
  - For a process: refreshment rate, enterprise-wide consistency
  - Supporting technology processes

- Service governance
  - Identify overall governance structure defining ownership and approvals required
  - Identify individual workstream activities, roles, and responsibilities
  - Key governance policies and controls
  - Metrics to measure the efficiency and effectiveness of the service

- Service resource strategy
  - Number and names of resources responsible for providing data service
  - Interaction with other organizations for service fulfillment, e.g., collaboration, hand offs, etc.
  - Roles and responsibilities of stakeholders in delivering the service

Figure 1.10   Service Delivery Model (SDM)

for designing the new data services proposed under the service catalog needs to be formally transitioned to the architecture team whereas the development team should be responsible for creating data services.

In cases where the organization has decided to engage an external vendor on a particular Data Services workstream, then the service level agreement (SLA) on timeliness, formal dependencies, and the interactions with other workstreams need to be finalized with the Data Services vendor. For example, the Data Services provider organization may decide to engage an external vendor to conduct data profiling and quality assessments for the underlying source systems that will be used to supply necessary data for publishing. In these situations, a clear understanding is necessary between the organization and the vendor on task dependencies, SLA, and timelines. The technology procurement, installation, and set-up activities also need to be undertaken during the deployment phase (Figure 1.10).

In addition to these activities, the service governance process also should be set in motion with a service governance council formally responsible for the Data

Services program. A comprehensive set of reporting metrics to monitor the various operational processes under the DaaS program (as well as progress made) is essential to track the progress made by various SDM workstreams during the deployment phase. Chapters 8 and 14 discuss Data Services performance and quality metrics in more detail.

Guiding Principles of DaaS

There are some key principles that may be useful to consider when any organization embarks on the road to become a data-driven organization.

Architecture not technology: DaaS is an architectural framework and not merely a technology or an application. In essence, DaaS can be defined as a framework for designing and developing a set of reusable data services that are designed based on enterprise-level standards. This standardization allows data services to be utilized by downstream applications for multiple purposes in the organization. Underlying these enterprise services are basic data services with well-defined functionalities that can be built as stand-alone modules (comprising reusable logic and/or data structures; Krafzig, 2007). The architecture needs to transition generations of technology.

Reusability over rework: The underlying foundation of DaaS is typically based on the concept of service reuse, enabling users to interact with their business using common reusable *services* over the web, the Cloud, and related technology. The reuse and flexibility associated with the Data Service components make it easier to leverage by businesses or by operational processes in an organization. Business services can be deployed as customized, functional modules of software stored in a centralized service repository, which can be run in a network. A real-life example of such a business service component is an online travel agent responsible for making airline bookings. During the airline booking and reservation process, the agent needs to know certain details about the passenger before proceeding with the booking. When the passenger requests a single reservation service, an internal call is made to the underlying data service components to gather the data requested or to make a subsequent request to process changes in the underlying corporate systems storing relevant data (e.g., customer profile, address change, etc.).

Foundational to enterprise capabilities: Past experience in organizations studied by industry analysts has shown that investment in any IT-based services can yield a limited return on investment (ROI) unless there is a solid enterprise foundation already in place. Data Service-based implementations cannot be expected to function well as a Band-Aid on top of unmanaged data structures. Thus, DaaS's focus has to be placed squarely on enterprise needs.

Looking outside the enterprise boundaries: Until recently, Data Services projects were focused on supporting internal business services and processes. However, as the profile of the data discipline has grown with the introduction of new consumer trends, things have changed. For example, consumers accessing and ordering company products in real time through online stores of the company (e.g., electronics retailer bestbuy.com). New DaaS projects are expected to respond rapidly to external events or requests sent from outside the organization's boundaries. To support these interactions, all of the data service users need to follow well-defined protocols as well as adhere to industry standards.

DaaS Drawbacks and Limitations

Recently, a host of *services* have also been deployed by many business organizations using on-demand software models such as SaaS, which are implemented over the web, the Cloud, and through related technology. In addition to this, to survive, it has become increasingly necessary for organizations to consolidate and form partnerships with external organizations to develop an innovative range of financial service offerings (e.g., banks and car insurance companies can develop a new line of products). All of these factors are becoming ever more complex due to the diversity of technology and data standards across partner organizations. The data integration challenges faced by IT departments in these financial organizations are universal and are not merely limited to a few sectors.

The need for enterprise-level data services with compatible data integrity, standards, enterprise models, and common definitions of data entities and attributes has increasingly become a necessity for most large organizations.

So far, we have seen many benefits from adopting DaaS frameworks. However, there are some limitations that readers also need to take into consideration.

- Because DaaS applications are hosted in the Cloud, far away from the application users, this could introduce latency into the environment. At times, the DaaS model is not suitable for applications that demand response times in the milliseconds (unless aided by performance improvement tools, which are discussed in Chapter 13).

- When data is being stored on the DaaS vendor's servers, data security could become a major issue faced by the organization. Security concerns are addressed in more detail within Chapter 10 of this book.

- When downstream applications require integration with commercial data provided by the DaaS vendor, integrating them with remotely hosted software can be costly or risky, or can conflict with data governance regulations. This is often seen when the volume of data transferred is substantial.

However, none of these drawbacks are insurmountable. There are several technology solutions as well as process and control mechanisms that can be implemented to lessen the impact of these issues.

It is most crucial to ensure that services are tied to the organization's present and future needs. We look at the underlying role of enterprise-data strategy, architecture, and data models in greater detail in Chapter 2.

Summary

DaaS is a data-distribution and publication framework that can be used by organizations to engage their customers in real time. The DaaS framework is expected to deliver data by leveraging reusable data services that meet enterprise and industry-wide standards. The need for EDS is already being used in a few industry sectors such as healthcare and insurance sharing data across healthcare exchanges.

DaaS's commercial market is also expected to grow, as more companies choose to become data service providers, with further demand from a range of data brokers for real-time access to enterprise data. Overall, as traditional businesses become more aware of the DaaS framework, they will identify an expanded set of data assets, which can then be offered to customers as a revenue-generating service.

This book gives readers an overview of why leveraging your organization's data has exciting possibilities as well as the economic value proposition of providing DaaS to your customers. It also provides a detailed overview on establishing a service delivery model to support a large range of on-demand service requests from data subscribers.

Chapter 2

DaaS Strategy and Reference Architecture

TOPICS COVERED IN THIS CHAPTER

- This chapter explains the significance of formally creating an enterprise data strategy in an organization while formulating a long-term roadmap to deliver Data as a Service (DaaS).

- A reference architecture is presented for the DaaS framework, which provides details on the various components required for publishing data services. Having a high-level and functional understanding of the various reference architecture components and best practices is crucial for implementing a successful DaaS program.

- The chapter also presents a few core principles and architectural patterns of the DaaS framework. These principles need to be adopted by data provider organizations to enable data sharing and interoperability across systems at the enterprise-level.

Any enterprise CEO really ought to be able to ask a question that involves connecting data across the organization, be able to run a company effectively, and especially to be able to respond to unexpected events. Most organizations are missing this ability to connect all the data together.

—Tim Berners-Lee
Co-inventor of the World Wide Web

While introducing the Data as a Service (DaaS) framework in the first chapter, the need for business organizations to deploy a DaaS framework to enable their businesses was explained. This often means providing decision makers with the means to conduct their analysis for business decision-making by leveraging enterprise data. The emphasis on sharing enterprise data is an underlying tenet of the DaaS framework,

Data as a Service: A Framework for Providing Reusable Enterprise Data Services,
First Edition. Pushpak Sarkar.
© 2015 the IEEE Computer Society. Published 2015 by John Wiley & Sons, Inc.

as opposed to maintaining huge amounts of isolated data. The DaaS framework can fundamentally transform an organization to a service-driven IT delivery model by utilizing reusable data services that facilitate information sharing and distribution with their customers. Chapter 1 also discussed how many organizations can generate business revenues by providing data as a service to their clients through fee-based subscriptions. However, in addition to helping monetize an organization's data assets, the DaaS framework can also significantly enhance reuse and exchange of enterprise data across large organizations internally, by distributing data to subscribers across the enterprise with the use of Enterprise Data Services (EDS).

Evolution of Data Services within the Enterprise

Within a large organization, the data landscape of a business is often complex. Due to their sheer size and complexity, these organizations may comprise of multiple lines of businesses (LOBs). These LOBs can individually develop and maintain a number of independent IT applications. However, there is often a lot of common data within each enterprise's information systems, and there is usually great potential for data reuse by employing a common architecture framework such as DaaS.

In fact, when the term *web services* became very popular, it usually referred to data from legacy applications delivered to users over the web. Typically, the concept of data services was also limited to implementing a series of database queries exposed as web services.

While these SOA-based applications offered a great deal of utility, they could not grow beyond a certain point. This saturation was caused largely because most initial efforts focused on application integration without putting much emphasis on the underlying data-centric components that can make data services a cornerstone of any enterprise.

Moreover, since these web services were not linked to an overarching enterprise strategy or founded on any enterprise architecture principles, they could not grow its usage across the enterprise beyond a certain point. More often than not, these tactical solutions were neither consistent nor were they reusable. They also could not cater to the growing demand from users with complex requests, requiring integration of data from multiple internal and external feeds (e.g., social media and twitter feeds).

To address these gaps, the DaaS framework recommends having a well-thought out enterprise-wide data strategy to ensure data published by data providers to subscribers is reliable, accurate, and consistent.

The following recommendations are a few shared principles and goals that will enable data sharing and interoperability using reusable data services across your enterprise, as part of the DaaS architectural framework (Figure 2.1).

ENTERPRISE DATA STRATEGY, GOALS, AND PRINCIPLES

The Enterprise Data Strategy outlines an organization's vision and goals for managing their enterprise data as an asset. The Data Management Body of Knowledge

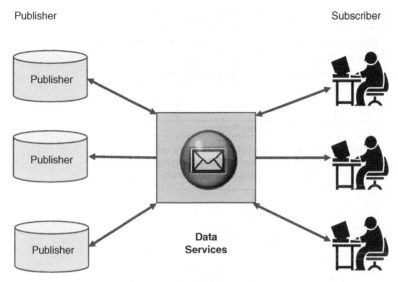

Publisher   Subscriber

Figure 2.1   Accessing and sharing data with Enterprise Data Services

(DMBOK) recommends "every enterprise should have a data strategy, driven by the enterprise business strategy and used to guide all data management activities."

The major benefit of adopting an Enterprise Data Strategy and its related planning activities is that it allows an organization to layout a formal roadmap for its future information-related plans at the enterprise level. While evaluating new IT project initiatives, such a roadmap is highly recommended for capital allocation, budgeting, and funding purposes by information domain. The roadmap should also formally reflect IT's projected priorities as well as the organization's business sponsor priorities. Overall, the roadmap should always be aligned to reflect multiple priorities and perspectives.

Having a well-formulated data strategy is especially crucial for an organization introducing enterprise-wide data services for the first time. Typically, an organization's data strategy is also impacted by IT-related factors such as underlying infrastructure environment, current application development, future technology trends, risks of obsolescence, etc. Moreover, the underlying business and technology scenarios affecting an organization can change over time. Having a rigid data strategy can slow an organization in responding to the long-term and fundamental changes in markets, geographies, and industries that impact the organization. In my experiences, the initial phases of setting up reusable EDS under the DaaS framework can resemble a business re-engineering initiative. Therefore, we recommend that the data strategy be kept flexible by IT leadership to meet the organization's evolving needs.

As mentioned in Chapter 1, DaaS is an integrated framework that helps an enterprise's clients by delivering information to them in real time, regardless of the type of information or platform(s) on which the underlying data is stored. DaaS achieves this key objective by ensuring consistent data formats as well as consistent application of rules to process data, data models, and centralized control and governance. Without

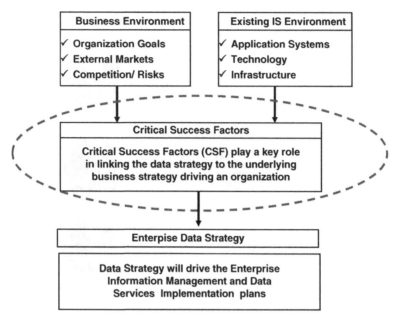

Figure 2.2   Identifying critical success factors

IT leadership formally defining the data strategy of a major DaaS program, it is highly unlikely that all the end user requirements will be considered and met when application teams start developing new data services.

CRITICAL SUCCESS FACTORS

Critical success factors (CSF) play a key role in linking data strategy to the underlying business strategy driving an organization (Figure 2.2). While formulating the initial data strategy, an enterprise assessment should be planned at the outset by the leadership to obtain a high-level understanding of the CSF, which reflect the priorities for sharing data as a service across business segments.

Enterprise Data Prinicples:
Recommendations for Adopting the DaaS Framework

Data Provider organizations that are interested in publishing data services to subscribers need to ensure their enterprise data meet the following principles of good practice.

- **Visible**: Users have the ability to discover the existence of enterprise data using common data services. All data assets are published or "made visible" by providing metadata, which describe the asset.

- **Accessible**: Organizations need to publish enterprise data by employing a "shared services" approach. Data assets are published or made available for access to users or applications, except when limited by policies, regulations, or security issues.

- **Understandable**: Users and applications can understand the published data in order to determine how the data may be used for their specific needs, both structurally and semantically.

- **Interoperable**: Services need to be in place that allow for exchanges of data between systems, through interfaces that are predefined and compatible for data exchange. Metadata are available to allow for the mediation or translation of data between interfaces, as needed.

- **Governable**: The data published by the services need to be executed according to agreed upon data governance processes, which describe the actions permissible on different sets of data, by whom and when, with a clearly laid out set of decision rights and accountabilities.

- **Open**: The distribution of data should follow industry-accepted open computing and data standards for timely and convenient exchange of data.

- **Secure**: Data providers need to ensure any enterprise data they publish is distributed securely and the entitlements, security level, and lineage of each data asset is known and available.

- **Trusted**: Regulators and other authorized users should be able to determine and assess the authority of the source of enterprise data whenever necessary.

- **Privacy**: Data providers should process confidential enterprise data in accordance with data subject's privacy rights and also cannot transfer consumer data to authorized third-parties without adequate protection.

Adapted from Enterprise System Architecture in Practice (Saha, 2005).

This assessment of CSFs should also help focus attention on the high payoff areas where exchange of data using data services can make a significant impact. The assessment should cover the following areas.

- High level understanding of the current IS environment
- Goals and strategies of the organization
- Management's awareness and vision on the strategic use of data
- Rationalizing the overall portfolio of enterprise data across teams

An effective data strategy identifies key components that must be done well by the organization to achieve its goals. A data strategy must therefore be aligned with an organization's business strategy and organizational needs. Any data strategy should therefore address major business needs, goals, and critical success factors (CSF) requested by the end users of DaaS implementation.

From a DaaS perspective, the enterprise data strategy at most organizations should normally focus on data visibility (i.e., data publication) and data accessibility. The strategy should also ensure strict compliance to data security and privacy standards. In fact, any data that is published over a data service has to be "fit for use" by a broad cross section of external customers, enterprise users, and downstream applications. Having a data strategy that prioritizes these underlying factors will be essential in terms of supporting *complexities* of system interoperability and data exchange in a service-enabled environment.

The next section explains how long-term data strategy can be implemented in real-life, within the context of DaaS. A reference architecture for the DaaS framework that provides details on the various components required for publishing data services is presented. Having a high-level, functional understanding of the various reference architecture-related components and patterns is crucial for implementing a successful DaaS program in any organization.

REFERENCE ARCHITECTURE OF THE DaaS FRAMEWORK

The reference architecture is a great starting point for exploring the foundations of any IT or software engineering or related discipline. A reference architecture can be thought of as a template that documents technology, processes, specifications, and configurations. It also provides a collection of patterns that is based on past learning experiences gained through past projects by experts in the discipline.

By using a reference architecture, a project team can potentially save time and avoid mistakes by learning from previous experience in other organizations. The reference architecture should be particularly beneficial to readers in terms of explaining foundational aspects of DaaS because it is independent of specific standards, technologies, implementations, or other concrete details.

The DaaS reference architecture typically can be represented at the following levels (Figure 2.3).

Conceptual Architecture: Translates business objectives into fundamental architectural concepts and IT capabilities at the conceptual level. At the conceptual level, business and IT leadership have to jointly set up the vision for DaaS within the organization. They should also identify their high-level objectives and key priorities with regard to data. Then this vision needs to be translated into a high-level reference architecture by enterprise architects for the delivery of enterprise-level data services.

Logical Architecture: The logical architecture is a lower-level decomposition of the conceptual architecture. It will specify major architecture building blocks in the form of a component model. The logical architecture also describes the functional characteristic of individual components and their relationship with other components of the architecture framework.

Physical Architecture: The physical architecture typically covers the operational characteristics of the design. It usually describes hardware, software, and network details of various components. This books does not cover physical architecture

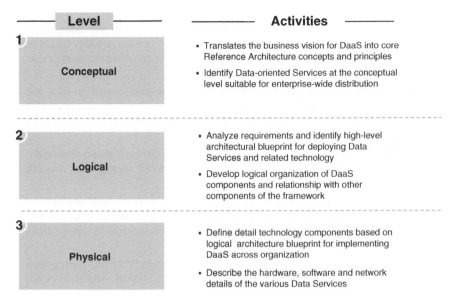

Level	Activities
1 **Conceptual**	• Translates the business vision for DaaS into core Reference Architecture concepts and principles • Identify Data-oriented Services at the conceptual level suitable for enterprise-wide distribution
2 **Logical**	• Analyze requirements and identify high-level architectural blueprint for deploying Data Services and related technology • Develop logical organization of DaaS components and relationship with other components of the framework
3 **Physical**	• Define detail technology components based on logical architecture blueprint for implementing DaaS across organization • Describe the hardware, software and network details of the various Data Services

Figure 2.3   DaaS reference architecture description

in the DaaS framework because details of this level should be specified by people within the organization who are closely familiar with their infrastructure environment.

At the conceptual level, DaaS reference architecture has to follow some fundamental architectural principles that can be used as an input to guide the solution design implemented by an organization. Consequently, there are several conceptual architecture principles used as guidelines for the overall design of the DaaS framework and reference architecture specified in this book.

DaaS Reference Architecture: Guidelines for Data Providers

We recommend that business organizations providing DaaS follow these core architectural principles while delivering data services to subscribers.

1. The data published by data providers should comply with industry-based data standards on data interoperability and sharing with reusable service components and service interfaces that leverage open computing standards.

2. The data provider should be capable of providing high service availability and performance while supporting Service Level Agreement (SLA) for uninterrupted operation of its published data services.

3. The data provider should provide the ability to distribute information updates to other systems in a standardized way, independent of underlying technology or application differences.

4. The data provider should be responsive and flexible to customer needs when presenting data as a service. Different perspectives of users, whether data consumers or data producers, are incorporated into the published data services, as necessary.

5. Providers need to incorporate customer feedback to ensure long-term value and satisfaction of the published enterprise data. Data providers should also be capable of supporting the analytical/reporting and visualization needs of downstream users.

6. Data providers should ensure that standardized and consistent data is made available across the organization by leveraging information management, reusable data models, interfaces, semantic vocabulary, etc.

7. Data services published by the data provider should be secure, fairly, and lawfully processed. The sensitive confidential data of customers should be processed only for limited purposes by the data provider, i.e., in accordance with the data subject's rights in the local country or region.

8. The provider should also be able to provide the benefits of easier integration by supporting different integration methods (web services, MQ/Middleware, or ESB).

By following these recommended guidelines, any organization can successfully start adopting DaaS as part of their business operations. These guidelines will also help build the architectural components (or component model) required for DaaS implementation.

By building the component model, under the DaaS reference architecture, an organization can establish a number of foundational components (usually at the function level) that are relevant for organizational needs along with specifying relationships and interactions between the various components comprising the reference architecture.

Under the reference architecture, the DaaS component model includes the following major components.

- Data Acquisition
- Data Management
- Data Distribution
- Data Governance
- Data Security
- Data Analytics
- Service Management

The next section provides a brief overview of the DaaS reference architecture's components at a logical level (Figure 2.4). However, these components will be covered individually in greater detail in later chapters.

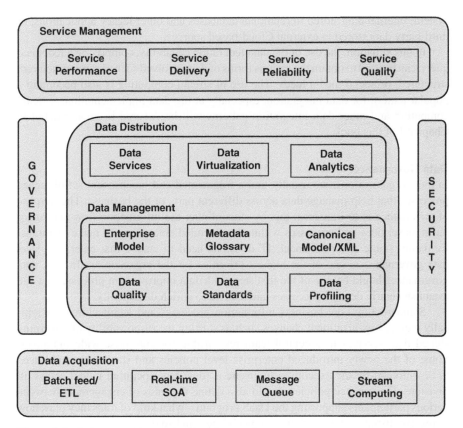

Figure 2.4   Reference architecture for DaaS framework

Data Acquisition

This layer enables the integration of data through the introduction of a reliable set of IT-based capabilities. It is responsible for physically acquiring data from a wide range of data sources and then consolidating them in the appropriate data storage format. The acquisition layer for DaaS could transport data in real time using multiple techniques – ranging from data services, Message Queue(MQ), data federation, stream computing, etc. In case there is no messaging component deployed, the organization can also pull in batch feeds using ETL tools. With the recent expansion of data feeds coming from cloud social media and mobile sources, the importance of efficient data acquisition has become especially vital to most organizations implementing Big Data solutions.

However, consolidation in such an environment can become very challenging and complex at times. This is because data from the underlying sources can send data in disparate formats. For example, an organization implementing a diverse set of applications may have to consolidate many different types of data such as semi-structured data from social media feeds; unstructured data from a content management system; internal data stored in relational databases and other legacy applications; or third-party data stored in external Cloud-based sources.

In this situation, the use of the data federation capability, comprising a federated query, can be used to obtain the various forms of data involved such as semi-structured, structured, or social media feeds. The use of stream computing is also becoming a popular pattern for data integration, especially at big data implementations. Stream computing and other data integration patterns will be covered in greater detail in Chapter 7 of this book.

Data Governance

In most organizations, we usually find a fragmented and inconsistent set of legacy processes that help manage data across different parts of the business. The purpose of governance is to transform this by streamlining the information flow and major business services and processes within the extended enterprise. To make this transformation stable and permanent, IT divisions need to ensure that enterprise-level data governance is one of the highest priorities for the organization. In fact, data governance should be one of the first steps in a data improvement process, as it can establish clearly defined processes and metrics to enrich data quality.

Standardizing core business-information processes and architecture may typically require organizational changes such as shifting the responsibility of governing shared data services to a central team responsible for enterprise-wide initiatives. Some of the newly introduced enterprise-level policies and standards would need to be enforced by the executives to ensure a consistent operating model across all divisions. Governance policies should also define the rules of engagement between various participants supporting the DaaS program – what kind of roles they play, how to resolve disputes, their various responsibilities, and so on.

Chapter 12 focuses on DaaS governance by discussing various data and business governance issues such as data governance and ownership in greater detail.

Value of Reusable Patterns in IT Architecture

One of the common concepts used in the DAAS framework is the use of patterns to drive reuse of IT assets (e.g., common data formats, enterprise models). Let us look at this term closely and understand why it is so popular among IT architects. Let us start by defining the term pattern. As defined by Dreibelbis et al., 2008, "a pattern is a solution to a recurring problem applied in a given context."

The problem for which the pattern provides a solution is usually difficult to solve and the solution can be applied in a given setting (or domain). Patterns are used by domain architects across multiple industries ranging from building construction, automobile manufacturing, financial engineering, and, of course, IT architecture. In the business world, individual architecture patterns should be selected only if it helps accomplish the specific business objectives of the organization. In other words, if a pattern does not resolve a specific problem, the pattern might not be the right fit. For example, if you decide to use a pattern originally developed to solve a structural problem encountered by buildings during earthquakes to predict forces and constraints in the event of a tsunami then it could lead to disastrous consequences.

For most business scenarios, we recommend Pareto's 80/20 rule for applicability of a given pattern to a specific real-life situation. This means that when we try to deploy a pattern in a specific organization, we can assume the pattern will fit out-of-the-box or be reused for 80% of the functionality in the pattern. However, minor adjustments or customization to organization-specific functionality will be necessary for 20 % of the pattern while deploying in a specific instance.

The following key benefits are gained by using these architecture-oriented patterns in an IT environment.

Reduced complexity: To reduce complexity of integration efforts, it is best to use an architectural approach that decouples functionality from technology platform constraints.

Greater reuse: Patterns will encourage reuse of IT components, data assets, components, and reference models that were tried and tested in similar implementations earlier.

Consistency and improvements in service quality: Patterns ensure the delivery of consistent data quality due to the usage of standardized architecture component and solution blueprints while publishing data services to consumers.

Accelerated deployment: Since new initiatives can reuse a significant amount of pattern components, they do not have to start from scratch. This could result in faster deployment, productivity gains, and cost reduction.

Improved flexibility: With the use of reusable patterns, the underlying IT architecture is designed to be modular, making it easier for the organization to quickly adapt its technology to changing business needs

In the context of DAAS, the following are a few major patterns that have been discussed throughout this book.

Extended enterprise data design patterns: Enterprise Data patterns define ways to standardize design to promote data interoperability and sharing across the extended enterprise. The architecture pattern defines various components in a reference model to describe the structure definition as well the relationships among the data components.

Data access patterns: Data access patterns define the most efficient ways an organization's users can access key types of data stored across the organization. The pattern also provides details on the nature of the application and how they can be deployed as data services (e.g., fine-grained).

Data integration patterns: Integration patterns define ways to effectively bring together data from multiple systems across the organization. The recurring problem that this pattern specifically tries to address is the integration of the data service bus with multiple data sources.

System deployment patterns: System deployment patterns provide guidance on service-implementation characteristics such as runtime performance, scalability, and availability of data services published by the data provider.

Data Management

While governance may be primarily focused on setting policies, the data management layer is more focused on realization and enforcement of policies. This is largely because having a policy without any means of enforcing it in the daily activities of the organization has no real utility. In the case of management policy, we rely on a management infrastructure to realize and enforce management policy.

The data management functional layer is primarily responsible for efficient organization, storage and management of data assets within the enterprise. There can be various types of data stored in a large organization. However, the major type of data residing in the data management tier may be classified into the following categories:

- Unstructured data, e.g., documents, graphics, images, files
- Semi-structured data, e.g., XML, SharePoint, e-mails, text files
- Structured data, e.g., databases, RDBMS, BI cubes

Underlying data management services provide an enterprise with business flexibility by decoupling the data sources, while keeping them logically consistent using various common data-related principles and best practices. Many of these capabilities need expertise in data- related disciplines, e.g., data architecture, data governance, data quality, data modeling. For example, this category often provides data quality services necessary to ensure integrity of the underlying enterprise data fed by the data sources.

Similarly, consistent data definitions and data mappings are made possible with metadata services, by covering the definitions and relationship between the various data objects. Data management services also include several data quality services to enrich the data from the underlying data sources. Data standardization would ensure that the data exchanged with consumers via data services are consistent across the enterprise and meet the established industry data interoperability standards (interoperability is the ability to make systems and organizations work together).

Recently, several vendors have been marketing the concept of data lakes (or data swamp) as an essential component to capitalize on big data. However, as industry analyst Gartner has warned, it is a common fallacy to confuse the data management tier with a data lake. Gartner says, " While the marketing hype suggests that audiences throughout an enterprise will leverage data lakes, this positioning assumes that all those audiences are highly skilled at data manipulation and analysis, as data lakes lack semantic consistency and governed metadata."

Data Distribution

Data Distribution (or data access) services refer to the process of organizations making virtual business views of enterprise data available, to enable demand-driven query access by live applications and business users. A properly architected data services layer is the foundation for the DaaS platform, which support data services over multiple platforms (e.g., web-based, mobile and the Cloud).

DaaS consumers are expected to be heavily influenced by the nature of their daily experience while accessing data. Even from an enterprise-centric view, building this access layer is essential to conveniently and securely providing access to data assets and related infrastructure of an organization.

This layer can help achieve efficient and timely distribution of data with a standardized set of published services that enable data subscribers to access and reuse data on demand, at the time and place of their choice. The data services tier typically can expose all the disparate data sources via the use of XML, Web services and other supporting technologies (e.g., data federation and data virtualization) as a single source of data. In some situations, the data services may also provide notification to users about certain data in the form of alerts to trigger actions in real time.

Data Analytics

The data analytics tier is perhaps one of the most important areas of growth for DaaS in the future. This growth trend is likely to grow further with the increasing demand for CAMS applications (Cloud, Analytics, Mobile, Social Media). Let us now look at a brief overview of data analytics and its significance in the DaaS framework.

Analytics is the discovery of meaningful patterns in data to help organization make predictions to support decision making. This process usually involves inspecting large amounts of data, observing them, and modeling the data with the goal of discovering useful patterns and making predictions to support decision making. Firms usually apply analytics to business data, to describe, predict, and improve business performance with detailed analysis.

The Data Analytics layer originated from providing a set of reporting capabilities to traditional users to help them gather information with queries and run reports. Most of this analysis was descriptive and happened after the fact. Over the last decade, analytical capabilities evolved further to comprise a range of BI tools that served as a useful aid for business users to diagnose various business trends and anomalies Figure 2.5).

However with the advent of big data, the scope of data analytics has now been enhanced dramatically to predict and improve business performance using a range of sophisticated analytical and statistical tools.

Predictive tools are expected to evolve further to help the business with actionable intelligence. Future-generation analytical tools will provide various sophisticated forecasting that can help businesses take decisions proactively to explore unforeseen opportunities and prevent them from business risks. DaaS can potentially become the backbone of real-time analytics enablement. It can allow decision makers to obtain the results of prescriptive data analysis in a fraction of a second. The organization's leadership can then leverage the results obtained from this data-driven analysis to foresee likely business scenarios. By knowing these scenarios well in advance, organizations can make their decisions more proactively and change the course of future events (instead of reacting after they happen).

The enhanced data visualization capabilities seen in several new vendor tools are helping to critically enhance data analytics' role. Most decision makers in the corporate boardroom are hard pressed for time. In such a scenario, "A picture is worth

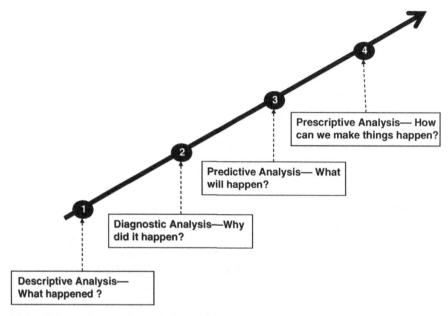

Figure 2.5   Evolution of data analysis needs within an organization

a thousand words" and data visualization plays a vital role in helping leaders arrive at decisions with greater clarity.

With new data visualization features, DaaS customers will have mechanisms for discovering and exploring their core data as well as reports in a visual form. Data visualization can help users filter through massive sets of consumer data with the help of dashboards, interactive bar/pie charts, and line or scatter charts. These visualization services can also be combined with data federation capabilities and use of in-memory data to provide real-time or near real-time analysis and reporting services.

Data Security

With increasing occurrences of cyber attacks and data security breaches, securing data environments is critical for any organization interested in implementing a DaaS framework. When a business organization encounters a data breach involving sensitive, protected, or confidential data falling into the hands of unauthorized individuals, the effect can be disastrous.

While introducing public data services offers a number of significant benefits to both the organizations and consumers (in terms of ease of data access and productivity gains), it also introduces several security and privacy related challenges. Using mobile, web, and online social networking services further increases these threats to organizations. There is clearly a trade-off between data sharing vs complying with privacy laws. This leads to most organizations providing data to external subscribers to face conflicting priorities. Organizations pursuing DaaS need to strike a balance between competing demands of data sharing and privacy (Figure 2.6).

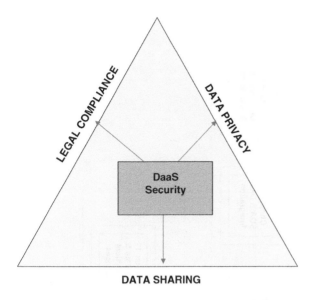

Figure 2.6 Trade-offs between data sharing and data privacy/legal considerations

The threat from data security and privacy to data providers can be greatly minimized, if an organization sets up a robust IT security framework. This needs to be accompanied by well thought-out data entitlement rules on privacy such as who can request access for a particular data element over the data service and who cannot.

Due to the competing priorities (or trade-offs) required between data sharing and data privacy/legal considerations, data entitlement policies should be gathered from business users and formally documented as part of DaaS security policy and procedures. These policies should be introduced under the general oversight of the data security team (details on data security are provided in Chapter 13). Regular security audits need to be conducted by organizations to proactively ensure there are no security or privacy threats to the DaaS infrastructure and related environment.

Service Management

The role of service management is critical for data providers so it can ensure that its ongoing service to customers exceeds their expectations. It also makes sure that providers meet all their service-level agreements with customers in terms of service delivery. We have already covered the key steps for implementing the service delivery model (SDM) in Chapter 1. This included defining how any organization can set up a formal roadmap and detailed blueprint for data services enablement.

However, even after the deployment of data services, data providers have to ensure they maintain a sustainable, high quality list of data services. In order to ensure this, regular monitoring of service quality using a metrics-based approach is an essential prerequisite for these organizations. They should identify appropriate key metrics and performance indicators (KPI) to track performance to ensure that they are consistently delivering service well beyond the acceptable level. For example, KPIs

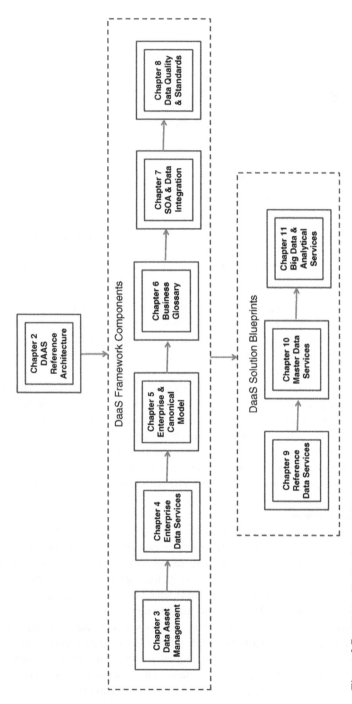

Figure 2.7 Linking DaaS reference architecture components

may include service availability, service fulfillment and service capacity utilization metrics.

We have attempted to define various steps which are required to meet specific goals and KPIs for DaaS implementation. The use of a data service performance scorecard to define performance targets is discussed in Chapter 14 of this book.

HOW TO LEVERAGE THE DaaS REFERENCE ARCHITECTURE

The successful adoption of DaaS in any project is based on several underlying technology and process components – data services, data models, data quality standards, and service governance. This book provides several best practices and guidelines for adopting DaaS into your organization based on the reference architecture presented in this chapter.

Throughout this book, several key patterns are introduced about the DaaS framework such as architecture patterns, SOA and integration patterns, data modeling patterns, data services, data governance, and security. The foundational components previously listed under the reference architecture for DaaS are discussed individually in later chapters of the book. (Please refer to Chapters 4 to 8 for architecture, SOA and integration, and data modeling. Chapters 12 and 13 cover data governance and security.) This chapter on reference architecture has merely attempted to link the technical architecture of the individual components comprising the DaaS framework.

The finalized solution blueprint is typically derived from the DaaS reference architecture, which provides reusable patterns to solve a repeating problem in a given business context. This book encourages using patterns provided in the DaaS reference architecture to develop data services that are architected to support enterprise-level needs. As part of the DaaS solution blueprint, several case studies are discussed from several leading organizations to learn how to successfully leverage data as a service (DaaS) framework for distributing reference data, master data, and big data.

Figure 2.7 depicts the major architecture-related components of the DaaS framework, linkages between the components, and how reference architecture can be used as input for development of DaaS solution blueprints for enterprise data services. Please also refer to the DaaS reader included in this book's Preface for a narrative on the topics covered within each chapter of this book.

SUMMARY

Enabling a business with the right data comes with its own, unique set of challenges for every organization. Consequently, having a proper roadmap and strategy is essential for the success of any DaaS initiative. This chapter described how an organization can build a solid architectural foundation to set up DaaS. Several core DaaS principles were discussed that can be employed by readers as they develop DaaS operations within their organization.

An overview was also provided of the DaaS reference architecture, which was has been conceptualized after working on multiple DaaS project implementations. For a successful DaaS implementation, it is essential to have a well laid out architectural blueprint that can promote the intelligent reuse of data across the organization.

The reuse of architectural patterns discussed throughout this book have been tried and tested in similar implementations and have been successful. They will minimize the risks associated to an organization that has limited experience in implementing DaaS. With the increasing size and complexity of information systems implementation, using architectural patterns is a vital part of DaaS strategy.

Chapter 3

Data Asset Management

TOPICS COVERED IN THIS CHAPTER

- This chapter looks at the significance of enterprise data and the foundational role it plays to make enterprise data services successful in any organization.

- Underlying principles of data asset management and why companies need to treat data as a corporate asset are explained. Major types of enterprise data and their features are also examined.

- The significance of enterprise information management are discussed along with the role it plays in improving data quality within an organization over the long term.

"Data really powers everything that we do."

—Jeff Weiner, CEO of a leading business-oriented social networking service

Chapter 2 explained the underlying factors that can drive organizations to deploy the Data as a Service (DaaS) framework to enable their businesses. This framework helps users conduct analysis for business decision-making by leveraging enterprise data.

Successful adoption of DaaS is based on three factors: the quality of data and content, underlying architectural principles used for management, and real-world experiences of how to distribute them to consumers in an effective manner.

An emphasis on sharing enterprise data is an underlying tenet of the DaaS framework, as opposed to maintaining silos of published data. This chapter provides a detailed overview of the major categories of data that can be considered significant and shared across the enterprise including master data, reference data, analytical data, and big data.

Data as a Service: A Framework for Providing Reusable Enterprise Data Services,
First Edition. Pushpak Sarkar.
© 2015 the IEEE Computer Society. Published 2015 by John Wiley & Sons, Inc.

Managing Data Assets

The role of data (and information) is pivotal to the success of any business organization. Whether customers place an order, search for a product from their online catalog, or fill an online survey form, their actions generate underlying data within the organization. All this data should be considered as organization assets, due to their intrinsic value to the business users for their role in day-to-day operational support, decision making, analysis, and business intelligence.

A data asset is a piece of data stored in any manner that is recognized as *valuable* within the organization. It has been argued that the most important factor in making a specific type of data a valuable corporate asset is the extent to which it can provide the organization with competitive advantage. Let us look at an example to illustrate this point. Many firms have invested in Customer Relationship Management (CRM) systems after recognizing the value of customer relationships in the sales and marketing of their products. However, these applications can be useless without safeguarding the most valuable asset supporting CRM, underlying customer data. Similarly, other firms have recognized the role of big data (BI) and data warehousing in predictive analysis and business intelligence. They too need to ensure they support their analytical users with high quality data assets that are reliable, accurate, and up-to-date.

The landscape of data assets within any enterprise is usually vast (often terabytes of data) and can be comprised of different forms of physical data storage (Figure 3.1). While organizations have traditionally focused on structured data formats

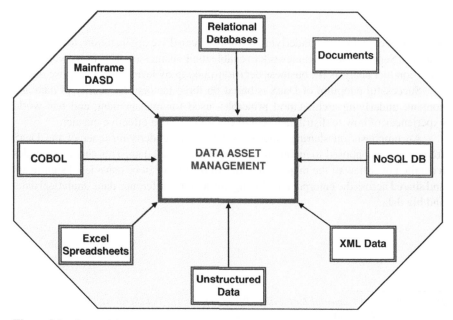

Figure 3.1   Scope of data asset management within a typical enterprise

(e.g., relational databases) as the primary mode to support their daily operations or business intelligence, there has been growing awareness on larger amounts of data content stored in unstructured (e.g., internet files, content received from social media applications, blogs) and semi-structured formats (e.g., No SQL databases, XML). Unless the information content in all these forms of data is properly managed as assets, there is limited chance of this data being exploited to its full potential and generating true value to the organization. Investing in data warehouse platforms, sophisticated business intelligence tools, or storing content in numerous files and replicating data will only increase costs with little perceptible gain. With explosive growth in data and proliferation in various uses (e.g., big data), organizations are finding it harder to manage their data assets. Moreover, this explosive growth of data is creating increased storage costs for organizations in their data centers. It is often difficult to know what data to exploit, where the data comes from, and what the content of data is worth to your enterprise unless you maintain a full inventory of your data assets along with their relevant metadata (Chapter 6 looks at this issue in greater depth).

Data asset management (DAM) ensures that all of an organization's data content gets treated as corporate assets with tangible value. While reducing short-term costs on database management operations by optimizing storage and data center costs is important, it is critical that organizations also look at the long-term ROI on their investments. For example, a data strategy that places emphasis on data virtualization (as compared to creating more databases) can drive greater business agility and reduced time-to-market. An optimized data strategy can therefore draw significantly more value out of data.

Data management should also ensure there is no improper use of data assets by unauthorized users. Data asset management should also include proactive risk mitigation measures to help avoid exposure to regulatory risks and penalties in the event of a data security breach (Figure 3.2). Moreover, managing data assets in a coordinated manner across the organization should also focus on improving data quality over the long term. Any organization that wants to successfully manage their data has to focus on planning, directing, governing, and supervising the utilization of data in an effective manner.

Managing these valuable data assets as an organization require using a common set of asset management principles that are no different from managing other types of corporate assets, including buildings, inventory, accounts receivable, cash, and equipment. An organization's leadership therefore has to ensure that all their data assets are formally controlled and managed often with the use of asset tracking and monitoring tools. Successful organizations create environments where their valuable forms of data are secure, reliable, accurate, up-to-date, and easily accessible. Often, achieving such an environment for data assets within an organization requires relentless focus on underlying data standards, data quality, and data governance processes.

To create a long-term roadmap and vision for enterprise data, areas of DAM and Enterprise Information Management (EIM) must be closely interlinked. The efforts of both these areas do often overlap, however, it is best to distinguish EIM and DAM. As discussed earlier in Chapter 2, EIM is typically concerned mainly with

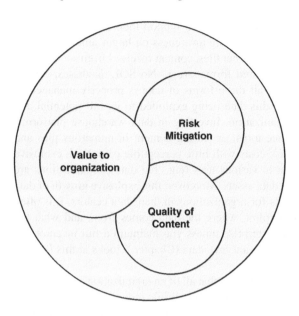

Figure 3.2   Key considerations for data asset management

information planning policies, governance, and quality related issues. The emphasis of DAM is on fundamental asset management concepts and processes to manage these assets (e.g., regular auditing, compliance to data security controls, and backing up data periodically).

Even for an organization that has developed and deployed mature EIM processes, there are still other aspects of the vision that need to be developed as part of governance efforts. These include uniform metrics as well as agreement on a single source of the truth across various business teams for each data subject area (e.g., CRM modules for customers, PIM module for Product). There also has to be a sincere attempt to reuse the single source of truth on major project initiatives across the organization, along with respect for the EIM governance processes and the need for information integrity, quality, and consistency by IT application teams and business partners.

In the context of DaaS, building data services leveraging EIM principles is expected to not only integrate different parts of the enterprise but also cover the extended enterprise. These include partners, suppliers, and customers as well as internal business units. Given this additional growth in coverage of data access, EIM becomes a critical enabler and foundation for Enterprise Data Services.

INTRODUCTION TO MAJOR CATEGORIES OF ENTERPRISE DATA

Let us now try to think of the data that we deal with in our own enterprises. Envision the types of data that you really care about. As an insurance-firm analyst are you interested in knowing what your most profitable services and insurance products are? Or do you wonder who the customers are that could pose a credit risk to your enterprise (if you are mortgage lender or bank)? Think about these issues in the context of your organization and then read the next section, which introduces the major categories of enterprise data.

Enterprise data can defined as data that is shared by the users across an organization, generally across departments and/or geographic regions. Enterprise data can also be shared outside the organization with other external users who depend on that data such as customers, suppliers, distributors, and regulators.

There is no precise criteria for what defines the use of enterprise data. However, one of the best ways to identify any form of enterprise data is that it belongs to the entire organization, not to an individual division, department, or application. Therefore, once data in an application gets to the point where some data needs to be shared across many operating units in different locations, it becomes a data asset that is critical for the organization. It also becomes critical for enterprises to spend time and resources to ensure that enterprise data is governed actively with effective standards on data modeling, data storage, data access, and data security.

A lack of adequate attention to enterprise data can result in significant financial losses, not only for the organization but for other external entities that depend on that data such as customers, suppliers, and distributors. Similarly, increasing compliance and regulatory reporting mandates from governments worldwide can be a challenge for organizations with no clear strategy on sharing enterprise data with regulators. For example, the United States Federal Drug Administration (FDA) has experienced multiple incidences in which the pharmaceutical industry has been lax in terms of regulatory reporting. Therefore, the FDA requested the pharmaceutical company submit reports, requiring a list of transactions that need to be compliant with a particular government policy (or environment standard). Failure to provide these compliance reports in a timely manner can lead to severe penalties as was witnessed during the Sarbanes Oxley Act of 2002 and in the aftermath of major corporate and accounting scandals such as Enron and Worldcom. Overall, organizations that govern their enterprise data proactively are better prepared to meet the growing compliance and reporting demands of regulatory agencies.

Guiding Principles for Enterprise Data

Data Ownership: Enterprise data belongs to the entire organization, not to an individual division, department, or application.

Data Standards and Interoperability: With greater use of standardized data formats, enterprise data provides the ability to allow systems and organizations to work together (interoperate).

Data Sharing: Enterprise data facilitates improved data sharing throughout the enterprise by providing a consistent, authoritative version of data.

Data Redundancy: Use of enterprise data also reduces data redundancy drastically as applications gradually prefer to reuse the authoritative version of data instead of building their own siloed version of data and eliminate disparity across systems.

Data Delivery: Use of standardized components leveraging enterprise data can help application teams with faster delivery on projects.

Data Standards: Usage of enterprise data encourages adoption of industry standards and specific reference standards mandated by the government in certain sectors (e.g., ICD 10).

Data Quality: Increased use of enterprise data and related standards can leads to improved data quality over long term.

Data Reuse: Use of enterprise data makes it possible to reuse data across different projects, instead of reinventing the wheel on every project.

Data Security: Enterprise data allows organizations to centrally secure and share sensitive or confidential data only with authorized users.

Figure 3.3 illustrates how data can be broadly classified into a number of different categories, based primarily on their popular usage in the enterprise (Chisholm, 2007). Let us start with *transaction data*, the category of data which is the most widely prevalent in the industry. This data form represents the transactions that most businesses need to use to support their daily business operations. It is usually encountered when making airline reservations, trading stocks, or purchasing items.

ENTERPRISE DATA

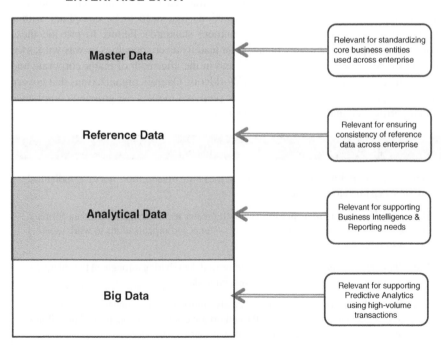

Figure 3.3   Key categories of enterprise data and their usage in the real world

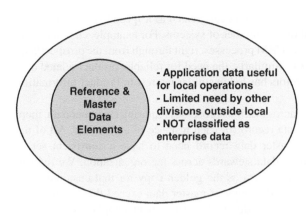

Figure 3.4 Differentiating between enterprise data and other types of data

The majority of transaction data (or any other form of application data) supports the specific processing needs of a single division or department. While transaction data could be mission critical for supporting business operations of a particular department, this form of data can have limited need from other divisions in the organization (or among external consumers). Strictly speaking, most transaction data used in organizations to run their day-to-day business is not considered enterprise data, unless the transaction data is needed by users across multiple business departments or divisions within an organization (Figure 3.4).

That said, transaction systems are increasingly being required to support storage of large amounts of historical data detailing individual transactions to support detailed data mining and predictive analysis needs. With its growing significance for supporting big data analytics, this area is popularly referred to as big transaction data. Big transaction data is required by users across the enterprise, not just for supporting users in specific departments.

Let us look at an example to illustrate how the use of big transaction data is used in an automobile insurance firm. This type of organization can hugely benefit by saving the history-related details of insurance claim transactions made by a customer. Claim history can be very useful to analyze and predict likely customer behavior while finalizing future insurance premiums from an underwriting perspective (i.e., driving behavior, propensity of future accidents, or making false claims).

In addition to the insurance sector, the detailed use of transaction history along with mining other analytical patterns is seen extensively in several other industries such as credit card firms, airlines, and healthcare. Big data analytics is discussed in greater detail in Chapter 11.

Master Data

Master data represent core entities that are critical to an enterprise. They are usually non-transactional but help to describe elements that interact when a transaction occurs.

For these reasons, master data have often been treated as a special type of reference data—as data that are shared over a number of systems. For example, customer data could be required across several CRM processes, right through from the prospect/lead generation to customer support. Similarly, the need for reliable, product related data in manufacturing and retail sectors has led to similar interest in Product Information Management (PIM).

To fulfill the requirement across various processes requiring customer data, there needs to be a unique master data record for each instance of a customer. All of the attributes that comprise the master data record need to have a consistent set of data definitions agreed upon by data stewards across the organization. We refer to this unique instance of the master data as the golden copy for that customer. The quality and correctness of the golden copy of master data exceed that of any other representation of master data within individual or departmental applications.

Master data typically need to be shared or exchanged across the organization for the business to function effectively. Although considered non-transactional, the term non-transactional is an unnecessary qualifier here. Master data are often required by several parties involved in making transactions within an enterprise and they are an essential part of every commercial organization from day one. For instance, master data that represent the product and customer must be present before the organization can complete a transaction to sell a product to a customer (Figure 3.5).

To summarize, master data are:

- Core data of an enterprise that are critical and shared across the organization.
- Representative of business entities (e.g., customer, account, product) rather than of transactions (e.g., claims processing).

Typical Master Data Elements

Parties: Represents all parties the enterprise conducts business with such as customers, prospects, individuals, vendors, partners, etc.

Places: Represents the physical places and their segmentations such as geographies, locations, subsidiaries, sites, areas, zones, etc.

Things: Usually represents what the enterprise actually sells such as products, services, packages, items, financial services, etc.

Financial and Organizational: Represents all roll-up hierarchies used in many places for reporting and accounting purposes such as organizational structures, charts of accounts, cost centers, business units, profit centers, etc.

Figure 3.5   Examples of master data elements

- Standardized and consistent values of data (often known as the golden copy).
- Conformed to business-specified validation rules.

A major requirement for establishing integrity of master data is the need to identify unique identifiers to match and reconcile records from different systems storing master data across the enterprise. Assigning global IDs to master data records across systems and storing them in a registry to link them can be essential for identity resolution. The impact of identification-related issues on master data (or analytical data) is probably the highest among the different categories of enterprise data.

Although several characteristics of reference data are different from characteristics of master data, they have a high degree of commonality and overlap in many respects. Therefore, master and reference data are treated as distinctly separate but interrelated types of enterprise data.

Reference Data

Reference data refers to the list of common codes (or values) used by different applications across an organization. Reference data are essential to consistently define the context for business transaction details. For example, a code for the abbreviation of country (or state) may exist in different application within the organization. However, in the event of different applications having different values for the same country code, the reporting across systems would be inconsistent and unreliable. Similarly, in the world of finance, stock trades would require financial reference data such as CUSIP (or security master used for the clearing and settlement process of securities in US). In other sectors, reference information can include industry codes (retail sector), airport codes (airline sector), or clinical diagnosis codes (healthcare sector).

Reference data often consist of a code and a description. The code is usually an acronym, which is actually very useful, because acronyms can be used in system outputs, even for views of the data, and they can still be recognizable to users. Thus, the acronym USA can be used instead of the United States of America. Some reference data sets are universal such as the list of NAICS industry codes, ISO country codes, ISO currency codes (Figure 3.6), and ICD codes for healthcare.

Some of these reference codes can also be covered by a global standard (in this case, ISO 3166-1 for country codes), industry recognized codes (NAICS industry codes), or by a sector (clinical diagnosis codes, ICD 10).

Code Value	Description
AUD	Australian Dollar
EUR	European Currency
GBP	Great Britain Pound
INR	Indian Rupee
JPY	Japanese Yen
USD	US Dollar

Figure 3.6 Reference data example for ISO-specified currency codes

Typical reference data are physical such as products, material, assets, customers, or locations. Reference data can also be virtual as in cost centers, planned buildings, currency, or accounts.

Reference data are usually non-volatile; that is, they do not change frequently over time via transactions (as described in the section on "Transaction Data"), but they are ubiquitous. Thus, when a change in a code does take place, synchronizing the value across multiple systems can become extremely challenging. For example, when a government changes a currency code, such as Europe did when they integrated currency to the Euro, the impact on different financial transactions or downstream reports that compute and store tax can be an onerous task (IBM, 2013).

In some cases, one can find reference data that change more frequently. An example of such a volatile set of reference data is the security related reference data used by financial organizations for security identification, creation, trading, and settlement. There are several DaaS providers (e.g., Bloomberg) who are already providing these reference data services to their clients (mostly banks and financial organizations). Users in these organizations can conduct their daily operations with confidence, when they know that their reference data (e.g., security master) is fully verified, error-free, and reflects the latest market changes.

However, in most situations, reference data change more slowly than volatile transaction data, or even slower than the changes seen in master data.

To summarize, reference data:

- Provides context for transaction data used during a business operation.
- Are critical to have accurate integration among applications across the organization.
- Changes less frequently (non-volatile).
- Are traditionally associated with lower data volumes

In contrast to master data, the impact of identification-related issues on reference data (or analytical data) is typically less. This is partly because volumes of reference data are much lower than for master data, and also because reference data change more slowly. For reference data, most challenges tend to revolve around the use of look up codes. Reference data such as gender, nationality, country code, or customer type often consist of a code and a description, probably little else. The code is usually an acronym, which is actually very useful, because acronyms can be used in system outputs, and even in views of the data can still be recognizable to users. Thus, the acronym NY can be used instead of New York.

Analytical Data

Traditionally, IT organizations have focused most of their analytical efforts on applications using structured data (sourced from relational databases and data warehouses) while largely ignoring unstructured data. In the world of data warehousing, one often replaces transaction and reference data with facts and conformed dimensions to support reporting and analytic needs.

Data warehouses were initially designed to meet the business intelligence and analytical needs of the entire organization storing historical data from a large variety of operational and external data sources. Every record in the data warehouse was considered accurate, relative to a moment in time (more like a snapshot). There were also no updates necessary in traditional data warehouses during normal processing cycles. Consequently, historical data stored in the data warehouse is often considered less volatile than operational systems.

For supporting the analytic needs of their business users, organizations often built departmental datamarts with feeds from the enterprise data warehouse. The focus of these datamarts was on supporting business intelligence, strategic decision making, and analysis by senior management.

Analysis by data warehouse and BI users is typically more ad-hoc in nature and involves asking a series of questions that meaning slicing data in numerous ways. In consequence, analytical data is represented through dimensional data models comprising facts and dimensions.

Fact tables represent common business measures that need to be tracked for analytical needs. Dimensions serve as the primary mechanism to link fact tables. They also are used as filter constraints while users run reports or queries. Therefore instead of using natural keys for defining codes in reference data, in the world of analytics, data mart designers like to use artificial keys known as data warehousing surrogate keys, due to the need to track slowly changing dimensions gathered from multiple operational systems over a period of time.

To summarize, analytical data:

- Primarily supports senior management and analytic users in the organization.
- Supports ad-hoc querying of business facts that need to grouped by different dimension flexibly to support BI and analytical needs.
- Stores large volumes of historical data gathered from a range of operational systems.
- Are largely nonvolatile with limited need for processing updates in data warehouses.
- Conforms to business-specified validation rules.

While historical data in data warehousing and data marts have been extremely beneficial for analytic usage in the last couple of decades, their heavy dependency on traditional database platforms employing structured data is now becoming a bottleneck for supporting other forms of data.

Too many organizations were unaware of the immense potential in using unstructured data, semi-structured data, and text data for predictive analytics. It almost never existed, until the advent of new big data platforms that could provide capabilities for dealing with high volumes and velocity to ingest unstructured data files that were massive in size. These data are generated in multiple formats ranging from human-generated feeds (social media, blogs, web postings, etc.) to machine-generated feeds (data collected from sensor readings, RFID, GPS, biometric feeds, etc.). Big transaction data such as healthcare claims, telephone call detail records (CDRs), and billing records were also only available in semi-structured formats.

With the explosion of data received over the web, enterprises now need to focus more heavily on unstructured data and semi-structured data being received from the external marketplace. Slowly but surely, there is growing realization that businesses can gain extremely valuable analytical insights by mining detail transaction data for predictive analytics and competitive intelligence purposes.

TRANSACTION DATA (INCLUDES BIG DATA)

Within any organization, every external or internal business event that gets recorded by its IT systems is a transaction meant for business processing. Transaction databases capture the events that take place as an organization conducts its business and stores them for further processing by their users. An example of transaction data being generated can be when a customer makes an online flight reservation with an airline. Each record in the airline reservation database captures the details of the individual transaction like reservation transaction identifier (PNR), flight number, flight date, originating airport, destination, passenger name, Age, fare charged, and so on.

However, the day-to-day transactions that run an organization can produce extremely large volumes of transaction data so storing their history data was often ignored. For example, tracking the status of every shipment may need to be retained for a limited time by a freight transportation company (perhaps until the customer receives the shipment). However, with the advent of big data analytics, organizations now need to store even those details to conduct predictive analysis of their optimal route to ship packages in future.

Big data is a popular term to describe specific types of transaction data that have the following characteristics.

- Extremely large volume
- Being captured at a high velocity/dynamism
- Usually comprised of a variety of structured and unstructured data
- A large section of the unstructured data gets sourced from external sources (e.g., web site logs, email, SMS, video, twitter, social media)

In the future, business users and decision makers are likely to move their focus from BI and warehouse environments, and depend more heavily on big data transactional engagement models. This will largely be caused by the realization that the raw computing power provided by big data platforms can be very effective for conducting predictive analysis on large volumes of structured and unstructured data.

Some of the fundamental success criteria while designing sophisticated big data, analytical applications are very different from those required for traditional data. For example, the police department in a large European metropolis has resorted to analyzing large amounts of data from confiscated hard drives, cell phones, and USB drives to perform text analytics that identify the most common words in emails and chats. To predict criminal behavior accurately, the analysis has to support real-time decisions. This form of predictive analytics often uses data mining patterns on huge amounts of data. This is very different from the traditional data warehouse or BI application, where these systems provide BI information based on historic data. Moreover, the prediction of consumer behavior (e.g., fraud detection) in big data systems has to be designed based on probabilistic models and needs to rely less on deterministic modeling.

Unfortunately, the majority of IT organizations have been slow to react to the demands of unstructured text mining and big data analytics. In some cases, they have made a huge effort to respond to demands from stakeholders to provide insights and analytical capabilities to leverage some of their unstructured text data.

However, it can be said that organizations that leverage both their structured and unstructured data together in a real-time, managed environment can gain the ultimate competitive advantage: they will find opportunities to optimize their business processes and strategic decision-making capabilities.

Chapter 11 looks at how companies can take a more holistic approach toward integrating big transaction data and analytics for supporting reusable data services. However, consolidation of these disparate forms of data can only be done by taking appropriate steps to have a comprehensive and balanced data management strategy across the enterprise covering structured, semi-structured, and unstructured data.

Comparing Various Types of Enterprise Data

In order to truly understand the significance of enterprise data, let us now highlight some of their key features and benefits to an organization. This section will also help readers identify major features seen among different types of enterprise data.

Enterprise data should be recognized as an area that is not homogenous by nature. As noted earlier in this chapter, different categories of enterprise data have their own unique characteristics. Unfortunately, projects that approach enterprise data as homogeneous fail to address the unique needs and challenges posed by each type of data, and may encounter problems in the long term.

In summary, there are a few major differences among the various types of enterprise data: reference, master, transactional, and analytical data. From an illustrative perspective, the table in Figure 3.7 shows a comparison of how various enterprise data categories can be used in a real-life environment.

After examining the differences between major categories of enterprise data, we can conclude that a single approach is never going to be sufficient to address

	Reference Data	Master Data	Analytical Data	Big Data
Business Purpose	Consistent use of reference codes	Improved data quality and integration drives reuse of core business data	Reporting & Analysis	Specific business function
System Orientation	Provides commonly used codes and values across enterprise	Provides official record for critical business object used across an organization	Provides historical data for Business Intelligence	Provides transaction details for predictive analytics
System Availability	Low	Medium	High	High
Volatility	Low	Medium	Medium	Highly Volatile
Typical Usage	Supports daily operation	Authoritative Source	Supports business analysis for decision-making	Supports long-term decision by strategic leaders
Level of Detail	Atomic level	Low	Summarized	Raw Detailed Data
Volume	Low	Medium	High	Extremely High

Figure 3.7   Example of real-life usage of enterprise data

problems. The challenges faced by different categories of enterprise data are unique and will be addressed separately in Chapters 9, 10, and 11 of this book.

However, while there are differences between enterprise data in some of these detailed features, there are also important linkages that can allow an organization to adopt common approaches toward standardization and publication services of various enterprise data types (data governance issues are discussed in Chapter 12). This is particularly true in enterprises where business operations are not well integrated with information delivery systems. The next section addresses how often most organizations lack a standard information delivery system in relation to sharing enterprise data.

SIGNIFICANCE OF EIM IN SUPPORTING THE DaaS PROGRAM

Data asset management typically involves long-term planning, directing, governing, and supervising the utilization of data in an effective manner. The implementation of data asset management is most effective within an organization when its supported by EIM policies that aim to improve data quality and governance.

In the context of published data services, a critical prerequisite for any corporate DaaS initiative is to provide a consistent view of their enterprise data that can be trusted by the business users. Without the presence of certain EIM capabilities and configurable components such as shared business vocabulary key terms, common enterprise models, and business rules, users cannot be expected to rely on the veracity of the data distributed by the DaaS provider.

In many internal DaaS programs, business sponsors rush to take tactical steps to ensure quick wins for deploying data services without resolving underlying data quality and consistency issues in their current data sources. They are often encouraged by some vendors to use their tools in hope they will provide an easy way out for the business to obtain integrated views that bring together disparate data from multiple sources. However, the reality is that usually these IT tools (based on data virtualization, data federation, data integration, workflow, etc.) cannot provide a comprehensive solution by themselves.

Ultimately, the capability of any tool can only go so far. The mess created by the lack of an enterprise system plan or governance in a large organization can lead to complex data quality and integration challenges that cannot be magically solved by a vendor solution. Subsequently, to resolve these concerns, organizations have to introduce EIM capabilities in a planned manner. They need to treat data and all other types of enterprise information as corporate assets (Ladley, 2010). The EIM program has to be viewed primarily as a strategic program, which should set up processes to preserve integrity, consistency, and security of data from the time it is entered in the authoritative source to the time the data is published for a data service subscriber.

The role of EIM in building the future DaaS roadmap is also crucial from a project planning perspective. It can show the key stakeholders and sponsors in a company how best to align their existing and future DaaS project initiative into their corporate business strategy (Figure 3.8).

ROLE OF ENTERPRISE DATA ARCHITECT

The enterprise data architect role in any IT organization can be compared to a city planner or urban architect who plans cities or builds buildings. In the domain of data specifically, the enterprise data architect (EDA) has a major role in identifying the enterprise data strategy initially as well as supporting the DAM-specific activities later on. Furthermore, a good EDA also enables stakeholders with their expertise in achieving the right balance between IT efficiency, business innovation, and risk mitigation.

Typically, any major business transformation within an enterprise calls for radical data infrastructure-related changes to the existing environment. More often than not, a major change driven by business requires IT to initiate a review of their underlying infrastructure to see if it can support the change. Often, key people identify the areas of change that are required in order for new business goals to be met. These people are commonly referred to as the stakeholders in the change process. These leaders know that effective management and exploitation of information through IT is a key factor to business success, and an indispensable means toward achieving competitive advantage. Thus, stakeholders often champion the initiative across the enterprise's leadership and build a case for funding purposes.

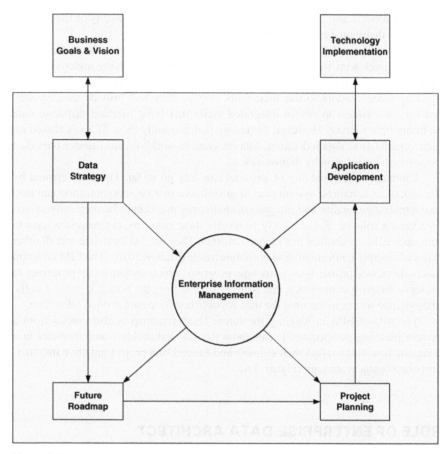

Figure 3.8   Role of EIM in building future DaaS roadmaps

The role of EDA is to address the DaaS stakeholders' concerns by:

- Identifying and refining the information flow and related requirements that stakeholders have.
- Developing views of the conceptual architecture with data models that show how concerns and requirements are going to be addressed.
- Showing the trade-offs that are going to be made in reconciling potentially conflicting concerns of different stakeholders.

Without the enterprise data architect formally defining the overall portfolio of enterprise data for a major program such as EDS, it is highly unlikely that all the concerns and requirements will be considered and met. These individuals need to have a broad range of skills ranging from business communication skills to an understanding of database design principles. To make a difference in this role, these architects need to be able to understand business problems from the business domain, and understand the ramifications from a long-term, enterprise-system planning perspective (often focusing on EIM and data governance issues). They should then translate these needs for the benefit of the technical architects and application development managers.

Ultimately, no matter how advanced or progressive an architecture structure laid out by architects, the success of the initiative comes from how well people collaborate to make it happen. Specifically, the technical architects responsible for the implementation of plans have to be able to understand the plans from the EDAs and build the appropriate systems.

However, the role of the EDA is still critical, as she/he needs to explain the technical possibilities to business people and the technology leads who are responsible for implementing the individual technology component of the proposed data solution and architecture. This is very similar to the field of civil engineering and architecture; it is the architect who has to explain the design to the building sponsor(s), the person who is funding a building or city. In reality, the architect typically presents multiple solution possibilities for the proposed building, explaining the various pros and cons of each design option.

After the sponsors indicate their preferred solution option and give the go ahead to start the building development activities, the architect eventually has to provide the blueprint to the builders, specifying what the owners of the building want in a language that the builders can understand.

However, deep technical experience and skills are a must for enterprise data architects, as they need to be knowledgeable on industry-wide data related design standards, and yet they need to be realistic enough to be able to listen to practical advice from the teams implementing the architect's solution.

SUMMARY

Organizations have to ensure that their data assets are well governed and managed over the long term. Ensuring data is being treated as assets in a finance and accounting sense helps organizations in several ways. A good data asset management plan can help an organization:

- Exploit the true value of their data assets.
- Mitigate risk of improper use of the data assets.
- Improve quality of data owned.

Data Asset Management typically involves long-term planning, directing, governing, and supervising the utilization of data in an effective manner. The implementation of DAM is most effective within an organization when they support EIM policies that aim to improve data quality and governance.

This chapter covered major categories of data that can be considered significant to the enterprise to support DaaS. These categories include master data, reference data, analytical data, and big data. It is important for a designer of data services to be aware of the distinctive characteristics of different types of enterprise data, as this results in different design specifications for EDS publication with respect to their initial publication, operational performance, and maintenance.

A special emphasis has been placed on understanding the challenges of managing unstructured and semi-structured data because of the increasing urgency felt in business organizations to utilize the content of these forms of data in big data analytic applications.

Part Two

DaaS Architecture Framework and Components

Chapter 4

Enterprise Data Services

TOPICS COVERED IN THIS CHAPTER

- This chapter provides a brief overview of how an organization can publish their enterprise data through a set of standardized service interfaces to enable data sharing and interoperability across systems. It discusses overarching principles required for developing standardized and consistent data services that enable data sharing, reuse, and interoperability.

- The various enterprise architecture (EA), enterprise information management (EIM), and service-oriented architecture (SOA) principles required to make a data service successful and relevant across the enterprise are also examined. These disciplines are mutually independent, although they often drive each other.

- A case study is discussed that illustrates how data-driven organizations can transform their business by enabling data sharing and interoperability across teams by using standardized data service interfaces across the enterprise.

- Finally, the foundational role of DaaS in supporting big data and analytics applications are briefly explored.

With data collection, 'The sooner the better' is always the best answer.

—Marissa Mayer, CEO, Yahoo

This chapter emphasizes the need for publishing common, reusable data services to distribute enterprise data to data consumers across an organization. Data sharing and reuse across an enterprise in a timely manner results in improved and effective decision making. Usage of shared data also results in improved quality of data and cost savings as existing data structures get reused.

By implementing data services as a virtual data integration layer between data consumers and existing data sources, most organizations can eliminate the need for physical data consolidation or replicate data in multiple databases. The virtual data

Data as a Service: A Framework for Providing Reusable Enterprise Data Services,
First Edition. Pushpak Sarkar.
© 2015 the IEEE Computer Society. Published 2015 by John Wiley & Sons, Inc.

integration layer becomes especially useful in big data environments. The virtual data access layer can extract data from multiple data sources on heterogeneous platforms (relational data, unstructured data like social media feeds, files, etc.) to provide an integrated view after aggregating the relevant data. The virtualization approach using well-governed data services is increasingly popular as it successfully hides the underlying complexity of data integration from end users while ensuring appropriate privacy controls.

EMERGENCE OF ENTERPRISE DATA SERVICES

In a business environment with increasing competition, the time to market is crucial for most organizations. Organizations need successful IT delivery to quickly meet business demands. Business trends like increased globalization are driving the need for organizations to support easier data exchange and access with customers, vendors, and regulators around the world. There are also several socioeconomic and techno-logical factors that make DaaS an increasingly attractive option to more people and organizations (Figure 4.1). For example, technological advances such as an increased use of mobile devices for consumer purchases and marketing efforts via social media are driving organizations to support a self-service model for consumers using reliable and secure data services across an enterprise.

In addition, the organizational need for electronic sharing of data with customers has seen a wider acceptance due to other socio-technological advances such as the convergence of the Cloud, analytics, mobile, and social media (CAMS). For example, Cloud computing encourages the use of externally hosted computing resources that

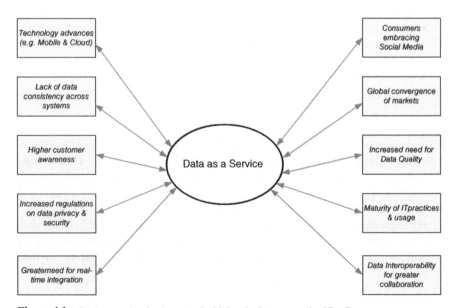

Figure 4.1   Business and technology trends driving the future growth of DaaS

are delivered as a service over a network (Monaco, 2012). Organizations that enable customers to access enterprise data (or analytical results derived from the data) over their mobile devices or social media can herald a new way of doing business. There are many subcategories of public Cloud computing that offer specific resources such as Platform as a Service (PaaS) and Infrastructure as a service (IaaS).

The downstream effects of creating these new products affect not only an organization's numerous departments but they also impact external partners. As if this is not a sufficient factor for motivation, many organizations are subject to increasing scrutiny by government agencies while releasing customer data. Frequent incidents of data breaches have highlighted the need for increased adherence to data privacy compliance and regulation, reporting, and risk.

NEED FOR AN ENTERPRISE PERSPECTIVE

Business organizations are increasingly driven to transform as providers of value-added services, often packaged to be useful and necessary to consumers to fulfill some of their daily needs. This concept is not entirely new or radically different from the traditional definition of a service. As per *Merriam-Webster's* dictionary, a service is defined as a "facility supplying some public demand." Therefore, a utility company provides households with water or electricity whereas insurance companies exist in the marketplace to fulfill the need felt by most people for security and well-being.

Similarly, DaaS helps an enterprise's clients by delivering trusted information to them in real time, regardless of the underlying platform(s) on which the underlying data is stored. DaaS achieves this key objective by ensuring consistent data formats, consistent application of rules to process data, data models, and centralized control and governance. To publish reliable data to consumers, there also needs to be agreement on data service characteristics and they must be commonly available. Definition (structure and semantics), data quality and integrity, and governance to ensure uniform and consistent changes of the service's underlying information needs are three of the most important characteristics.

Defining an Enterprise Data Service

The term *service* is not a new concept and has been used extensively in many business sectors. Defined by *Merriam Webster's Collegiate* dictionary as "a facility supplying some public demand," allows any utility or system that is responsible for supplying a public need such as transportation services or utilities like water or electricity to be considered a service. Even within the IT sector, we have seen the emergence of various types of services.

In the context of DaaS, think of an enterprise data service as a remotely accessible, self-contained application module (Krafzig, 2007) that provides virtualized access to any form of enterprise data. Enterprise data services are not designed for a specific consumer or a select group of consumers. Instead, they provides data-related functionality that is reusable across the enterprise. Some data services can also provide access to external consumers who are authorized to access the data assets of a company.

From a technical perspective, enterprise data services help clients of an enterprise identify, access, manage, secure, and deliver data in real time regardless of the type of information or the platform on which it is stored. The DaaS framework achieves this by ensuring consistent data formats, data models and common vocabulary, consistent application of rules to process the data, along with governance of underlying data services.

Many organizations also need to understand customer sentiment by keeping their ears close to the world of social media. They need to read and respond to their Twitter posts and blogs, and measure customer feedback using sophisticated natural language processing. Analyzing customer sentiments (often their likes and dislikes) can help generate predictive insights for companies. Decisions can then be made in a timely manner after mining these huge amounts of gathered data.

To support this new user segment, IT departments supporting business operations have to provide enterprise data (and analytics) as a service to internal and external data consumers, sooner rather than later. These trends are illustrated throughout this book with examples drawn from a range of industries covering retail to finance to healthcare providers. As discussed previously, the widely held belief of industry professional is that most organizations have to embrace these trends to support increasing pressure from stakeholders to support data and analytical needs for the foreseeable future (and perhaps forever).

Similar to public utilities, banks, or insurance firms, most IT organizations also need to view themselves from a new perspective as a service provider. They exist primarily as service providers responsible for providing high quality information accompanied with innovative analytics as services for their consumers, both inside the company as well as to external consumers and agencies. Moreover, just like new categories of financial products are being created on a regular basis by investment banks, IT service providers also have to provide innovative ways to analyze information gathered over various channels. The latest analytic models and technologies to help mine all this underlying data can help decision makers with real-time intelligence in order to stay ahead of their market competitors.

EMERGENCE OF ENTERPRISE DATA SERVICES

Traditional data applications had a preference toward building monolithic applications with data stored in silos across a disparate environment. Often, the concept of data services was limited to implementing a series of database queries exposed as web services to access data from legacy stores. However, since these services were not found through any enterprise information management (EIM) or data governance concepts often these tactical solutions provided limited value as the services were neither consistent nor reusable across the enterprise.

In contrast to this, the DaaS framework leverages enterprise data services (EDS) that are tied to underlying enterprise and canonical models. It also provides organizations with a set of data governance principles to ensure the data published is reliable, accurate, and consistent.

Data as a Service helps clients of an enterprise identify, access, manage, secure, and deliver information in real time regardless of the type of information or platform on which it is stored. DaaS achieves this by ensuring consistent data formats, consistent application of rules to process the data, data models and centralized control and governance. To publish reliable data to consumers, one needs to agree on a number of characteristics and have it commonly available: (1) definition (structure and semantics), (2) data quality and integrity, and (3) governance, changes to the service and the underlying information need to be governed in a uniform and consistent manner.

The key underlying feature that DaaS leverages is the usage of several newer techniques (e.g., data virtualization and stream computing) that can help improve access performance by reducing the underlying complexity involved in consolidating data from multiple systems. Use of data virtualization tools can also allow users to access data from structured and unstructured data sources (enabling support to big data implementations). By implementing DaaS as a virtual data integration layer between data consumers and existing data sources, an organization can also eliminate the need for physical data consolidation or replicate data in multiple databases. The virtual data integration layer becomes very useful in the big data environment as the federated layer can extract data from multiple data sources on heterogeneous platforms (relational data, unstructured data like social media feeds, files, etc), providing an integrated view and aggregating the relevant data. The virtualization approach is increasingly popular as it successfully hides the underlying complexity of data integration from end users.

Chapter 7 covers in more detail on various technology components specified in the reference architecture that need to be considered while setting up a DaaS program. However, having a functional understanding of EDS components is crucial for implementing a DaaS program. The next section provides a function-based overview of some of the key EDS building blocks (Figure 4.2).

Architecture and Strategy

The architectural blueprint plays a key role in enabling effective management and distribution of data within an enterprise leveraging data services. The blueprint translates DaaS principles in the context of an individual organization, allowing it to achieve a competitive advantage against other competitors in its industry. An enterprise data strategy addresses this need for DaaS by providing a strategic context for the evolution of data services requested from service consumers in response to the constantly changing needs of the business environment.

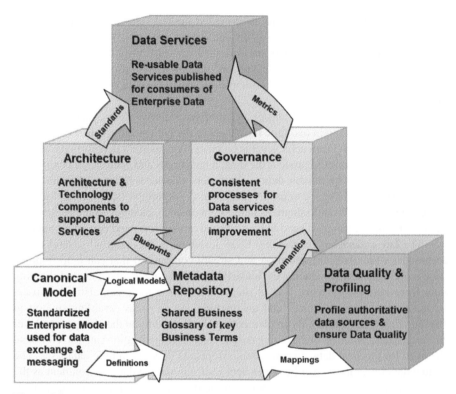

Figure 4.2 Building blocks of a typical enterprise data service

Governance Process

A fragmented and inconsistent set of legacy processes (both manual and automated) can often be found across different parts of many businesses. The purpose of governance is to streamline information flow, major business services, and their processes within the extended enterprise. Focusing on governance can enable a DaaS program to successfully engender an integrated environment that is responsive to change and supportive of delivering business strategy.

Reusable Data Services

A properly architected EDS layer means a fundamental shift away from traditional development. It leads to a more nimble use of semantic vocabularies, data virtualization, and security components. This approach brings other standardizing aspects that act as a foundation for the DaaS platform. It replaces point-to-point connections with a standardized set of published services that enable data subscribers to access and reuse data on demand, at the time and place of their choice. The use of data virtualization technologies can further support performance and scalability needs that are essential for large organizations to enhance customer satisfaction.

Service Delivery

Successful execution of DaaS strategy largely depends on technology architecture, design, and integration solutions being adopted to implement the DaaS roadmap in an effective manner that meets the needs of an enterprise's major stakeholders. Several key technology deployment patterns play a crucial role in a DaaS provider meeting the SLA requirements of their stakeholders after DaaS implementation (e.g., service availability, runtime performance, and scalability).

To publish reliable data to consumers, DaaS stakeholders and architects need to agree at the outset on the three most important characteristics discussed earlier and have them commonly available. However, to successfully implement data services, all source applications generating any form of enterprise data (for use across the organization) have to transform their enterprise data elements identified for publication to a standardized data model designed for data exchange. The process on how to go about creating this standardized model (also known as a canonical model) and how to use it for publication of EDS is discussed at length in Chapter 5. The critical enterprise data elements identified by the organization for publication also need to adopt common semantic definitions that are formally agreed upon by data stewards. The significance of maintaining a common business glossary while setting up publication services for enterprise data is discussed in more detail in Chapter 6.

The other feature that EDS implementation can leverage is use of increased data federation techniques that can also allow users to access data from structured and unstructured data sources (enabling support to big data implementations). By implementing data services in the form of a virtual data integration layer between data consumers and existing data sources, organizations also eliminate the need for physical data consolidation or replicate data in multiple databases.

Let us now look at the detailed process associated with publishing enterprise data using a data service.

PUBLICATION OF ENTERPRISE DATA

This section focuses on the need for standardization of enterprise data to enable data reuse and sharing across an organization (as well as with external subscribers). The publication of enterprise data require organizations to publish standardized data services that leverage underlying service-oriented architecture (SOA) and EIM principles to make them reusable and consistent across the organization. Authorized data subscribers can then obtain the latest version of enterprise data by accessing enterprise data services.

To summarize this approach briefly, each source application publishes enterprise data across the organization leveraging enterprise data services. Then the service takes critical data elements from different source applications within the organization and

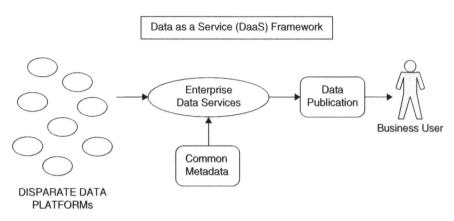

Figure 4.3   Publication of enterprise data services within the DaaS framework

makes it available to consumers who need enterprise data using a standardized format for delivering data (Figure 4.3).

The following items are key criteria for assessing publication and delivery of enterprise data to subscribers using data services.

- The data service must supply data to all consumers or subscribers of the data service within SLA and timelines that are predefined and agreed upon by key stakeholders and consumers.

- The data service provider should ensure that data provided by the service has data integrity, follow consistent data standards, and data definitions.

- The delivery infrastructure must be robust and allow data exchange between various kinds of applications, hosted on various system platforms.

- The publishing mechanism of the service provider should ensure that information published by the service meets data and messaging/xml standards to ensure system interoperability.

- The data publication and delivery mechanism must be scalable and be able to ensure service levels as the number of service subscribers increase.

- The information published via the Data Services component has to be delivered in a secure manner to subscribers authorized to access it, based on enterprise data security and privacy policies.

When evaluating the quality of an enterprise data service, an organization needs to assess not only the service delivery mechanism used for publishing but also ensure that the enterprise data published by the organization meets the expectations of data subscribers (both internal and external).

The significance of on-demand data services to customers has increased with the ever increasing shift toward Cloud and mobile computing. Most organizations now need to make data available to consumers at the time and place of their choice by publishing services that deliver information quickly. Leading companies like social media trendsetter Facebook have clearly shifted their development efforts toward the mobile computing platform. There are also find several vendors promoting IT software products on the Cloud such as Salesforce.com. Consequently, IT leadership in these companies feel more pressure to offer some of their enterprise data as a service on a diverse range of platforms.

To summarize then, the goal of EDS is to introduce a virtual data access layer supported by electronic messages that are reusable and meet overall governance standards to reduce the complexity of data integration faced by many organizations. The role of EDS is going to continue expanding within more organizations into the future. This will be caused largely by new technology factors driving change in organizations' interactions with business partners and customer base. The reference architecture, principle, and technology components suggested for EDS in this book are based on my own practical experiences in developing EDS components at several large organizations.

For example, at United Healthcare I led efforts to introduce the use of EDS to share provider data with customers online, using the DaaS framework components described in this book such as the enterprise canonical model, business glossary, XML schemas, etc. These components can play a pivotal role for allowing physicians, nurses, and other healthcare professionals to access electronic medical record (EMR, also known as electronic health record). In contrast to current scenarios in which the exchange of information can be extremely time consuming and frustrating, because EDS was set up by the healthcare organization medical data consumers can now share information quickly. This enables healthcare professionals to work more efficiently and make better quality decisions collectively.

There is also a recent trend seen toward greater use of data virtualization and related technologies to improve access to data through services. Currently, some of the software tools available in the market help aggregate data from various sources. These data virtualization tools can abstract the physical implementation details stored in underlying data repositories and make them appear as a single physical data store for consolidated EDS services to publish a virtual, unified view of the enterprise. The separation of logical and physical layers by using reusable data services enables IT organizations to make future application enhancements faster and easier.

Currently, in most organizations, data are difficult to access largely because various forms of enterprise data are typically buried across multiple applications, often on disparate platforms. Most IT professionals are familiar with the challenges faced because of data integration to support consuming applications or users trying to access enterprise data. They can also appreciate the potential of data virtualization as technology matures to support both conventional structured data sources with new forms of semi-structured or text data generated for data mining and big data analytic applications (Figure 4.4).

To summarize the value and benefits discussed earlier in this chapter, one can safely conclude that introducing reusable EDS can reduce application development and maintenance costs. It can also make it easier for IT departments to comply with increasing government regulations on standardized reference data and code sets.

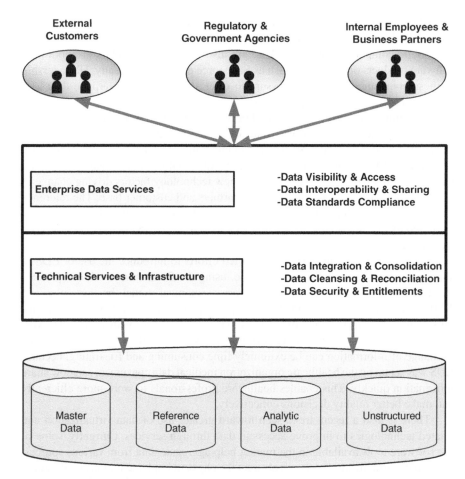

Figure 4.4 Getting virtual enterprise access with data services

---

Major Drivers for Adopting Reusable Enterprise Data Services

– Provide a consistent enterprise view of data across an organization

– Use a common and shared business vocabulary for usage

– Make data available to consumers easier and faster

– Ensure compliance to industry standards on privacy of sensitive data

– Facilitate data interoperability/sharing with major partners

– Reduce maintenance costs through reuse and less rework

– Prevent investments in redundant systems

– Ease of administration and compatibility among diverse platforms

– Facilitate consistent reporting

INTERDEPENDENCIES BETWEEN DaaS, EIM, AND SOA

From a technology perspective, it is important to understand organizations that are interested in providing DaaS often end up with limited success if the development teams build data services without aligning their efforts to an enterprise data strategy and its key components such as data models, metadata, enterprise SOA standards, etc.

Figure 4.5 illustrates the multiple disciplines necessary to build reusable data services. Organizations need all of these specialized components to work together as pillars of the DaaS framework. Only by adopting a multidisciplinary approach can the finalized solution be suitable for meeting a large organization's information publishing and distribution needs. For instance, some organizations can deploy data services based solely on an SOA solution with no data integration, governance, or master data management (MDM) strategy in place. This can make the overall solution untenable for enterprise usage in most cases due to the inconsistent data quality. The problem is further accentuated in organizations when dealing with huge volumes of data or with no consistency in data governance practices across the enterprise. Therefore, using complicated queries to link data across multiple systems on a thin messaging layer is often not scalable. It also fails to meet the performance expectations of data service consumers when they try to access the data service concurrently. DaaS can improve the overall quality of data because it is a framework that leverages best practices and technology components from multiple disciplines.

Given this context, it is clear to most IT architects and enterprise application planners that there is practical necessity in focusing on building enterprise data models, a shared business vocabulary, and standardized XML messaging formats in the initial phases of implementing DaaS. These foundational components are absolutely essential for achieving a successful implementation that meets the long-term business needs of users. This chapter discussed enterprise disciplines (EIM, SOA, and EA), all of which are relevant to DaaS.

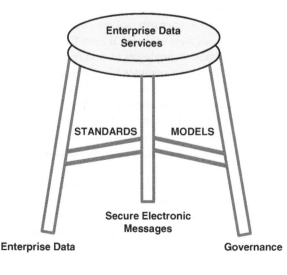

Figure 4.5

Multi-disciplinary approach to building reusable data services

Next, this chapter explains how data sharing and interoperability capabilities of the DaaS framework can improve prospects of big data and predictive analytics initiatives.

Role of Enterprise Data Services in Supporting Big Data and Predictive Analytics

With the explosion of data, enterprises see a growing need to focus more heavily on unstructured data, text, and semi-structured data being received from external marketplaces and social networking sites.

Amidst these increasing data volumes, diversity, and complexity of data sources, IT managers are being asked to address requests to process and distribute several forms of data including:

- Structured data, e.g., relational databases.
- Semi-structured data, e.g., text files.
- Unstructured data, e.g., images, sounds, and videos images, etc., which are actually structured with some internal "metadata" and a documented, standard structure.

Some of the drivers while designing these big data applications can be very different from those for traditional data. However, there is growing realization that businesses can gain valuable market insights by mining this voluminous data for predictive analytics and competitive intelligence purposes. Figure 4.6 illustrates the evolving role of big data analytics.

For instance, some retail-based companies are using social-networking data—Facebook and Twitter—to carry out sentiment analyses. They are using word count analytics involving customer interactions to predict future behavior. In many situations, big data streams are combined with the data received from internal business applications, data warehouses, as well as from other external information providers selling information for a particular market segment (e.g., D&B from Chapter 1).

Several companies are leveraging the latest technologies to modify their business model with sentiment analysis. A recent article in *Computer World* noted that a leading international hotel chain had earlier launched the first version of its social-media analysis platform (Twentyman, 2011). One of the most important goals of this collaboration was to gain useful insights into how the hotel's brand was perceived online, what kind of sentiment surrounded the brand, and who the brand's followers were across the world in terms of demographics (e.g., age, income, gender, travel and lifestyle preferences).

There has also been much interest in predictive analytical services across sectors such as financial services, insurance, and healthcare. In the healthcare sector, for instance, many organizations are moving beyond early experiments in predictive analytics. Some organizations have invested heavily in a big data platform that can support a range of predictive analyses and data mining tools. As such, the healthcare

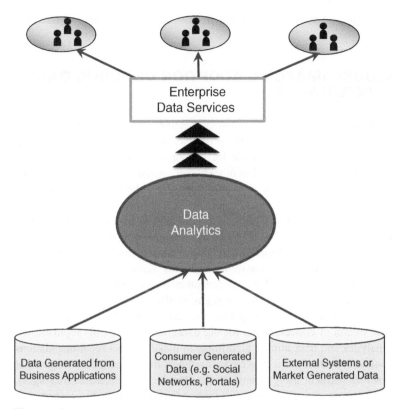

Figure 4.6   Evolving role of big data analytics

community of clinical data scientists is trying to determine answers to key questions such as:

- How to use genetic and clinical data to develop more effective therapies and personalized medicine?
- How to unlock the insights stored in massive amounts of observational data from the healthcare system?
- How to establish which individual treatment will work for which group of patients?

Due to the complexity and immense processing power required to analyze big data, many organizations still have not utilized the power of these new untapped data sources for predictive analytics. Yet social media, big data, and predictive analytics will continually become more important to businesses. Therefore, organizations' IT departments will have to provide enterprise data (and analytics) as a service to internal and external data consumers to support future business needs. As shared earlier, the widely held belief of industry experts is that most organizations will have to embrace these trends to support increasing pressure from stakeholders to support data and analytical needs.

CASE STUDY: AMAZON'S ADOPTION OF PUBLIC DATA SERVICE INTERFACES

This chapter closes with the real-life example of Amazon, an organization that clearly understood the significance of using enterprise-wide services (both data and functionality) as their company grew larger for supporting application programming interfaces (APIs). Amazon's leadership quickly recognized the need to set up public data services to support reliable data exchange across the enterprise and for its customers.

What differentiates a leading online retailer such as Amazon from its competitors is its intelligent use of data collected from its consumers on the web and social networks, and its reuse of this information for innovative customer loyalty, marketing, and online promotions to specific consumer segments. Each click on their website is collected and organized to understand consumer buying behavior, pricing, and product preferences. The retail bookstore segment also analyzes text available on social media for sentiment, readership choices, and other consumer preferences. Based on this wealth of collected data (or big data), the retailer runs sophisticated predictive analytics and data-mining algorithms to make product recommendations to specific online consumers or it runs customized advertising campaigns targeted at a select consumer segment using a range of data services (or electronic messages). Figure 4.7 shows an overview of Amazon's range of services offered to customers.

Some of the key sets of data gathered from customers often include:

1. Pre-sales product recommendations to customers.
2. Price comparisons with competing products.
3. Price alert messages for a product that the customer has saved on their shopping cart but not purchased.
4. Post-sales support to customer.
5. Customer survey on their online experience shopping with Amazon.

Amazon can then reuse all the collected data for supporting innovative customer loyalty programs and targeted online marketing promotions to specific consumer segments. Often, the retailer sends messages to Amazon Prime Customer with offers on selected products, targeting them if their profile meets the criteria set by the big data analytics algorithms created by data scientists. They can also receive follow-up messages with a promotion code to remind them to stop by the store if they want to take advantage of the offer by a certain expiration date.

After the consumer complete his or her online purchase, Amazon solicits direct feedback from the customer on his or her shopping experience with the product a few months after the purchase. In some cases, the retailer conducts surveys on a select line of products. The comments received is the feedback used by the company for future product catalog decisions.

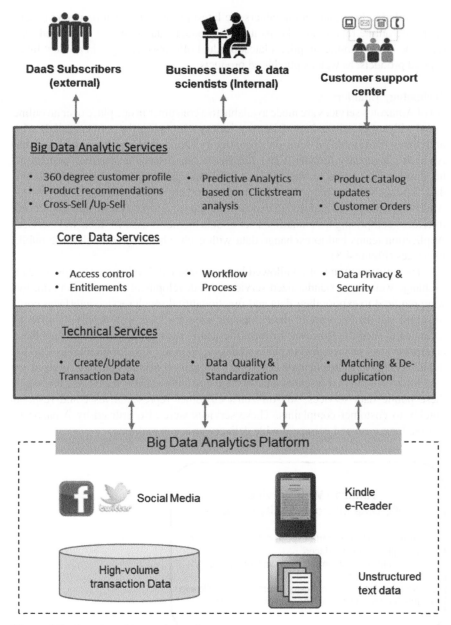

Figure 4.7   Overview of data services at Amazon

Updated real-time information on consumer preferences on books, videos, and games are based on the latest activity feeds from social media, and the data gets published at regular intervals for Amazon Prime Service and other authorized subscribers.

Similarly, the organization gathers the latest product information from the supplier. The online retailer also keeps its own product catalog, which is updated on a real-time basis with the supplier's latest product offerings, changes in product lines, expired products, as well as purchased products.

Technology Enablers

All of Amazon's services are made available to a consumer in one place over an online portal with a sophisticated set of data services synchronizing the portal regularly with underlying data stored on Amazon's proprietary Cloud platform. It was reported that Amazon's legendary founder, CEO Jeff Bezos, also issued an internal mandate to his development teams around 2002 or 2003 that the use of standardized web and data services was mandatory to support the company's APIs (Furrier, 2011). All of Amazon's teams were required to expose their data and functionality through service interfaces comprising a standardized set of data elements used for their web service. Application teams had to exchange data with each other only through these public interfaces (Figure 4.8).

The only communication allowed between internal development teams for data exchange were these standardized services. All development teams within Amazon were required to expose their data and functionality through service interfaces comprising a standardized set of data elements used for their web service (similar to a canonical model). However, in turn, the teams responsible for developing these enterprise-level services had to plan and design them not only for internal use but for public APIs used by application developers and data consumers outside Amazon.

Amazon's internal research analysts and customer support teams also leveraged these public data services, so Amazon's customer representatives could respond quickly to customer complaints. These services were also utilized by Amazon to resolve long-term and company-wide delivery issues in real time.

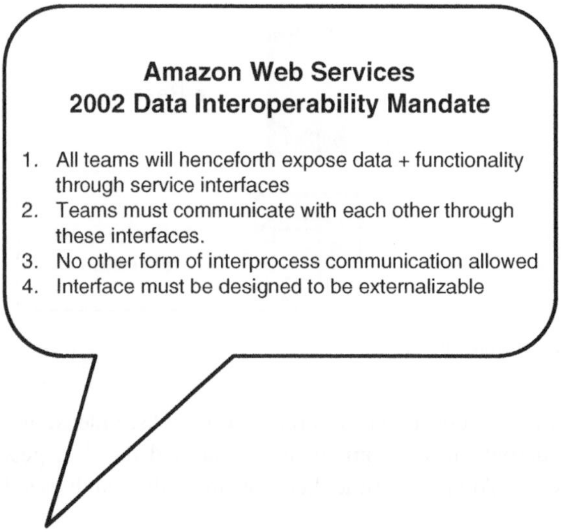

**Amazon Web Services
2002 Data Interoperability Mandate**

1. All teams will henceforth expose data + functionality through service interfaces
2. Teams must communicate with each other through these interfaces.
3. No other form of interprocess communication allowed
4. Interface must be designed to be externalizable

Figure 4.8   Amazon's use of standardized data services to exchange data

For over a decade, deploying public data services and APIs was a great stepping stone for Amazon's success as a pioneer among online retailers. Based on their initial success, Amazon would later go on to transform itself into a company that introduced Amazon Web Services on the Cloud platform for clients to renting their infrastructure. This move would fundamentally change how companies viewed Amazon, establishing them more as a technology company as opposed to an online bookseller.

Amazon's innovative data-driven culture combined with the zeal and vision of its founder for surpassing customer expectations makes the company stand out among its competitors.

SUMMARY

This chapter explained why it is essential for an organization to define their enterprise data strategy clearly while preparing to offer data as a service. It also defined what components are essential for formulating an enterprise data strategy. The basic emphasis of the DaaS framework is that an effective enterprise data strategy must be aligned with an organization's business strategy, organizational capabilities, and current IT environment.

To support this vision, achieving a single view of an enterprise should be one of the fundamental goals of any organization. With the increasing size and complexity of information system implementation, the role of DaaS in exchanging data across disparate system platforms has also become vital for most organizations.

For successful DaaS implementation, it is essential to have a well laid out architectural solution blueprint that can promote the intelligent reuse of data across an organization. The finalized solution blueprint is typically derived from a reference architecture that provides reusable patterns to solve a repeating problem in a given context. Using the patterns provided in the DaaS reference architecture is encouraged to develop data services that are architected to support enterprise-level needs.

Chapter 5

Enterprise and Canonical Modeling

TOPICS COVERED IN THIS CHAPTER

- This chapter explains the significance of the Enterprise Data Model (EDM) as the foundational component required for building a robust and mature set of data structures, which can be reused across an entire organization.

- The concept of a canonical model is also introduced as well as its enabling role to promote consistent and reliable data exchange across disparate systems spread out over an organization(s).

- The detailed approach to designing and developing data services are explored, which can be reused across an enterprise by using common design components and standards.

The most profound technologies are those that disappear. They weave themselves into the fabric of our everyday life until they are indistinguishable from it.

—Late Professor Mark Weiser (Father of Ubiquitous Computing)

A robust and scalable DaaS strategy can only be sustained by an organization when their data service development efforts are built on the strong foundation of architectural principles and standards. The next few chapters look at several of the foundational components comprising the DaaS reference architecture.

This chapter explains the significance of the canonical model as a foundational component for underlying data services and the critical role it plays in the efficient exchange of data across systems. The focus is on explaining why the canonical model needs to be regularly kept in alignment with the underlying enterprise data modeling and governance efforts of an organization.

Data as a Service: A Framework for Providing Reusable Enterprise Data Services,
First Edition. Pushpak Sarkar.
© 2015 the IEEE Computer Society. Published 2015 by John Wiley & Sons, Inc.

A MODEL-DRIVEN APPROACH TOWARD DEVELOPING REUSABLE DATA SERVICES

Data services can liberate the data in an enterprise from being held captive in silos. If designed correctly, data services can ensure that different applications share and reuse them. For any organization interested in deploying reusable data services, many essential planning, design, and preparation activities are required. The emphasis in the planning stage needs to be on setting up the appropriate foundation for reusing common data. Enterprise modeling can be used as a technique for defining, relating, and validating the underlying data stored within an organization (referred to as data-at-rest).

When offering data as a service, the canonical model is one of the popular design techniques used by organizations to share data between multiple systems. A canonical model is a shared model primarily used to exchange data-in-motion between multiple business applications. It facilitates sharing data by using standardized data formats and commonly agreed data definitions, for all data elements that need to be shared across disparate systems. Figure 5.1 illustrates the role of canonical models in promoting data access and exchange.

Currently, data services are the most popular method of data exchange across systems using XML payloads. However, in recent years, enterprise service-oriented architecture (SOA) principles and data standards have also transformed the usage of externalized data services. Data services have truly become a key mode of information delivery to business customers of most enterprises. By following enterprise SOA principles, data services can also be used more extensively for data integration and sharing outside an enterprise.

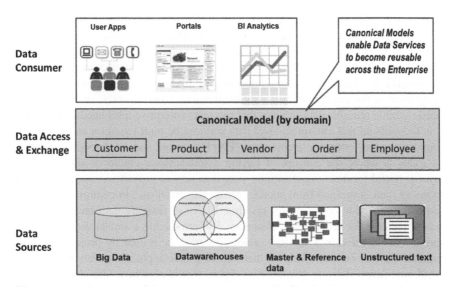

Figure 5.1   Role of canonical models in efficient data access and exchange

As discussed earlier in the Chapter 2, the enterprise roadmap and strategy phase is a critical step for an organization to ensure that their service-related blueprint meets both enterprise and divisional needs. The purpose of this chapter is to further refine the enterprise data strategy and provide direction and guidance to support implementation of needed changes. By providing direction and guidance, organizations will be in a better position to determine the long-term impact of DaaS on their organization. Overall, it is critical that an understanding is reached by all of the stakeholders in the organization regarding what an enterprise solution means and how it impacts their individual areas.

As illustrated in Figure 5.1, the underlying enterprise data services layer, apart from being a stable foundation, is also a useful artifact for IT managers and architects during future projects, while enhancing their enterprise data services with additional data, or building new functions in big data or analytics. Reuse of enterprise data services common components, such as the canonical model or data definitions, will not only reduce the architectural complexity associated with point-to-point data integration, but can also reduce development costs in the long run.

The remainder of this chapter explains how to approach enterprise canonical modeling in the SOA environment as well as the reference framework and architectural principles of setting up enterprise data services (EDS) in your organization. A detailed understanding of these individual modeling components should help most readers to appreciate the underlying factors that make an enterprise data services initiative tenable over the long-term in any organization.

DEFINING A STANDARDS-DRIVEN APPROACH TOWARD DEVELOPING NEW DATA SERVICES

For several years, XML has been extensively used by organizations to build web service applications. However, a lack of available XML schema standards have made it difficult to integrate systems. Even vendors who have provided XML interfaces have frequently maintained their proprietary XML schema and document-type definitions (DTDs). This has made the import/export of data using XML and large-scale integration at the enterprise level very challenging. Consequently, an organization needs to build reusable data services that can meet enterprise-level needs. Therefore, it is recommend that enterprise-level data services be built based on an underlying foundation of an enterprise-architecture (EA) framework and data/service standards.

This is where the concept of having a standardized enterprise data services layer is useful for most organizations. Any data service provides virtual aggregated views of data, leveraged from sources across the enterprise, in contrast to a point-to-point connection between two systems. EDS can simplify data integration and access patterns for all service consumers. By introducing a standardized message format once created in a service catalog, they can be reused by project teams in separate lines of business, helping them develop new applications very easily with rapid application delivery (Figure 5.2). There should also be a formal governance approach laid out under the DaaS framework to manage the reuse of data services.

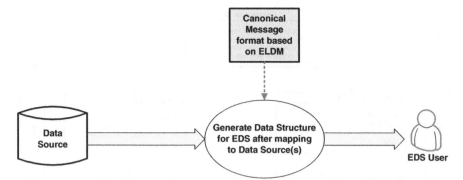

Figure 5.2   Mapping a standardized data exchange model to the XML messages used

Finally, as discussed, the EDS governance model should be agreed on by all of the identified DaaS stakeholders across the organization.

ROLE OF THE ENTERPRISE DATA MODEL

The canonical model should be developed in close partnership with business stewards and the enterprise information-management (EIM) team. There are several benefits in developing the canonical model based on the underlying Enterprise Data Model (EDM). The organization has to maintain the model over the long term with a formal data governance program for daily reference and usage by data subscribers across the organization.

The EDM is primarily used to provide a high-level enterprise view of an organization's data and of the relationships that the data have with various business segments and core entities. It is important to note that maintaining a canonical model should be viewed as a key component of the EIM division in any organization (Figure 5.3).

Even from a data service perspective, the importance of having a standardized data model is essential for data exchange and interoperability. This is a crucial consideration while defining canonical data formats and is extremely critical for the success of an EDS program. The individual data elements in an enterprise model have to be mapped to the underlying data sources, even if they cannot be integrated into a single physical integration platform such as a MDM hub or data warehouse.

At the outset of the program, having an EDM as the foundation of enterprise data services is essential. It can be compared to a town planner preparing an architectural blueprint before proceeding to build a new set of apartment buildings in a city. Even after the building is complete, the blueprint remains useful for the building owners, especially when they need to make changes to the original design, for example, when they add a few extra floors or new apartments to increase their occupancy revenues.

Similarly, in the absence of an EDM, the IT organization can struggle to understand what the impact is of extending or modifying some of the data services to meet new business requirements (or to meet newly introduced government regulations).

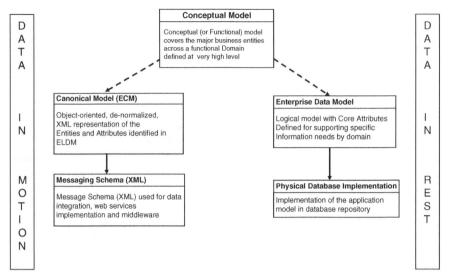

Figure 5.3 Overview of an enterprise and canonical model in a DAAS environment

To support the deployment and use of EDS, organizations need to use the enterprise data model as a reference for developing the canonical model to support enterprise-level data services.

DEVELOPING THE CANONICAL MODEL

This section looks at how to develop the model components to implement canonical models and data services in more detail. Three major modeling components are necessary to represent the enterprise at different levels of granularity. These three levels of abstraction are where the enterprise's data model can be captured and include the conceptual data model, enterprise data model (EDM), and enterprise canonical model. Each are essential for supporting data exchange and sharing.

Conceptual Model (or Functional Model)

Conceptual models represent the business functions within an organization. The conceptual model usually covers high-level concepts or business terms that are significant to the business. It provides the common business language that is used to define structural business rules, agreed-upon data, and metadata explicitly. The primary audience for the conceptual model are not well versed IT practitioners, but business teams.

The conceptual model is hierarchically organized into functional domains or subject areas (e.g., customer, product, organization). The domains also need to be associated with each other according to a pervasive ontology defining all associations within and across all structured data dictionaries. Every change to the conceptual model (or a functional domain under it) needs to be reviewed by a group of business or data stewards before the model is modified.

The primary audience for the EDM includes business team representatives, data stewards, data governance teams, and senior executives.

ENTERPRISE DATA MODEL

The enterprise data model (EDM) is a logical data model that is independent of technology, implementation, and application-specific data and rules. It primarily represents the state of persistent data stored in database repositories across the enterprise as a whole.

The EDM identifies and describes the complete list of approved organizational entities (data) and their relationships. However, it should be clarified here that no EDM can cover every detail of all possible data entities and attributes within an organization. Therefore, this form of data model represents data at a high level (core entities and attributes only) and embodies major structural business rules that are essential for EIM and data planning activities.

The EDM is typically normalized to some extent, but not to the same level of detail as the logical data model for an application (DAMA, 2010). Therefore, the EDM is not expected to strictly enforce data integrity rules, as the objective for this model is to communicate with the business leadership and validate their understanding of key concepts that need to be included as inputs for the enterprise-logical data model.

The primary audience for the EDM includes data architects, data modelers, and enterprise architects.

CANONICAL MODEL

Canonical models are foundational components of the DaaS framework because they act as a key enabler for sharing and reusing information. The canonical model represents a standardized and consistent way of representing data so that they can be used for data exchanges across multiple applications. The canonical model also provides common business language, including specifying business rules, agreed-to data, and metadata (Figure 5.4).

The canonical model is usually derived from the EDM and should be independent of any individual application's implementation. It usually provides a common format for the application and service-development teams, which is at a higher level of abstraction when compared to the individual application team's data formats. Having a generic format helps in enabling usage of the canonical format by all applications, although there is usually some mapping/transformation required to convert the data from the native formats in a particular system to the enterprise canonical format.

While developing the canonical model, the model should not be designed to support tactical needs (e.g., to support a single web service application team's needs). Instead, it should be designed for generic reuse by multiple projects implementing the model over a period of time. For this reason, a recommended approach is to use

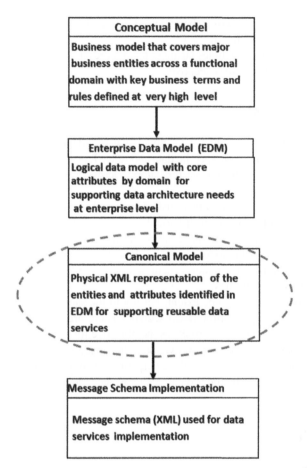

Figure 5.4 Developing the canonical model

the universal modeling approach to develop the canonical model. An example of this is to use a common object such as a party to represent multiple entities (e.g., customer, prospect, and supplier) because they all represent a person, and thus share many similar attributes (name, address, gender, date of birth, etc.).

The canonical model is typically implemented in XML format, which has several, inherent benefits. Let us now briefly look at the scope and coverage of the canonical model.

Enterprise Canonical Model Covers

- The critical data entities an organization uses repeatedly.
- The core entities impacting the major business processes and that need sharing across many business areas and external customers, partners, etc.
- The relationships and hierarchies among these business entities.

- The canonical model is not designed to support local applications that do not need to be shared with other areas (however, some canonical model components can be reused if necessary).

As mentioned, it is recommended that the canonical model be regularly kept aligned with the EDM. This is necessary as the canonical model also has to reflect the entities, attributes, and relationships finalized by data stewards. A detailed mapping is necessary to ensure the canonical XML model is aligned to the EDMs. These de-normalized, object-oriented, XML structures are also very useful for promoting data sharing and interoperability across various applications through a common data and messaging format.

Standardization of the canonical model and the XML messaging schema formats is also essential for the governance of data services at the enterprise level. For large enterprises with many web service-development efforts running simultaneously (often as stove-piped systems), governance overheads and change management issues can be a challenge for IT departments. These challenges are significantly reduced by having a canonical model in place (Figure 5.5).

To summarize then, the benefits of using EDS with a canonical model that is reused across development projects are as follows:

- Accelerating the development of reusable services and integration procedures.

- Decoupling information from processes when building data sharing services.

- Reducing the downstream application-development costs and compliance risks.

- Building a controlled vocabulary to support the portfolio of business applications.

- Improved governance.

- Simplifying the service integration patterns (Figure 5.6).

In the introductory phase of EDM development, only a select group of critical data entities and attributes that are considered important for the business have to be included in the canonical model so that they are published for use by consumers of the EDM. The criticality of each data element included in the canonical model has to be judged by the extent to which it is required in running the daily operations of the business.

	Canonical Model	**Enterprise Data Model (EDM)**
Representation	ER diagrams with XML schemas	ER diagrams and/or DDLs
Perspective	Application-centric	Data-centric
Purpose	Standardization of message formats	Alignment to business model
Drivers	System interoperability and data sharing	Structural completeness and data integrity

Figure 5.5   Comparing the EDM with the canonical model

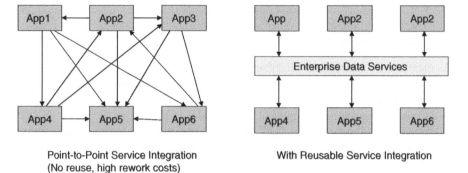

Point-to-Point Service Integration
(No reuse, high rework costs)

With Reusable Service Integration

Figure 5.6   Service integration and reuse with and without a canonical model

The approach of starting with critical data elements in the initial phase of the data-service build is usually more effective compared to the alternative approach of conducting an extensive assessment of all EDM elements, because it is usually time consuming and costly.

The major benefits of developing a canonical model is that it allows for:

• Faster delivery by application teams.

• Promotion of data sharing with greater use of common data formats.

• Easier adoption of industry standards and specific reference standards mandated by the government in certain sectors (e.g., ICD 10).

The canonical model should be developed by a group of architects representing various applications, under the guidance of the EIM, EA, and business domain teams. The primary audience for most canonical models include service delivery teams such as application developers, SOA/integration architects, and data analysts.

Best Practices for Implementing Reusable Data Services

• For any organization, the canonical model provides the building blocks, i.e., XML message formats when data services are implemented by providing an agreed-upon base vocabulary for interactions between application systems. It does this by using core data entities and attributes of the EDM in a domain (customer, address, product, etc.).

• The major benefit for teams consuming data services is to avoid complexities involved in accessing information from back-end data sources. The canonical model helps standardize data access and exchange mechanism. It reduces overall complexity by eliminating the need for point-to-point transformations between application-specific message formats.

• The canonical model should have core blocks that are standardized across the organization. However, individual application teams can extend the canonical model with XML extensions (modeled as extensions in generated schemas), if they need something beyond the core model. However, these extensions need to be maintained locally by each relevant domain, minimizing the impact to other domains with any of the extensions.

- The canonical model and related data services should be owned, governed, and managed by an enterprise team within the domain. A central group should also manage mapping legacy/source systems into the canonical model. Centralizing these concerns in a Center of Excellence or architecture group is, overall, the more economical thing to do.

- Consuming applications are continuously changing and being extended to meet new business requirements, and they are in the best position to manage change and know what makes the most sense for them locally. However, organizations cannot centrally manage mappings to implemented Web Services Definition Language (WSDL) schemas supporting local applications. The responsibility for mapping out to endpoint applications that will consume information off the service bus (or information-access layer) lie with the concerned application team implementing the service.

- Applications that consume information from the bus should only take what they need. That way they are only exposed to changes in those elements. This means there are more versions of the message coming off the bus, but they are all subsets of a larger standard message, or more precisely, all different projections into XML Schema of a larger, single logical model. The logical model is important to support the full range of relationships within data that can exist, and not be constrained to modeling in hierarchies.

IMPLEMENTING THE CANONICAL MODEL

Developing a canonical model includes the process of identifying, modeling, and documenting data requirements that have been agreed upon by business stakeholders across various parts of the enterprise. This section examines how to go about developing a canonical model in the initial phase across various information domains in partnership with domain subject-matter experts using an iterative, rapid application-development (RAD) process. Figure 5.7 illustrates critical success factors for developing canonical models.

The data relevant to an individual domain (e.g., customer, product, etc.) are separated into entities (things about which a business needs to record information) and relationships (the associations between the entities). The RAD process is especially recommended because it promotes a strong collaborative atmosphere and dynamic gathering of requirements. The business owner actively participates in prototyping, writing test cases, and performing unit testing.

In the initial phase, the canonical model should be developed in partnership with business domain SMEs using an iterative process. The use of joint action-development (JAD) sessions could also be very useful when developing the Enterprise Data Model (EDM) because it also promotes a strong collaborative atmosphere and dynamic

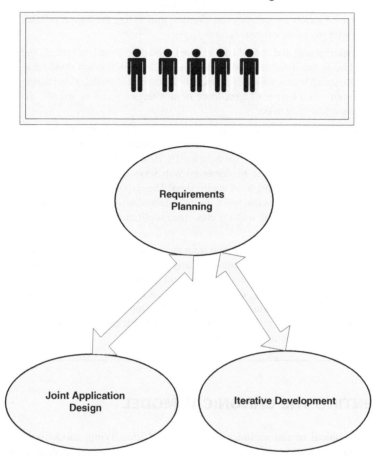

Figure 5.7 Critical success factors for developing the canonical model

gathering of the requirements. A JAD session typically captures customer voices by involving them in the design and development of the application through a series of collaborative workshops called JAD sessions. Even after the initial canonical model requirement gathering phase, it is also recommended that business SME teams stay engaged and actively participate in prototyping, writing test cases, and performing unit testing for the development of the subsequent EDMs.

When developing the canonical model, it is recommended to use techniques that capture the business SMEs' voices (treating them as internal customers), by involving them in the design and development of the application through a series of collaborative workshops and JAD sessions. Their input can be likened to the voice of the customer—a market research technique that produces a detailed set of customer wants and needs, organized into a hierarchical structure, and then prioritized in terms of relative importance and satisfaction with current alternatives.

Joint Application Development (JAD)

Let us now look at some popular techniques to gather information from business SMEs to develop the canonical model.

- Provides a detailed understanding of the customer's requirements
- Establishes a common language for the team going forward
- Gathers input for setting appropriate design specifications for the new product or service
- Provides a highly useful springboard for product innovation

There are many other possible ways in which to complement information gathered from business SMEs to develop the canonical model such as through focus groups, individual interviews, and surveys. These techniques involve a series of structured in-depth interviews, which focus on the business team representative's experiences with current processes or alternatives within the category under consideration. Statements that are recorded during individual interviews with various SMEs are then organized into a more usable hierarchy and prioritized by customers.

Customer stakeholders must take the lead in defining the topic, either by conducting or observing and analyzing interviews, designing and validating the data models, providing the data definitions on key entities and attributes, or by reviewing the shared business vocabulary (Wood, 1995). The use of agile techniques can also help minimize feature creep by developing components at short intervals and releasing the canonical model in phases. To define the canonical model for each individual functional domain, the organization's enterprise modeling team should conduct JAD sessions under the business stakeholders' guidance.

Team Roles During the Canonical Model Development Process

The enterprise modeling team, business stewards, EIM team, data administration, and respective application-development teams are responsible for the following roles during the initial creation of the canonical model along with the related policies, standards, and procedures. Figure 5.8 shows RACI details for developing a canonical model.

Data Steward

The role of the data steward is to:

- Represent the business stakeholders while defining the future state of EIM.
- Act as the SME in their respective data subject area.
- Define the key terms in the enterprise data glossary by information domain.

Tasks/Roles	Enterprise Modeling Team (EIM)	Business/ Data Steward	Enterprise Data Services Development Team (project)	Data Management & Adminstration
Enterprise Data Model & Business Glossary	R	A	C	C
Data Model for Individual Projects	C	I	A	R
Enterprise Data Model Mapping	A	I	R	

Figure 5.8 Responsibility assignment matrix for canonical model-related tasks

Enterprise Information Management

The role of the EIM group in the context of enterprise modeling is to:

- Create the canonical model and business metadata/glossary based on inputs from all the business stakeholders across all divisions.
- Assist the application owners and data administration teams throughout the organization to leverage and reuse the EDM. They also guide these teams to comply with established EIM policies and standards.

Enterprise Data Service Development Team

The role of the Enterprise Data Services (EDS) development team is to ensure that their individual data models reflect individual project requirements and to ensure those models are in alignment with the EDM, by ensuring that the application data are mapped to the canonical model and/or that the data reuse the common DaaS implementation components like Web Services Definition Language (WSDL).

Mapping between the EDM and the application models has to be regularly monitored by the data governance council and the respective sub-committees responsible for EDS implementation.

Data Management and Administration

The data administration team is responsible for continued maintenance of data modeling, physical database design, and implementation efforts that are necessary to support EDS development projects.

RACI Notation

R—Responsible: Doer of the task, author of the artifact. Implies consulted.

A—Accountable: The individual who owns the task and outcome. Not necessarily doing it themselves.

C—Consulted: Consulted for subject-matter expertise, to review and provide feedback.

I—Informed: Is made aware that a certain activity has taken place, receives finalized document.

Given the diversity of stakeholders who need to be involved during the planning and requirement-definition phase, it is important to establish a good communication mechanism among stakeholders.

PUBLISHING DATA SERVICES WITH THE CANONICAL MODEL AS A FOUNDATION

As mentioned in Chapter 4, the first step suggested in deploying an EDS is to study the requirements of potential data subscribers to the service. The data service project team needs to finalize definitions to be published on the data service by engaging with the various stakeholders of each subject area to gain consensus on the key business terms during the onboarding phase of new projects. The focus should be on creating a unified view published via the data service. In addition to business inputs, the IT department can study the existing state of data assets and start preparing a current-state data asset inventory.

The process of deploying a standardized data service for use by projects across the enterprise typically include the following steps (Figure 5.9).

Capture Requirements

At this stage, the DaaS team has to conduct detailed sessions with stakeholders and user teams to gather the initial scope and requirements for the canonical model:

- Define source systems (data providers) for web services.
- Identify key entities and critical data elements that need to be included in the canonical model.
- Identify resources from various teams who can validate the design artifact of reusable data services.

Gap Analysis

After user requirements are agreed on by data stewards and SMEs, there has to be a thorough mapping exercise, which should be carried out jointly by business analysts and ETL teams to collect and analyze the metadata from different source systems

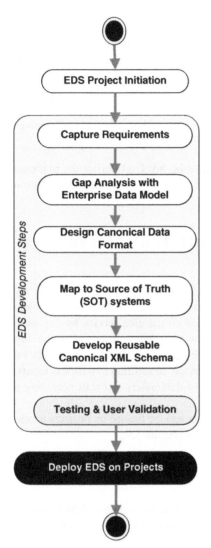

Figure 5.9   Standard process for deployment of
reusable data services across the enterprise

through empirical analysis and/or the use of data profiling tools. This needs to be
followed by an evaluation of differences between the underlying data structures stored
in multiple data sources and the EDM. The steward team should also try to resolve
any differences between data elements that have conflicting business usage.

Mapping to the Source-of-truth Systems

For most large organizations, a critical step necessary for implementing enterprise-
level data services is to identify the authoritative (or golden) data sources that can

provide reliable information to users across the organization. The DaaS stakeholders and service architects have to determine jointly which data sources can be considered as the authoritative Source-of-Truth (SoT) systems for various data attributes that are identified for publishing over the EDS layer.

Testing and User Validation

Before deploying the services into a production, there has to be a rigorous quality assurance (QA) exercise conducted from perspectives of technical development and business. Since information-privacy security is a real concern for many external, customer-oriented applications, the business user also needs to validate data visibility and access aspects of the data service thoroughly before they are made available to external consumers.

Deploy Data Services

This step deploys data services with runtime XML/XSD using the enterprise canonical message formats. For the XML schema to be used during runtime and message payload development, the enterprise canonical model is often found to be too large for effective use in message development. Consequently, a subset XML schema that only contains what is required by the specific message while maintaining alignment to the enterprise canonical message format model is required. Valid message payloads are developed in a fraction of the time by using the reusable canonical XML components.

Using this approach ensures that data exchanged between various applications and consumers that are leveraging runtime enterprise data services all follow a standard format, thus making data sharing and interoperability possible. The compliance of the implemented service with an enterprise's canonical message format can be limited only for the critical data elements that need to be exchanged across the enterprise applications, and not necessarily for the elements of local application relevance. This ensures that there is consistency in terms of semantics, when possible, regarding critical data elements, while differentiating between the terms, as necessary, when there are subtle variations in meanings between the EDMs and local application needs.

IMPLEMENTING THE CANONICAL MODEL IN REAL-LIFE PROJECTS

During a data service deployment, the canonical version of the model needs to be translated by the application team as an XML message that represents the actual interface (or the WSDL schema) deployed for a data service. The canonical versions of XML models in real life are often large and complex to understand, as they are designed to meet the integration needs of an enterprise, business line, or subject area. The key to their widespread reuse across an enterprise is the ability to build subset XML schemas easily and quickly from a model for use in payloads and WSDL (Figure 5.10).

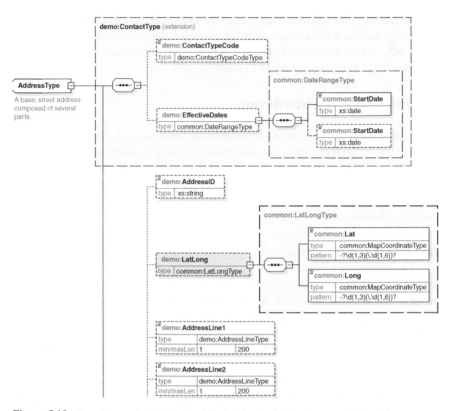

Figure 5.10 Sample canonical model-based XML schema of an address messaging block

This challenge can be addressed with a simple web interface built for data service consumers using a canonical message format with component definitions that are reusable across the enterprise. Following this approach can help in several ways. For example, business analysts are able to navigate the model while using the service and data integration architects can understand data lineage, as well as specify which parts of the XML model should be reused for a specific project implementation for web integration developers. The integration developer can also search and navigate the model very easily to pick the components that they need, and they can automatically build runtime-optimized subset schemas from the model. If the model has the correct vocabulary relationships added, they can even navigate to required components using the shared business vocabulary.

The final outcome is a model-derived WSDL schema that only contains what is needed for the XML message requirements along with mapping and service definitions.

Some vendor-based tools have been introduced that are able to eliminate the manual process required by the data service team when creating canonical model sub-schemas for the service-application messages by using an easy-to-use web interface that allows anyone to search and navigate the enterprise canonical message format schemas (directly or through the application vocabulary that is familiar to them), to find components within the model that meet their message requirements and to generate a runtime-optimized XML schema. Valid message payloads can be expected to develop faster due to reusability, which reduces subsequent overall project timelines and costs.

Service Catalog

Enterprise canonical message formats contain standard patterns to model complex relationships between various entities within the organization. These XML messaging formats can be stored in a design-time service repository (also called a service catalog). Messaging blocks contain simpler structures that serve as building blocks for messages. The recommended practice for development teams building new web services is to reuse an XML block from the service catalog hosting the canonical model as much as possible during design time. As an example, let us discuss the case of an address block in a canonical model. Assume that multiple web services such as a customer, distributor, or employee all require that you include the address for the publication of their service. Using the common, reusable XML block stored in the service catalog would help to deploy web services quickly while ensuring consistency with overall enterprise-governance standards.

Apart from the simple service patterns listed earlier, there can also be composite data services designed to combine data from multiple sources into a common composite view. A complete portfolio of data services has to be stored in the service catalog. This enables users to find the data service needed (i.e., search/visibility) as well as to ensure that the data conforms to a registered (and publicly available) schema (i.e., understandable). The service catalog also ensures that the services hosted are both current and correct (i.e., authoritative and trusted).

Moreover, you can expect changes to the data service interface over time. This might happen because projects requirements are likely to evolve and change. Often, the underlying business model for organizations in a sector may also change due to larger environmental factors such as new government regulations, mergers, etc.

DATA SERVICES ROLL OUT AND FUTURE RELEASES

Data services should be rolled out within the organization in multiple phases in accordance with an adoption plan. For each of these phases of data service expansion and development, care should be taken to involve the data governance steering committee and business stakeholders. An adoption plan has several components:

- A distribution package that consists of standard service-interface specifications, developer guides, training material, and reference implementation documentation.
- A strategy for identifying and reaching key users and implementers.

- A support and governance plan for assisting implementers and ensuring implementation conformance to service-interface specifications.

- A maintenance plan for controlling change of services to meet new requirements and to correct issues.

Consequently, it is important that implementation teams have plans, policies, and processes to draw upon for guidance and the resources to deliver results if something changes. For example, a release plan includes information such as release schedules and release documentation requirements (e.g., change logs, release notes, impacts). The objective of such a plan is to provide service developers with clear direction and guidance on how to change the service easily to meet new standards or requirements.

Even after the data service has been implemented, there needs to be proper version-control and release-management policies set up by the central team responsible for making enterprise-wide release enhancements.

Finally, some automated vendor tools can help organizations build canonical models as well as implement version-control and release-management processes at the service level for XML messages built from the enterprise's canonical message format.

CASE STUDY: DaaS IN REAL LIFE, ELECTRONIC-DATA INTERCHANGE IN U.S. HEALTHCARE EXCHANGES

Let us now discuss DaaS in a real-life case study from the healthcare sector within the United States. As per provisions from the recently introduced reform legislation (ACA, 2009), new healthcare information exchanges (HIEs) have been set up for consumers to provide healthcare insurance plans. However, healthcare services to patients under these plans are provided by individual insurance firms.

An HIE facility provides the ability to electronically exchange information between different stakeholders such as the physicians' offices, community hospitals, insurance administrators, and patients. HIEs are expected to offer a number of advantages to the existing U.S. healthcare system. For example, they can facilitate the continuity of care when patients move between providers. Even claim processing for a patient can operate more efficiently, especially if there are multiple parties (general practitioner, specialist, labs conducting tests, etc.) involved in supporting the patient on a claim for a complex condition.

With new reforms leading to healthcare exchanges, HIEs will extend the concept of a single view of a healthcare claim or a patient across a community or state, not just within the organization. Individual organizations (say an insurance firm) now need to exchange data electronically with other agencies in the new U.S. healthcare ecosystem such as physicians, hospitals, public health agencies, government, and individual members/patients who use medical services from these providers.

DaaS can play a big role in achieving a seamless exchange of patient or claim data across healthcare exchanges by leveraging a common, standardized set of messaging services for electronic data interchange (EDI). The message formats for exchanging

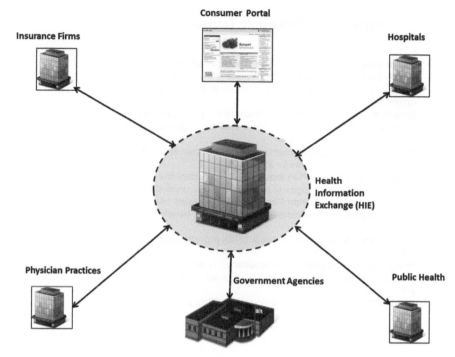

Figure 5.11   Evolving role of healthcare information exchanges

specific data have to be governed centrally by the HIE administrators. All of the organizations participating in healthcare exchanges have to follow standardized data formats for individual healthcare transactions (Figure 5.11).

To meet the specified EDI requirements for individual healthcare transactions, every participating organization needs to develop an enterprise-wide canonical model for the different subject areas they are involved in when conducting their daily operations. For example, a health insurer would certainly become involved in supporting transactions such as processing claims received from patients in their healthcare plan. The data services used for exchanging claim data should use standardized message formats (WSDL) that are derived from the canonical model for these claim-related entities.

A good starting point for a standardized data format used for EDI is the EDI X12 standard format provided by the healthcare standards body ASC X12, chartered by the American National Standards Institute more than 30 years ago. ASC X12 is a standards' organization that develops and maintains EDI and CICA standards along with XML schemas, which drive business processes globally.

More specifically, EDI X12 is primarily used to exchange specific kinds of healthcare data (known as transactions) between two or more healthcare organizations involved in a transaction such as providers, healthcare exchanges, insurance organizations, and third-party payers.

Major HIPAA Electronic Transactions

- **Health Care Claim** (837): providers use to submit claims to payers.
- **Health Care Claim Payment/Remittance Advice** (835): payers use to make claim payments or send Explanations of Benefits remittance advice to providers.
- **Benefit enrollment and disenrollment** (834): employers, unions, government agencies, associations, or insurance agencies use to enroll members in a health plan.
- **Health Plan Premium Payments** (820): health plan sponsors use to make premium payments for insurance
- **Eligibility for a Health Plan Inquiry** (270): providers use to inquire about the benefits and eligibility of a subscriber or dependent.
- **Eligibility for a Health Plan Response** (271): payers use to respond to providers' requests about subscribers' benefits and eligibility.
- **Health Care Claim Status Request** (276): providers use to request the status of a claim.
- **Health Care Claim Status Notification** (277): payers use to notify providers on the status of a claim or to request additional information.
- **Referral Certification and Authorization** (278): providers use to transmit pertinent health care service information for review/preauthorization of a medical procedure or service.

Figure 5.12 Major list of healthcare EDI transactions

HIPAA 5010 provisions specify major categories of electronic transactions for data interchange (EDI X12) among healthcare organizations, including healthcare claim submissions, claim eligibility and payments, benefit enrollment, provider referral certifications, and authorizations. Figure 5.12 provides some of the major categories of electronic transactions that are specified for data interchange (EDI X12) among various healthcare organizations under the HIPAA 5010 provisions as well as other data standards that have been defined for the healthcare sector.

Another real-life example is healthcare claim processing. The process starts when a healthcare service provider (e.g., a physician) submits an EDI 837 transaction for a healthcare claim. The 837 transaction sends details of the service that the physician provided to the patient (based on the patient's insurance plan).

In turn, the insurance organization uses the EDI 835 transaction set to send their payments and notify the coordination of the benefits' information back to the physician, including information on the charges that have been paid or denied, that are deductible, co-pays, and payment details on various claims. The EDI 835 is important to healthcare providers to track what payments have been received for services that they have provided and have billed clients for. The 835 transaction set can also be used to make a payment, send an explanation of the benefits (EOB) remittance advice, and to send EOB remittance advice only from the health insurer to the physician either

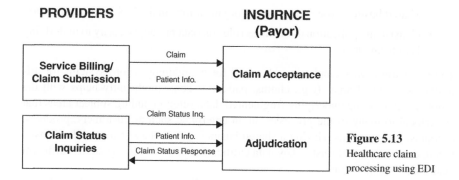

Figure 5.13
Healthcare claim
processing using EDI

directly or via a third-party financial institution. Figure 5.13 illustrates EDI Claims processing in the healthcare insurance sector.

For example, when a healthcare service provider needs to submit a healthcare claim for services it rendered to a patient (a member of an insurance plan), it will then use an 837 transaction specified under X12. The receiving insurance organization will need to know the transaction number (message numeric name), release version, and the member's plan details. All these details can be found inside the EDI file. After the receiving organization has validated the information sent by the provider, it initiates a separate transaction to make the payment to the provider electronically. The insurance organization then uses the EDI 835 transaction set to send details on the payment for that claim, including information on the charges that have been paid or denied, deductibles, co-pays, payment details on various claims, and so on.

Role of the Canonical Model for U.S. Healthcare Exchanges

One of the suggested measures for the U.S. healthcare exchange sector in the future is the use of standardized data/messaging formats. Healthcare exchanges can utilize a canonical model for exchanging data across different organizations participating in the healthcare exchange's network of hospitals, patients, and insurance firms. This would make the overall U.S. healthcare exchange system more timely, responsive, and cost-efficient.

Implementing a canonical model for healthcare exchanges judiciously will ensure overall improvement and efficiencies due to:

- Data exchange based on standardized formats reflecting the canonical model.
- Improved system interoperability and related efficiencies due to greater consistency.
- Improved oversight by U.S. regulators with planned system controls and safeguards.

- Shared business vocabulary across organizations in the U.S. healthcare sector.
- Consistent application of business rules on data privacy/security to underlying healthcare data.

The DaaS framework emphasizes the need for maintaining record systems for different data subject areas (e.g., claims, patients). This significantly helps with the rationalization of the underlying fragmented data, often including subject areas that are critical to many of the processes in an enterprise such as customers, products, accounts, and locations. Having a shared business vocabulary also provides consistent understanding and trust of key data entities and consistent usage across different healthcare organizations.

The goal of DaaS should be to put more capabilities into the hands of the end users so that they can decide what information they really need, and so they can become self-sufficient in terms of obtaining this information. Introducing DaaS components such as a healthcare canonical model along with a shared business glossary can play a major role in making the EDI more efficient and helpful for organizations to exchange data within U.S. healthcare exchanges.

SUMMARY

One of the key objectives of any DaaS program is to ensure that all EDS subscribers use a standardized version of enterprise data. An canonical model provides a foundation for an efficient form of data exchange across multiple systems.

This chapter explained the detailed process of developing a canonical model. Also shown were the various steps required for developing the canonical model in an organization, including gathering functional requirements from business users (by domain or subject areas), and mapping the canonical model to data sources. Suggested guidelines were given to roll out the canonical model, deploying it in EDS development projects and an overall release-management strategy to coordinate changes affecting multiple application-development teams using EDS.

Finally, a case study was provided on using canonical models within U.S. healthcare exchanges. The case study also illustrated how individual exchanges can benefit from using a canonical model as a foundation. The canonical model can help to create reusable, standardized EDS that can enable healthcare organizations to share information within a healthcare exchange and with other participating organizations. This reuse of published information can not only help reduce future development and maintenance costs, but can also make data access easier for healthcare consumers in the long term.

Chapter 6

Business Glossary for DaaS

TOPICS COVERED IN THIS CHAPTER

- This chapter provides an overview of the underlying reasons why organizations need to develop a standardized business glossary for their various data services published for user consumption.

- DaaS projects need to ensure that a business glossary of shared business terms and definitions is maintained. Using common business terms that are consistent and updated can also help DaaS users spend less time struggling to understand the data that they consume. This can provide a better understanding of data to users across an organization.

- Finally, the rationale for storing a glossary in an enterprise metadata repository is discussed. Having a common, shared vocabulary across an organization can improve the overall productivity of both the business and external subscribers of data services.

"Technology alone is not enough. It's technology married with the liberal arts, married with the humanities, that yields the results that makes our hearts sing."

—Steve Jobs

Metadata in most enterprises today is a bit of a catchall term, with many generalities emphasized by those looking for a quick fix. Notwithstanding this oversimplification, business organizations cannot overlook the strategic importance of metadata. In fact, some may argue that metadata is similar to a lens through which data is filtered and turned into real information. This is because data is meaningless and even misleading at times, without context. Metadata makes it easier for users to understand data in a holistic manner. Metadata does this by creating a kind of conceptual synthesis that helps us understand one business concept in the context of another. All of these key business concepts and terms are maintained in a *business glossary*.

Data as a Service: A Framework for Providing Reusable Enterprise Data Services,
First Edition. Pushpak Sarkar.
© 2015 the IEEE Computer Society. Published 2015 by John Wiley & Sons, Inc.

In the DaaS context, the business glossary can be compared to a formal contract between data providers and subscribers who need to access specific data provided by the DaaS organization to them in real time. Therefore, having a metadata repository that stores an up-to-date business glossary of key terms with data services publishing them across the organization is essential in terms of supporting consumers as they access information in the DaaS environment. For example, the glossary can be a good system of reference for online customers of retailers. It can aid consumers in making purchase decisions by clarifying product-related questions in real time using data services. However, to support this objective, the data provider has to publish standardized data definitions that are agreed upon by business stewards across the entire organization.

Investing in a business glossary (metadata) provides business teams throughout the organization with a shared business vocabulary with which to clarify business meanings and enable reconciliation on semantic differences between common data elements used across multiple divisions. This chapter analyzes and explains some of these concerns, along with the detailed processes that are necessary to achieve larger goals of consistency in enterprise-level information semantics (Ferguson, 2012).

PROBLEM OF MEANING AND THE CASE FOR A SHARED BUSINESS GLOSSARY

As shown in Figure 6.1, metadata can be found in several places within the organization such as business documents, files, or spreadsheets, database definitions, application code, and even someone's head or written notes.

Having metadata is of limited value to business users if they have no context in which to understand what the underlying data actually means from a usage perspective. For example, when looking at a series of financial data, if a user encounters the number "12," it could mean several things, such as the number of months in the year, total body weight increase over the last year (as in the author's case), or the number of items sold today. Most users will have no idea what that number means without a business context or definition.

Clearly, data and information with context are not the same thing. A business glossary can help users within the organization to resolve differences because they all share a common vocabulary. It helps them to answer important questions on key business and data-related issues.

- What data or information exists?
- What is the business definition of a term?
- Where are the data being used?
- What other names has the data been called or what are the data currently being called?

Metadata

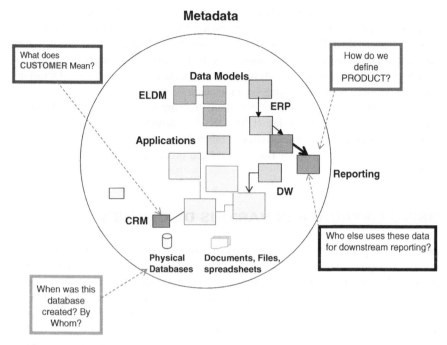

Figure 6.1 Role of the business glossary in the organization

- How are data interrelated to other information?
- Who is using the data?
- When were the data last updated?

In achieving the true reuse of information at the enterprise level, it is of critical importance to deal with issues of semantic differences, not just syntactic differences or structural differences—that is, one needs to understand what information is being exchanged, and not just how that information is transmitted as data or stored in the database. For example, in an organization, the answer to the question "What is a profit amount?" can be interpreted differently across various business units, depending on the underlying business rules used to calculate profits. Therefore, a change to the profit amount cannot be published, unless the business rules are stored and governed by a central team responsible for metadata-governance issues. Only when there is semantic consistency can an organization achieve the goal of implementable data services for enterprise data. Having a reliable business glossary of terms that can be shared by users across the organization is the anchor point for any information-management project in the organization.

The varied use of commonly used business terms in a large organization is mainly due to the traditional distribution of work through the line of business, geographical division, or a combination of the two. To facilitate information sharing and make data interoperable, there must be consensus on the key terms used by stakeholders. If there is no consensus, then the executives/custodians/owners of data representing different segments of the business organization need to formalize this as part of the data-governance steering committee. Achieving consistency in terms of data definitions can only be successful by focusing on a metadata strategy.

With regard to the definition of metadata, there are several definitions. However, the DAMA Body of Knowledge (DMBOK) has defined metadata as, "data that defines & describes the characteristics of other data, used to improve both business and technical understanding of Data and related processes" (DAMA International, 2009).

USING METADATA IN VARIOUS DISCIPLINES

Metadata are popularly used in the fields of information management, information science, information technology, librarianship, and Geographic Information Systems (GIS). While the traditional definition of the term *metadata* is generally common across various disciplines, there are some specific differences in metadata used in individual fields. The types of metadata objects used can also change with the context of the data or background environment. For example, metadata objects in data management can be very different from those used in the world of library science. Traditional library cataloging also contains forms of metadata with extensive taxonomies that were developed to describe several types of textual and non-textual objects (e.g., archival materials, visuals, geographic information) (Hodge, 2001).

In some disciplines, metadata can also be considered as data in their own right because they contain sensitive contextual data regarding the underlying record, unlike in the IT field. For example, a national agency recently gathered telephone metadata records from telephone carriers for surveillance purposes. However, they did not actually screen the telephone conversations. It is a matter of interpretation as to whether those telephone records should be viewed as metadata or as classified security data. Consequently, as discussed earlier, without a context and a point of reference, it can be impossible to identify and use metadata identically.

These abstract concepts can be somewhat confusing so let us look at an example to illustrate the point further. Perhaps you come across a bar code containing several numbers, all of which are 13 digits long. Like most people, who have no context, one might conclude that these numbers are randomly generated as the result of a scientific calculation. These numbers will not have any significance at that point to anyone. However, if you were additionally given some background context that this database stores information on a publishing organization, those 13-digit numbers may now be identified as ISBNs, unique numeric book identifiers that are used to identify a book across publishers, websites, etc.

The ISO IEC 11179 standard introduces metadata and defines certain domain-independent standards for various aspects of data, including standardized data elements, value domains, data element concepts, conceptual domains, and classification schemes that are essential to understanding this set of standards and that provide context for associating the individual parts of ISO IEC 11179 (ISO Publication, 2004).

Metadata are often stored and managed in a database, called a metadata repository. The repository stores a whole range of information about an organization's data assets including data definitions, relationships, business rules required for data validation, and valid codes for reference information. The metadata repository solution is often treated as a data asset inventory (DAI) because it stores and integrates business metadata, technical metadata, and operational metadata into consistent, consolidated views of enterprise, division, and application level data assets. The enterprise metadata repository can be maintained as the primary infrastructure for physical storage and catalog maintenance of all data assets within the enterprise.

It is crucial to note that prior to publishing any DaaS, the utmost effort should be made by the whole organization to ensure that data definitions for key enterprise terms such as customer, agent (or broker), or organization are consistent and actually refer to the same thing. For example, in financial services, many financial advisors cannot distinguish between their accounts and the actual person who owns the account. It is difficult to detect any fraud or suspicious activity unless all of these accounts can be traced back to the same account owner (or client).

Most investment banks and other financial institutions have gradually started to understand the difference between the account and client-centric view of data, especially when implementing know-your-client (KYC) initiatives or attempting to become more profitable with more cross selling and up selling to clients (and not accounts). This difference in metadata has made it challenging, cumbersome, and costly to transform core operations from being account-centric to client- or customer-centric.

An IT project initiative will never be accepted, unless the user knows that they have meaningful, complete, and accurate business information that they can trust and rely on for use in their daily work, no matter how reliable underlying data sources are. Having a shared business glossary as part of a foundational layer can help many of these business concerns.

Major Classifications of Metadata

Metadata can be classified into three broad categories: technical metadata, business metadata, and operational metadata.

- *Business metadata* include a glossary of key information terms used by business teams within an organization or by external subscribers. Business metadata are primarily descriptive in nature. Business metadata advise business users on what data they have, where the data come from, what the data mean, and what the data's relationship is to other data in the organization. In a DaaS environment, online customers who browse the data services for more details on a product they intend to purchase are primarily viewing business metadata. All terms published for business consumption in the DaaS environment would therefore need clear definitions, as they analyze some key terms. Business metadata is particularly critical for business users who access reports or for customers who access information published in a data service.

- *Technical metadata* define the objects and processes in an individual application from a technical point of view. This form of structural metadata can be helpful to technical users for detailed understanding, especially during data integration across multiple platforms and environments. For example, details on database schema names, tables, and data types can help IT support teams understand the physical data model and the way it is displayed for users in regard to reports, schedules, distribution lists, and user security rights.

- *Operational metadata* are used to capture details on various operations that occur while processing data. For example, in a DaaS environment, operational users can capture information regarding metadata details for ETL jobs, total number of customer records loaded in a table, or runtime statistics. Operational metadata are of interest for operational and business users in the organization, as they can use the data to identify systems users, which entities they are using, and what level of service they are receiving. Some other examples of operational metadata include access time, CPU processing time, and a count of the rows processed.

Broadly speaking, business metadata and operational metadata are primarily descriptive in nature, whereas technical metadata are primarily prescriptive (or definitional). One should also keep in mind that these categories of metadata can sometimes overlap.

ROLE OF AN ORGANIZATION'S BUSINESS GLOSSARY

As discussed, the business glossary is similar to a formal contract between data providers and subscribers. In a real-life setting, an authorized subscriber may need to clarify the meaning of a particular product-related characteristic as they browse data provided by the provider in real time. Figure 6.2 serves as an example of a subscriber who is shopping for a snowblower while browsing on the Internet, a tablet, or smart phone.

Often the best approach for enterprises to achieve semantic integration across the division is founded on an enterprise level business glossary with standardized metadata, agreed upon by key business and IT teams. This glossary can act as the shared business vocabulary across a large organization. Figure 6.3 illustrates the major components usually stored in a business glossary.

The common business vocabulary can provide the following benefits to business and IT users.

- Provide the business context and agreement on key terms to different data stakeholders across the organization. In the long term, this can help align various IT efforts with the business's goals.

Product Description

Toro 38371 15 Inch Electric 1500 Power Curve Snow Blower

Product Details

Product ID: 008FHFK1AO

Category: Snow Removal Equipment

Product Dimensions: 18 x 24.5 x 25.5 inches

Shipping Weight: 31 pounds

Shipping: This item is also available for shipping to select countries outside the U.S.

Shipping Advisory: This item must be shipped separately from other items in your order.

Item model number: 38371

Average Customer Review: 4.2 out of 5 stars. See all reviews (53 customer reviews)

Best Sellers Rank: #11,646 in Patio, Lawn & Garden

Figure 6.2   Example of metadata required by DaaS consumers in the online retail sector

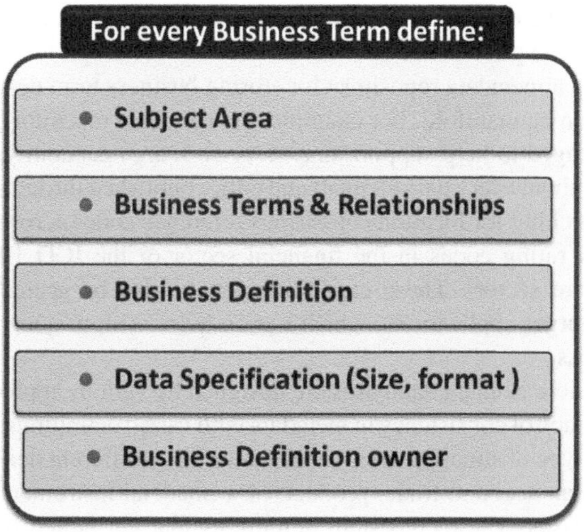

For every Business Term define:

- Subject Area

- Business Terms & Relationships

- Business Definition

- Data Specification (Size, format)

- Business Definition owner

Figure 6.3   Major components stored in the business glossary

- Ensure semantic consistency across various divisional and localized applications in the organization. Overall, bringing consistency to major data subject areas can reduce the total cost of operations in the IT budget. This is due to an expected reduction in redundant IT initiatives as well as efforts to reconcile inconsistent legacy systems.

- It can also act as a common vocabulary between business and technical users. The shared business vocabulary can provide business meaning to the key IT artifacts managed and created by other IT applications.

- From a data service user perspective, common business vocabulary can be very useful for sharing data across applications and with downstream users of shared data services.

Let us look at an example of how not clarifying business terms can impact a company's business operations in a significant way. While the accounting and finance departments can define customers only as those individuals or organizations that have done business with the organization (and have customer accounts), the sales department may define a customer both to include existing customers as well as future prospects or leads. Having this diverse set of business term definitions can impact users when they try to run an enterprise-wide report. Should they include customers limited to the accounting division view or should they go with the expanded definition of a customer as defined by the sales division? In fact, this seemingly simplistic difference in semantics can lead to a future situation in which sales and finance cannot share customer data between the two divisions. Usually what happens is that both divisions build redundant applications for their business users.

Resolving differences among business divisions while coming up with a common business vocabulary should ultimately be taken care of by the business/data stewards who own a particular set of data, not by the IT team supporting the organization's data governance efforts. If the different data stewards cannot agree on a particular definition for a business term at the enterprise level, then these kinds of issues have to be resolved by an enterprise data governance council.

The benefits of investing in a metadata repository for storing business term definitions across the enterprise can be manifold. For example, the metadata repository in an organization can be leveraged to help support an *enterprise search* capability, providing detailed information about every data element and entity published through EDS. It can also help when searching for locations of various reference codes across the enterprise (e.g., Basel risk rating codes in the financial sector or the ICD 10 diagnosis code in the healthcare sector). These capabilities could also be geared toward searching for specific target applications, which may require custom query development for metadata access.

The alternative scenario where isolated databases are designed by various application teams lead to a complete lack of consistency in metadata with varied definitions, formats, and semantics. In this type of situation, every application has a different definition for key entities such as an account, trade, product, or a financial instrument and this can lead to potential risks. The inconsistent definitions that get pulled in from multiple systems can lead to difficulties in achieving a consolidated enterprise level definition. For example, a financial system within an investment division may define various kinds of financial research or advisory services offered by its wealth advisory department as a product (e.g., financial research reports for ultra high net worth customers or global investment firms). However, their banking division could decide to exclude these types of services as being outside of their definition of a product. These types of differences in semantics can lead to major catastrophes in a financial institution's performance reporting.

Why a Business Glossary is Crucial for Enterprise Data Services

No DaaS initiative is likely to be effective as an information delivery mechanism for end-users, if it is unclear to them what type of information the data service delivers or what the meaning of that information is. Service-oriented architecture (SOA) and web services is especially significant for this reason. The business glossary should be considered the enterprise artifact that officially defines and controls the common vocabulary shared across an organization. The successful implementation of a glossary therefore drives the semantics of all the key terms and related taxonomy.

The business glossary also plays a crucial role in guiding data integration efforts across systems as well as in SOA initiatives to ensure that various roles within business and IT across the organization have the same understanding, not merely regarding which terms are which, but of what terms come together in an SOA context to form reusable information structures (Bryne, 2008).

Let us look at an example of an organization interested in establishing a well-defined business glossary centered on an account opening process in a bank (Figure 6.4). The definitions could evolve over the project lifecycle. Consequently, there may or may not be full definitions and values for all of the terms at the beginning of a DaaS project, e.g., early on in the identification phase. However, the glossary will mature as the project crosses the various systems development lifecycle (SDLC) phases. As more is learned about the business terms, more information will be updated in the DaaS business glossary.

Having a shared business vocabulary that is maintained/stored in an enterprise metadata repository with up-to-date definitions can be relied on by business and IT users across the organization as the anchor point for any DaaS project in the organization. The shared business vocabulary should be treated as a foundational component of DaaS, as it can be an anchor point for sharing data across applications and with downstream users consuming information published over data services. Therefore, developing a shared business vocabulary in the organization trying to implement reusable data services is essential. This is because of the simple fact that having key business terms (such as customer, product, or organization) formally named, comprehensively defined, and properly structured in a metadata glossary helps build semantic consistency and generates confidence among business users.

Subject Area / Domain	Business Term	Definition	Format	Domain Owner/Data Steward	Last Revision Date
Account	Account Id	This is the numeric categorization for the type of account	Varchar (4)	Controller's office	19/12/1992
	Account Type	This is the numeric categorization for the type of account	Varchar (4)	Controller's office	14/10/1986
	Account Description	This is the description for the type of account being used for this customer	Varchar (50)	Controller's office	19/12/1987
	Account Balance	Balance amount held in this account	Numeric	Controller's office	07/21/1987
Customer	Customer ID	This is the numeric identifier of the customer	Varchar (4)	Marketing	19/12/1992
	Customer Type	This is the numeric categorization for the type of customer, e.g., prospect, lead, existing customer	Varchar (4)	Marketing	14/10/1986
	Customer First Name	This is the customer's legal first name	Varchar (50)	Marketing	19/12/1987
	Customer Last Name	This is the customer's legal last name	Varchar (50)	Marketing	19/12/1987
Demographics	Address Type	This is the numeric categorization for the type of address such as ship to, mail to, contact, etc.	Varchar (2)	Marketing/Customer Operations	07/21/1987
	Street Address	This is the legal street address	Varchar (50)	Marketing/Customer Operations	07/21/1987
	City	This is the legal postal city address	Varchar (35)	Marketing/Customer Operations	01/21/1998
	Postal code	This is the legal postal code or zip	Numeric (9)	Marketing/Customer Operations	08/22/1989
	State Code	This is the legal postal state	Varchar(2)	Marketing/Customer Operations	07/11/2014

Figure 6.4   Real-life example of a business glossary

It is recommended that while developing an enterprise metadata glossary for the first time in an organization, the pragmatic approach is to leverage the definitions gathered while defining the enterprise logical data model (ELDM, which was discussed earlier in Chapter 5) jointly with the business and data stewards.

Standardizing Business Term Definitions and Business Rules

A business term is usually a word, phrase, or expression that has a particular meaning to an enterprise. As discussed earlier in this chapter, organizations can benefit from having an enterprise data glossary with standardized business term definitions. The glossary clarifies business meanings within an organization's many business areas, which can drive a common view of data definitions across the enterprise.

A rich business information glossary with a rich vocabulary of business terms can be very useful before, during, and after data quality and governance initiatives planned by business leadership. It also ensures greater semantic consistency across different parts of the organization by encouraging the use of *business terms* as a way to connect one world to the other. Over time, the glossary is expected to reflect the shared business vocabulary of how users look at a particular term. Figure 6.5 depicts a real-life organization where business terms and their definitions differ widely across individual divisions.

Definition Number	Business Term	Definition	Subject area Context	Business Owner/Steward	Revision Date
1	Product	Any goods produced by labor, typically comprises products of manufacturing units and factory	Manufacturing	S.K. Bose	19/12/1987
2	Product	A chemical substance used in the treatment, cure, prevention, or diagnosis of disease, or one that is used to otherwise enhance physical or mental well-being	Pharmaceutical/ Bio Tech	P. Hennigan	21/07/2000
3	Product	Refers to securities or other financial assets and instruments used during a financial trade	Banking & Financials	S. Devraj	15/09/2012

Figure 6.5   Example of varied business term definitions across multiple divisions

Since business terms have to be precisely defined in an enterprise wide glossary, it is recommended that an organization's key business teams become involved in coming up with the business term definitions in major subject areas. The largest objective when conducting the initial sessions is to gather definitions from business and data stewards, which should include the following steps:

1. Define the data.
   (a) Define a shared vocabulary for all key business term definitions.
   (b) Identify key data classes and entities in the business.
   (c) Identify critical data attributes and understand which of the attributes identify information.
   (d) Determine valid domain values.
   (e) Finalize data type and size specifications for data elements.

2. Define the business rules.
   (a) Data relationship rules
   (b) Data mapping rules
   (c) Data validation and constraints
   (d) Data matching rules

After various business stewards agree on a comprehensive glossary of key business terms required for use by the entire organization, the glossary has to be physically stored in a metadata repository solution implemented to hold these artifacts. The enterprise data glossary can be classified by functional domain (finance, customer, product, etc.). It should identify key data subject areas and the major entities and attributes under each subject area. It should also formally document the major business rules used with data elements for future data create, read, update, and delete (CRUD) activities as well as for validation purposes.

ENTERPRISE METADATA REPOSITORY

This section discusses various components of the metadata program, primarily from the larger perspective of the enterprise that is running a DaaS program. Each individual component needs to be discussed in detail to ensure that the right type of information is captured in the enterprise metadata solution while setting up the DaaS program.

The major benefit of having an underlying metadata repository is to provide an organization with a shared business vocabulary (or glossary) of key terms and their associated meanings. The glossary standardizes the different types of business metadata used across the organization, which should store these terms in an enterprise metadata repository. The metadata repository needs to be supported and maintained as an enterprise asset, not just for individual programs such as MDM, data warehousing, and DaaS.

This standardization can help to bring much value by providing *consistent* business definitions across the organization's business and IT user community. They can also be used to align the organization's business and information governance policies with application development and implementation project phases.

Data Definition of Data Entities and Data Attributes

This section focuses on defining definitions of data entities and attributes. Often, large organizations feel this need more, as different divisions often develop many distributed systems over time with no common standards. This leads to different divisions using the same term in different ways.

Figure 6.6 shows that there can be varied definitions of data elements for the product entity across different divisions in the organization. This inconsistency can be because products in the investments division may contain different component

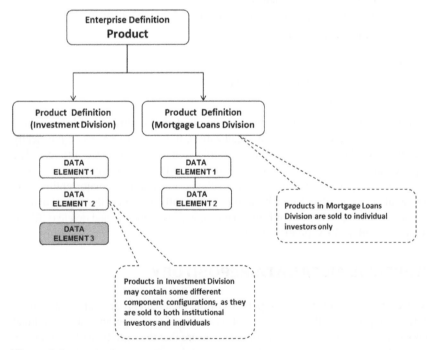

Figure 6.6 Varying instances of product definitions

configurations, as they are sold to both institutional investors and individuals. However, the mortgage division may sell products only to individual investors. Even the business rules across two divisions can be very different, reflecting a valid difference in business processes. These differences can cost organizations dearly as they cannot share information across applications because of differences in data structure, metadata, and business rules when a published data service is handling products across both lines of business.

Clarity of Relationships and Hierarchies

By focusing on building the underlying metadata layer, an organization can help remove inconsistencies across the underlying data architecture (DA). This not only ensures that data elements are defined to represent real-world objects, but also takes into consideration the relationship between various data entities stored across the enterprise. Similarly, if there are hierarchies involved among different information classes, then these are clarified in the metadata layer. As an example, in the pharmaceutical sector, the hierarchy of products can be rather complex. It is difficult to design any DaaS program without understanding the underlying hierarchy. Having this hierarchy information available as part of the business metadata to a business user can be extremely beneficial.

Service Integration-Related Metadata

This category of metadata is required for maintaining the definition and mappings of various EDS employed by business teams across client applications, their data lineage, and mapping information, which are related to every service from every client application. Service metadata would also reflect and capture the various lists of definitions stored in the canonical XML messages. For example, all of the process details related to individual data services such as "update a product" or "get a customer" need to be captured as metadata.

Standardizing metadata representation at the enterprise level can simplify the integration efforts that normally take place when applications do not have any shared data structure or canonical format. This collection of metadata can also assist during the post-implementation phases of the DaaS program project. Let us now briefly look at the process of implementing a enterprise metadata solution so that it can support DaaS needs.

IMPLEMENTING THE ENTERPRISE METADATA REPOSITORY

Delivering an enterprise metadata repository solution that holds all of the ELDM definitions can provide a comprehensive picture and description of an enterprise's data assets. The key benefits of having such a metadata repository solution for the

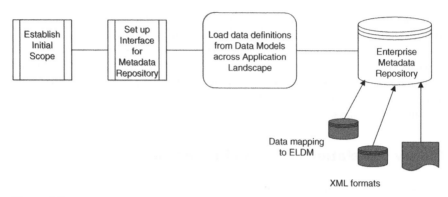

Figure 6.7   Metadata repository: Initial setup

business area is that it can help in capturing, sharing, and leveraging knowledge held by critical and disappearing business subject matter experts. It also helps IT teams during complex integration processes by making impact analysis possible during rapid implementation of managed system changes, which are required to support and integrate new business functionality. Metadata and profiling tools can provide developers with a quick understanding of data sources as well as of downstream systems (data lineage) and system component relationships.

Because few organizations have business glossaries in place, it is often necessary to populate the business glossary from existing databases (Figure 6.7). Most enterprises have multiple types of data stores. Because of this, the enterprise metadata repository solution needs to scan multiple types of data stores, as there can be various types of data sources in the organization with relevant metadata information. Most of the metadata tool vendors provide scanner software to facilitate importing metadata from disparate source platforms.

Periodic assessment to review the status of documentation (structured and unstructured) in the metadata repository as part of a metadata governance program should be conducted regularly. The recommended approach is to build a current state Data Asset Inventory (DAI) to act as a baseline for action on data governance. The next section covers these governance aspects in further detail.

METADATA STANDARDS FOR ENTERPRISE DATA SERVICES

In addition to the traditional metadata collected as part of EIM efforts to build an enterprise metadata repository, there are a few additional components related specifically to service metadata components that need to be considered for the DaaS environment. For example, efforts need to be taken to collect information on various lists of data services that are operational and hosted in the service repository.

The metadata team of data analysts helps the project team prepare this information so that it can be loaded or scanned into the metadata repository. These analysts also help identify metadata sources, determine whether they have been "scanned" or loaded into the repository, obtain any permissions that may be necessary if the source(s) is managed outside of the organization, and work with the data governance group to ensure the proper linkage of scanned items to business term definitions and details. As a result, the data service users are able to view extensive details through data lineage diagrams stored in the metadata repository, which are supplemented with detailed backgrounds, definitions, and supporting hierarchies.

The consensus among most IT practitioners and small and medium sized enterprises (SMEs) is that achieving consistency in terms of semantic and structural definitions across an organization is the most difficult challenge. Often, there are several underlying reasons that cause this disparity across divisions in organizations. While many of these roadblocks are caused by human factors, a major portion of these pain points can be alleviated by following a process-driven approach to metadata with active support from business users. While a complete state of nirvana (or bliss) is neither feasible nor realistic, achieving success in some key areas can go a long way toward reestablishing business users' trust toward the data they receive from published data services.

Let us now look at some major components to consider in order to achieve semantic consistency across the organization.

Semantic Definition of Data

These characteristics relate to the underlying meaning of a core entity in the EDM that needs to be resolved with the domain SME. For example, for the customer account support team in a bank, the customer is someone who has an existing account with them (Figure 6.8). However, for the marketing team, the customer is typically someone who either has purchased a financial product/service from the organization or is likely to purchase a product in the near future. This means that the total count of customers is higher when the marketing team counts the total number of customers (due to prospective customers being counted by marketing business users). It is fairly obvious that due to this discrepancy in the number of customers, using two different definitions of a customer could lead to inconsistencies in reporting across the enterprise.

Structural Definition

These characteristics relate to the structure of the ELDM's data entities and attributes. Some other characteristics that form part of the definition include the data type and column size of a customer identifier, the social security number (SSN), or tax identifier, which has to be both consistent and agreed upon by the team developing the ELDM.

A data type is a way of identifying different types of data by classifying the data values into distinct sets. For example, one could classify a set of integers with 5 digits or a set of decimal numbers with 6 digits, with 2 of them following the decimal point or a set of character strings with a length of 9 digits.

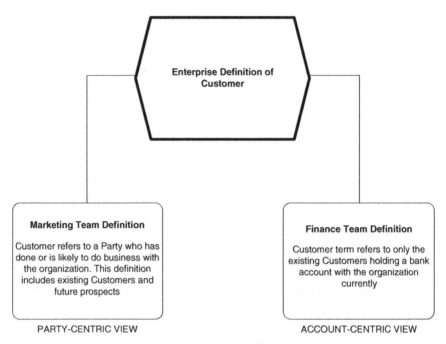

Figure 6.8 Mapping semantic inconsistencies across customer applications in an enterprise

The implementation models and exchange models used by XML canonical messages will use these definitions later and translate them into XML message schemas for data exchange with other systems.

Standardize Data Definitions

The individual subject area glossary should contain the following types of information for every business term.

- Data element definition: The definition should clearly describe what the data element represents. This is referred to as the structural definition of data. The definition should be unambiguous and it should also avoid using abbreviations as much as possible (Figure 6.9).

- Data format: Every data element should have specified the data size and type reviewed by the IT team and implemented across the physical databases in a consistent manner for data entry (e.g., varchar, number, integer, etc.).

- Profiling and lineage analysis: The relationship and hierarchies across the enterprise also need to be clearly identified and documented as part of the metadata gathering exercise.

- Business rules for each term.

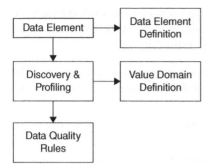

Figure 6.9   Structural definition of data

- The following business rules for each term must be gathered as part of building:
  - Data relationship rules
  - Data constraints
  - Data derivation rules (e.g., hierarchies).

Determine List of Valid Value Domains for Some Data Elements

A value domain is a set of valid values for a data element. It is a specific collection of representations of values for a particular data element, based on the organization's business rules, industry standards, or a regulatory authority (Figure 6.10). The rule specifies a restriction on the values within that data type that are allowed for a specific data element. For example, in the United States, a particular location can only have a specified and finite number of zip codes. The entire list of values for the 50 state codes in the United States can be considered as a value domain. For these data elements,

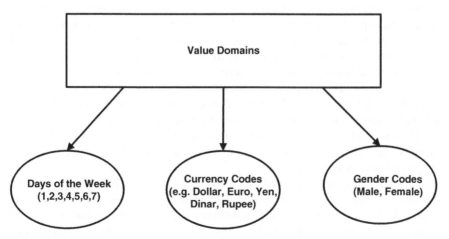

Figure 6.10   Illustrative example of value domains

the specific list of domain values that are allowed (as per business rules) have to be defined and stored as part of the metadata definition. Some other commonly found examples of data domains in a U.S. setting include the following:

- SSN: Has a base type of character 11 and is composed of five parts, i.e., the area denotation, a hyphen, the group number, and hyphen followed by the serial number.

- Corporate email address: An alphanumeric string concatenated with an @ string followed by the string.

- Zip + 4 code: Has a base type of character 10 where characters 0–4 must be numeric digits followed by a "-" and the four digits must be numeric digits.

Other universal examples include:

- Gender code: Has a base type of character 1 to represent male and female gender codes.

- Month of the year: Represents a domain with values ranging from 1 to 12 to represent the various months in a year, namely, January, February, March, April, etc.

Business Rules

Business policies are official statements that define or constrain some aspect of business behavior. They are intended to assert business structure as well as to influence or restrict the business's behavior in a particular way. Business policies are converted to implementable workflow processes to complete the job. While business policies guide the business processes, organizations need to formulate EIM specific policies that dictate how various information-related controls can be implemented across the organization separately.

In the context of EDS, business and information rules are an essential component because they specify the business specified constraint or directive associated with a data element that needs to be exchanged across the systems. An instance of such a business rule-driven constraint can be to trigger certain privacy alerts in case of a data attribute value that is noncompliant to a certain privacy regulation mandated by the government (e.g., PHI in the healthcare sector or KYC in the banking sector). Similarly, in the context of information domains, there can be rules specifying the list of allowable values by the business under a data validation rule.

However, unless the business uses a rules engine to centrally manage and enforce business rules, the behavior of business users could be completely unpredictable in any given business situation.

Therefore, it is recommended that a business rules engine be set up to ensure that business rules are centrally created and maintained. These rules also need to be periodically reviewed by the data governance council to ensure that there are no major discrepancies in the approach taken by different parts of the organization in a particular situation.

METADATA GOVERNANCE

The metadata governance process should be focused on managing quality, consistency, and usability of the shared business definitions of terms and business rules. Since metadata are typically stored in an enterprise metadata repository, metadata should be treated as a corporate asset. The governance of metadata should be viewed as a key component of the data governance strategy across the enterprise, not just of the DaaS environment. Investing in a metadata glossary can provide many advantages and result in several long-term benefits.

It is worth emphasizing that there are some disadvantages associated with running an enterprise's metadata program as a stand-alone IT initiative. If IT and data professionals follow a myopic approach that essentially translates into, "build it and they will come," then often times failure occurs. To ensure the DaaS metadata program's long-term success, it is critical that business users need to not only see the value of metadata, but also to champion its benefits to other business teams and likely users.

To overcome these obstacles, focus on building a continued metadata governance effort to ensure that any changes in the business systems are updated in the official metadata definitions in the business glossary (stored in the enterprise metadata repository). Metadata governance, change, and release management should be considered as a sub-component of the overall data governance council agenda. There also needs to be a formal list of data owners appointed on the business side who are accountable for these processes in their respective data domains (or subject areas).

In conclusion, metadata procedures need to be periodically reviewed by the organization's stakeholders and owners and changes in direction may be required from time-to-time to ensure that the program objectives stay aligned to business users' real needs. For example, if any data definitions change than this change needs to go through the data governance council and data stewards for review and formal approval. The governance of metadata needs to continue over the entire lifecycle of a data service published under the DaaS framework.

SUMMARY

This chapter focused on metadata, which creates a kind of conceptual synthesis in which one business concept is understood in the context of other related concepts. All of these key business concepts and terms need to be maintained in a business glossary. In the DaaS context, the business glossary can be compared to a formal contract between data providers and subscribers. The glossary can clarify the meaning of a particular term to DaaS users as they access the published enterprise data services.

In the context of the larger enterprise (not just in terms of DaaS), there are several major benefits of building enterprise-level metadata capabilities as part of the overall strategy to support the deployment of shared, reusable, enterprise-wide data services.

Having a metadata glossary offers the following major benefits:

- Providing a better understanding of data to users across the organization by providing a common business vocabulary. This includes a glossary of shared business terms and definitions.

- Storing this glossary in a metadata repository is expected to improve the overall productivity of business and IT users, as the agreement on common business terms can help them spend less time struggling to understand data and more time using data to support daily business operations.

- Having a centralized version of a business metadata glossary with definitions that are reviewed by the business stewards and other data stakeholders at regular intervals can help build semantic consistency for the terms used as the organization's core data assets.

- Facilitating easier compliance of reference data that need to comply with government and industry standards (e.g., adoption of domain values such as NAICS industry codes by banks or for complying with ICD-based diagnosis codes in the U.S. healthcare sector).

Finally, the metadata program and its continued support/governance should be aligned to the overall vision and scope of data governance for the organization as a whole. Gathering metadata should not be considered as a stand-alone IT initiative. If only IT and data professionals see the value of metadata and not business users, the chance for failure is very high.

Chapter 7

SOA and Data Integration

TOPICS COVERED IN THIS CHAPTER

- This chapter provides a high-level architectural roadmap for delivering on the promise of offering data services to end users in the real world.
- It explains how service-oriented architecture (SOA) principles can be leveraged to make enterprise data services reusable across projects in an organization.
- The concept of a data service is introduced and provides details on individual components of a data service.
- An overview is provided on key technologies (such as data virtualization, stream computing for big data, data federation, and visualization) that can be leveraged by the DaaS framework to publish data services with enhanced performance and scalable architecture.

"We shape our buildings; thereafter they shape us."

—Winston Churchill

Recently, Data as a Service (DaaS) has become popular as an information-distribution and delivery mechanism that can be used by organizations to provide convenient, on-demand access to their customers. This chapter explains in greater detail how underlying enterprise SOA principles can be leveraged to make data services reusable across projects in the enterprise. As previously discussed, one of the foundational blocks of DaaS architecture is service-oriented architecture (SOA).

From an enterprise view, building a data service access layer is a convenient way to access an organization's functional data assets and related infrastructure. Deploying data services have been more successful in real-life scenarios when organizations have also applied enterprise SOA principles while designing data services for downstream users and applications. This chapter explains how enterprise SOA principles can be leveraged to make data services reusable across projects in the enterprise.

Data as a Service: A Framework for Providing Reusable Enterprise Data Services,
First Edition. Pushpak Sarkar.
© 2015 the IEEE Computer Society. Published 2015 by John Wiley & Sons, Inc.

Also, this chapter looks at the benefits of leveraging data virtualization technology while publishing data services to meet enhanced performance and scalable architecture to consolidate structured and unstructured forms of data.

SOA AS AN ENABLER OF DATA INTEGRATION

The foundation to the DaaS reference architecture is enterprise SOA. As per the IEEE standard 1471-2000, SOA is defined as follows:

> SOA is an Integration Architecture in which components are available through services. These services are available through platform-neutral interfaces and communication protocols. They also encapsulate application functionality to be delivered to the service consumer. They are loosely coupled and based on a formal definition (or contract).

The approach toward building EDS leverages many underlying principles of SOA (e.g., service modularity and loose coupling, service granularity, service reuse, platform neutral interfaces) that were implemented successfully by practitioners on real-life projects. Having said that, the emphasis throughout this book is that for SOA to be successful, simply building services is not sufficient, unless they are based on a strong foundation of data. However, this point was not fully realized in the early days of SOA. This chapter explains in greater detail how underlying SOA principles can be leveraged to make data services reusable across enterprise projects.

Most experts agree that SOA is not a technology *per se*, but is an integration architecture framework that provides a rich set of foundational layers comprising standard blueprints to decompose the enterprise application layer into distinct functional modules that can be exposed as services by service providers. SOA became popular among organizations as a way of organizing business and software processes so that companies could swiftly respond to the global marketplace's volatile requirements.

The underlying foundation of SOA was typically based on the service reuse pattern concept, enabling users to interact with their business using common reusable services over the web, the Cloud, and through related technology. Business service components were considered customized functional modules of software stored in a centralized service repository that can be run in a network.

SOA Integration Patterns

As discussed, SOA integration patterns define ways to effectively bring together data from systems across the organization. They also provide guidance on message-implementation characteristics such as runtime performance, scalability, and availability. The following are two major patterns to support the delivery and access components of SOA and enterprise data services.

Publish-Subscribe

The publisher of a data service generates a message and publishes it. All subscribers to the service receive this message. The publish-subscribe pattern therefore establishes a one-to-many relationship between the publisher of content and service subscribers who receive messages simultaneously.

Point-to-Point

The publisher of a data service generates a message and posts it in a queue. The consumer can access the posted message from the queue. The point-to-point messaging pattern establishes a one-to-one relationship between the publisher of content and a specific application or subscribers who receive content from the message queue.

When there are multiple downstream applications receiving messages, using the point-to-point messaging pattern may be unsuitable as the multiple downstream system may result in high resource consumption. This may result in a performance issue for the underlying server hosting the message services. Consequently, in most situations, the DaaS environment follows the publish-subscribe pattern. Most of the examples in this book are also based on the publish-subscribe pattern.

The emphasis on reusable service components is an important advance seen in SOA-based implementations. There is also growing maturity among IT designers and SOA architects working in this area. Therefore, the essence of the service component is that more complex metadata regarding the SOA service provider are stored within the service container, making reuse by service consumers easier.

While SOA tries to integrate the application landscape through enterprise-wide messaging based on standards, it is not a realistic expectation to homogenize the disparity in existing application areas entirely because of the risks involved. By staying away from stringent measures for enterprise standardizations, the SOA framework allows the organization to design certain components by keeping in mind the local-level differences while simultaneously trying to achieve global integration at the enterprise level. By taking this balanced approach, most enterprise SOA initiatives can avoid any unnecessary turf wars among the organization's different stakeholders.

Figure 7.1 shows the basic functional components seen in a typical SOA environment.

Service

A service is a software component that encapsulates a high-level business concept comprising a distinctive set of functional features. In the SOA context, a service typically contains the service contract, which provides a formal, working specification of the purpose, function, constraints, and usage of the service. The functionality of the service is exposed by a service interface for clients using a network.

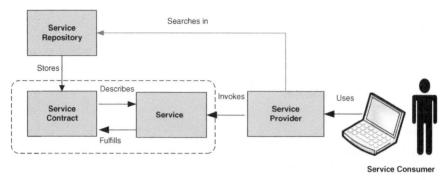

Figure 7.1 Functional components of SOA

The typical web service implementation includes the required business logic and data layer (Bean, 2010). Further, typically, enterprise data services can fall into two categories from an interaction-behavior perspective.

- Transaction notification: The service reports an event and causes something to change. Any complex data operation or request to update or delete a database element would be treated as a transaction service.

- Observational notification: The service reports an event but does not directly change anything. The requests to read or access data would be considered observational notifications.

Service Repository

The service repository is responsible for making web service interfaces and implementation access available to the service's potential requestors. Organizations have to establish and centrally manage their service repository in order to store the catalog of data services as well as provide consistent access to user applications that want to use data services.

Under the SOA environment setup, the service repository makes it possible for data services to be reused by any business team, authorized external entity, or by consumers. The service repository is a vital component of SOA in the long term, as it not only stores services but also provides the infrastructure and facilities to discover services or to acquire all of the information required to store services. Often, the service repository can store metadata about the service provider, contact person, usage details, security/technical constraints, and fees based on the service levels.

Although some service implementation teams may have the view that the larger goals of SOA can be accomplished without having a service repository, building this repository to support cross-enterprise service integration is highly recommended.

Service Provider

The service provider is the official entity publishing the service by providing an implementation for it, which potential consumers can access. Typically, the service provider also maintains detailed information about the service provider, contact person, security/technical constraints, usage details, and fees based on service levels.

Service Consumer

The service consumer is the client-facing component of the SOA. This component can use the service description directly or optionally it can also find the service description by using the service broker. It can then bind to and invoke the service from the service provider. Services can be consumed by any business team or external entity, as long as they are authorized to use the service (Krafzig, 2007).

A portal is typically a web site designed by a service provider (or organization) as the front door through which a user can access links to relevant sites. However, a portal site can also be used to entice people into using that site as the main point of entry for enterprise data services. For example, to find a service that shows the nearest physician to you in your neighborhood, the web portal offered by the insurance provider may be the front door that is used by the health-insurance consumer.

ROLE OF ENTERPRISE SERVICE BUS

In the real world of service implementation within any large organization, it is difficult to find all the systems in the application landscape using one set of software tools, databases, or networking. Instead, very often, the system is configured based on individual application needs. From a practical standpoint, many vendors have started addressing this concern by providing middleware known as an enterprise service bus (ESB), which can support an exchange between an organization's different systems. In an enterprise that makes use of an ESB, all applications communicate via the service bus instead of having point-to-point connections. By reducing dependence on point-to-point connections, it is easier to reduce the complexity of communication among multiple applications. This makes it easier to monitor for failure and to change individual components without impacting the remaining applications.

The major duties of an ESB include:

- Monitoring the routing of message exchange between services.
- Resolving contention between communicating service components.
- Controlling deployment and versioning of different services.
- Specialized functions such as event handling, data transformation and mapping, message queuing, security, or exception handling (Chappell, 2004).

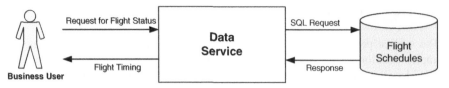

Figure 7.2   Data service to check airline flight status

WHAT IS A DATA SERVICE?

As mentioned, a data service is a specialized kind of web service implementation. The concept of data services originates under the SOA framework and the data service inherits a number of properties from original SOA characteristics (Figure 7.2). It can be viewed as a specialized type of service that addresses user data access needs by using predefined information-delivery patterns. Typically, data services are designed to respond to service requests that involve accessing data from one or more source applications (also known as the golden source) storing certain parts of the requested data.

The data services layer can be viewed as a virtual data layer, enriched by a relevant data model to support messaging needs (known as the canonical model). It is used for standardizing information that is collected from disparate data repositories spread across the enterprise. As Chapter 4 covered, the canonical model is part of an enterprise integration-design pattern, which provides a common view of enterprise data to data consumers. The need to standardize agreed upon data definitions associated with integrating business systems on disparate platforms is critical for the success of DaaS. The canonical model can ensure common data naming, definitions, and reference-data domain values for all data published under the DaaS framework. From a messaging context, the role of the canonical model is significant in building data services, which can be used to communicate between different formats of data being exchanged.

Having a virtual layer can insulate the IT organization against any impacts to underlying data sources. This is because the data service layer can greatly restrict the relevance of a particular platform on which a particular category of data resides. As such, data services should be considered an essential component of the reusable SOA infrastructure.

The following features are minimal requirements for a DaaS system as a delivery mechanism to distribute data to authorized service subscribers.

- The framework has to ensure that the information it distributes via enterprise data services is consistent across the enterprise and can meet data quality standards in case a data audit or review is necessary for regulatory authorities.

- The data delivery mechanism must distribute information to all subscribers in a secure and timely manner. Sufficient safeguards need to be in place to ensure that data are secure from unauthorized online usage by international rings of cybercriminals and sophisticated hackers.

- The system should also comply with all of the existing regulatory/industry standards on customer data privacy and the organization's other external partners.

- While DaaS may use reusable SOA-based components, the underlying technical architecture of the systems that DaaS needs to interface with regularly may be completely different. The DaaS infrastructure that is chosen should be able to operate with a varied set of data sources often hosted on different system platforms.

- The DaaS system must be scalable and users/subscribers of the data service should be able to get a response within a pre-defined service-level agreement (SLA) that is acceptable to the business.

Let us now discuss a real-life example from an airline to illustrate how data services can be reused by multiple business processes under the SOA framework (Figure 7.3).

In this example, various customers and travel agents have to use the airline web site (application frontend). This public service then invokes process-enabled services to carry out the airline's respective functional module with detailed workflow processing following business-specified rules (e.g., flight reservation or customer check-in). The process-enabled service in turn invokes basic services such as data

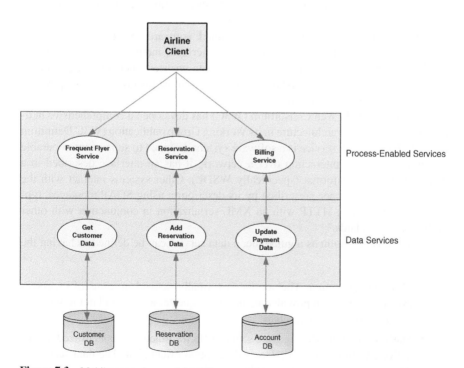

Figure 7.3   Multilayer services used for airline reservations

services to create/add/update the underlying customer database or business logic services.

It is worth highlighting here that in a real-life DaaS environment multiple process-enabled services can leverage the underlying data service (get customer data) for check-in, customer complaints, or the reservation process. Therefore, reuse and consistency are clear benefits obtained from service enablement of data services.

Next, let us overview the SOA components that are required as part of any typical data service. In its most fundamental form, every service involves three entities: service provider, service consumer, and service. The service provider (often a webserver) performs a task at the request of a service consumer (who can be a user or a calling function). The service binds the two parties together based on a service contract between them.

A service consists of a contract, one or more interfaces, and a service implementation. These services can be broadly classified into two forms of basic services, data-centric services and process logic-centric services. These services have become very popular because they are agile and reusable.

The data service typically provides users with an abstracted, logical view of underlying databases, files, other content, and so on, as necessary for carrying out a business operation. For a typical data service, extracted data are then placed on messages to be transported back for use by other consuming applications. While other composite types of services often manage data for an entire system(s), the data service usually deals with one specific business entity or domain (e.g., account, customer, product) in the physical repository.

Data services is defined as loosely coupled, software objects that are used to publish and consume data using standard web interfaces and protocols. Similar to the previous example, airlines can use enterprise data services when a passenger needs to get the latest flight-status updates (or times) from the underlying set of physical databases that store flight schedules.

The World Wide Web Consortium (W3C) has developed a comprehensive definition of web services architecture in its Working Group publication (W3C Definition of SOA, 2004). "Web service is a software system designed to support interoperable machine-to-machine interaction over a network. It has an interface described in a machine-processable format (specifically WSDL). Other systems interact with the Web service in a manner prescribed by its description using SOAP messages, typically conveyed using HTTP with an XML serialization in conjunction with other Web-related standards."

Using this definition as a guideline, a data service can be defined as having the following properties:

- Message orientation: The service is formally defined in terms of messages exchanged between provider agents and requester agents, and not in terms of agents' properties themselves.

- Platform-neutral: Messages are sent in a platform-neutral, standardized format delivered through the interface's description orientation. The data service is described by machine-processable metadata.

- Network orientation: Services should be planned assuming they will be used over a network, although this is not always an essential or necessary requirement.

- Granularity: Data services may tend to be designed using a small number of operations with relatively large and complex messages (known as coarse-grained services).

Certain specialized, enterprise-level data services can also support the management and governance of internal data across the enterprise. A complete portfolio of data services is needed to:

- Enable finding the data needed (i.e., search/visibility) across a wide range of repositories.

- Ensure that the data is both authoritative and trusted.

- Validate that the data conforms to a registered (and publicly available) schema.

- Transform the data into a usable format.

- Help create, update, and delete data.

Finally, in practice, sometimes many services deal with both data and process logic. Thus, for a claims' processing service, the data service stores the claim data. In this respect, the claims' processing service is a data-centric service. However, the user can require validation checks to determine the data set represents valid claims to bona fide parties. In this scenario, the service can be classified as a logic-centric service. That being said, this combined interpretation of a service does not make the separate premise of services being centered on data contradictory or untenable at the basic, atomic level.

FOUNDATIONAL COMPONENTS OF A DATA SERVICE

This section provides a high-level overview of foundational components comprising a typical data service (Figure 7.4). In its most fundamental form, every service involves three entities: service provider, service consumer, and the service. As shared, the service provider (often a webserver) performs a task at the request of a service consumer (who can be a user or a calling function). The service binds the two parties together based on a service contract between them.

A service consists of a contract, one or more interfaces, and a service implementation. These services can be broadly classified in two forms of basic services: data-centric services and process logic-centric services. These services have become very popular because they are agile and reusable.

The data exchange format and their underlying data services definitions are maintained in an enterprise model. The canonical model represents a common data format that is used for data exchange (and XML messaging) across the organization's different systems. The data format stored in the canonical model is independent of any individual application's implementation. It usually provides a common format

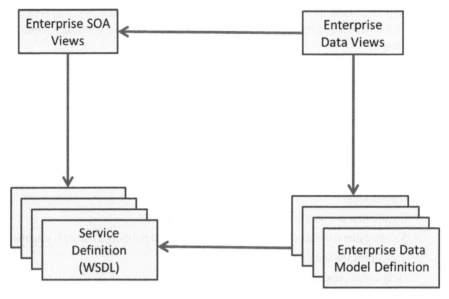

Figure 7.4 Data service interface is deployed based on enterprise-data definitions

that is at a higher level of abstraction from various applications' native data formats. Having a generic format helps to enable use of the canonical format by applications in multiple platforms. However, there is usually some mapping/transformation required to convert data from native formats in a particular system to standardized format in an enterprise's canonical model.

Data services is defined as loosely coupled, software objects that are used to publish and consume data using standard web interfaces and protocols.

What Happens as a Data Service Processes a Consumer Request?

- The request message from the service consumer is received.
- The service layer checks the user's entitlements and sends an internal request to extract the requested data from the data store (for unauthorized consumers, a denial response is sent instead).
- The data layer then processes the request and sends a response.
- The service layer inserts the response data in the message.
- The response message to the data service consumer is sent back.

Chapters 9 to 11 discuss this area in more detail from an enterprise data service implementation perspective. For now, let us look at the major categories of services.

SERVICE INTERFACE

The service interface layer allows services to be decoupled from underlying data sources as well as consuming business and application services. This approach provides the flexibility required to exchange data with each layer in the most effective manner, as well as the agility to integrate quickly across layers as applications, schemas, or underlying data sources change.

As discussed, XML schemas are used to specify the various terms and conditions of a service contract. However, in context of operating the service interface, recognize that these schemas only address the individual components of the message.

XML schemas alone are not sufficient to enable deployment of a web service, as they do not represent the overall service interface. To address this issue, another interface component is needed, known as the web services description language (WSDL), which is required to create the technical service artifact at implementation level. The WSDL specifies the web service interface between the service provider and service consumer. Any user who invokes a web service must adhere to the format and definition specified in the WSDL. Recently, WSDL specification has been approved by the W3C as a formal specification to define overall service interface and contract.

While the WSDL can be considered the XML component representing the overall service interface and contract, it can also reference the externally created XML schemas for individual areas with their own defined message structure and type definition. Consequently, there can be separate XML schema defined for individual components of the message, e.g., a request message, reply message, or error message. Each of these XML schema definitions specifies some part of the web service interface contract.

In any interaction during a web service, individual XML schemas for particular message components (request, reply) are referenced (or called) by the WSDL as part of the service interface contract. However, no correction takes place by validating the parser in the web service applications. This is because any error handling or remediation in the message component can require detailed analysis. Therefore, it is the responsibility of the consuming application to fix the service interface errors later.

As mentioned, implementing service definitions (WSDL) that are aligned with enterprise-data definitions can ensure that data is shared across the enterprise (refer to the section on canonical models in Chapter 5).

MAJOR SERVICE CATEGORIES

Data services enable an organization to be agile when reacting to changes in the business environment. It also allows an IT organization to be flexible when there are changes in backend systems storing master data or introduction of new reference codes (e.g., New ICD diagnosis codes resulting in decommission of older legacy system values). As such, it is crucial to understand and classify the major service types, just as it is critical to understand the distinctive features of different kinds of

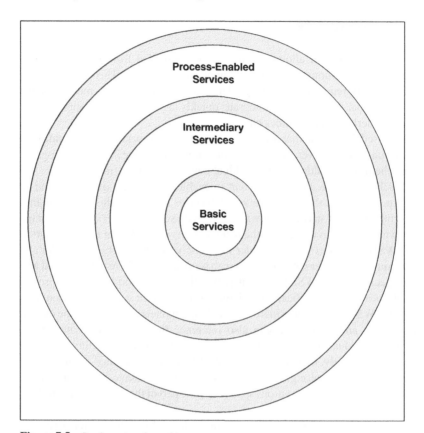

Figure 7.5 Service categories and types

service categories under the DaaS framework. This can help build enterprise data services that are consistent with underlying SOA principles within a unified DaaS framework (Figure 7.5).

Basic Services

Basic services can be considered the foundation layer of an SOA and usually data services and the logic-centric component reside in this layer. Many people refer to these as coarse-grained services because most of these services are simple and easy to implement. However, data-centric services do encapsulate all of their underlying data entities and related definitions. Characteristically, services at this level only deal with one major business entity or process, making the design modular more flexible. This is an example of a data service that enables different applications to read or update customer profiles in a consistent manner, irrespective of the individual platform where customer information resides within an organization (or externally of an organization). Similarly, a service to calculate a discount on a sale item can be treated as a basic service that is process oriented. Other services related to data quality, such as data parsing and standardization of domain values, are also good examples of basic services.

Intermediary Services

Intermediary services often act as the go-between (or middle layer) to help frontend applications access services in the basic layer. Intermediary services also can be used to add functionality to existing services. The intermediary layer of services is comprised of different categories such as technology gateways, adapters, and facades. The following are real-life examples of intermediary services.

– A technology gateway is used when an organization translates a web service request to a terminal data stream in order to communicate with a legacy mainframe.

– The facade category of intermediary services can commonly be seen when they are used to provide an aggregated view of one or more basic services.

– Similarly, the adapter category of intermediary services can be used to map message formats of an underlying service to the requirement of a client.

From a DaaS perspective, these services can also handle a range of core data functions such as the following:

• Access control and security management services.

• Audit services to manage access logging as well as an analysis of access history.

• Alerts and notifications.

These examples demonstrate that an intermediary service usually can play a significant role in the DaaS project's access layer.

Process-Enabled or Business Services

The process-centric layer contains the most advanced type of services because they typically encapsulate the organization's business processes and related knowledge.

Process-enabled services are usually designed as fine-grained services with complex logic built into them. They often function as enablers for interaction between cross-enterprise processes and integration services. An example of process-enabled services is a service that calculates an insurance premium for a customer based on several of their personal demographic factors such as their age, medical history, etc.

Process-enabled services can enable load-balancing between different basic services. These features make it very useful when a process-enabled service can improve user interface responsiveness by distributing a basic services work load on different servers to speed up processing.

This feature is especially helpful in a big data analytics environment, if there is a need for running a sophisticated algorithm and several predictive models to provide the user with a final result in a matter of few seconds, e.g., compute a consumer's overall credit risk. In such a scenario, it is recommended to assign core business logic (like running a complex algorithm) to the base service while a process-enabled service manages the organization's business processes. Separating core logic from process-centric logic is highly recommended to develop lean applications under the SOA framework.

Public enterprise services are a separate sub-category of process-enabled services that organizations commonly use to offer services to external partners and customers. Most organizations offering DaaS are also expected to provide some public enterprise services for external consumers. For example, if an airline offers services to their customers to track their flight reservation status, they would need to build a public service that can be accessed by customers to track any modification to reservation status.

It is important to note that unlike the other category of services discussed earlier, public services are not limited for use within the boundaries of an enterprise only. However, crossing boundaries can increase the risk of data breaches and significantly raise security concerns.

All the service types that have been defined are suitable based on the specific requirements of the web service applications through which they are likely to be deployed. The following are some major considerations to keep in mind while choosing appropriate technologies for a data-centric service.

- Performance (response time)
- Service availability (SLA)
- Number of data sources to be accessed
- Complexity of the underlying data sources
- Scalability, i.e., the volume of data involved
- Information-security requirements

Finally, to enhance customers' experience in terms of query and reporting performance, companies can also look at running data services in combination with data virtualization components, especially when the company has a disparate set of tools in its technology portfolio. Let us turn to some recent and major advances in data virtualization.

OVERVIEW OF DATA VIRTUALIZATION

The Data Virtualization design pattern is expected to be more commonly used for data integration, data services, SOA, Cloud computing, and enterprise search domains as vendors gain an increasing understanding and maturity of this technology. Data virtualization tools provide the opportunity for organizations to set up a set of standardized views and data services. The logic necessary to access, source, and deliver these views/services to the user are centrally encapsulated by the data virtualization tool. However, data formats and functionality of key data elements that are shared across applications get captured in a canonical data model that is defined for data exchange across enterprise applications (Chapter 5 discusses this concept in detail). The data virtualization tools can also map the canonical data model and its individual elements to the organization's underlying data sources.

In some situations, organizations that adopt DaaS may find that their external consumers face huge performance issues when trying to integrate data. Often, this is because their operations involve high levels of integration complexity or latency issues, which lead to slower response time. The delays become worse when large volumes of data are being transferred to and from the data provider's data center at slower Internet speeds (as compared to higher speeds while accessing a firm's internal network). In these situations, complementing DaaS with other virtualization technologies can be a great option.

Data virtualization tools support user information requests by providing data services and views that extract, transform, and aggregate data from an organization's multiple data sources. These tools drastically reduce users' waiting time even if they issue complex requests that may need data retrieved from multiple data sources. Users of a virtualization tool often may be completely unaware of any underlying complexity while requesting data that resides across multiple platforms. Data virtualization tools reduce system latency and improve data access performance by supporting advanced techniques such pre-fetching (anticipating the need for data input requests) and extensively storing data in cache storage components so that future requests for the same data can be retrieved faster.

In the traditional world of batch computing, organizations often used extract transform load (ETL) tools to move data physically from multiple legacy data sources and to consolidate them physically in a data repository. This form of data integration is reliable, but also time-consuming when consolidating data from multiple platforms. This is more prevalent when data is consolidated across disparate data sources within the enterprise or when it involves external data sources. In contrast to traditional data, integration approaches such as data virtualization does not require data to be copied and moved from pre-existing sources to a physical data virtualization repository. Instead, a virtual or logical data view is created after abstracting all necessary data from various legacy data sources supporting current business operations (Figure 7.6).

From an end user's perspective, data virtualization technology significantly improves the ability of a customer to access critical data using enterprise data services. The tool achieves this capability by abstracting data from multiple data sources (databases, applications, unstructured and semi-structured data, files, websites, etc.) into a single, logical data access layer (an abstract layer). The final data view provided by the data virtualization platform to the end user can provide clients with data in a standardized format. The data virtualization platform uses the standardized canonical model and XML exchange format for consolidating data from different platforms into a unified view. This view is termed the virtual consolidation layer and it can be reused by other customers interested in viewing similar data later on.

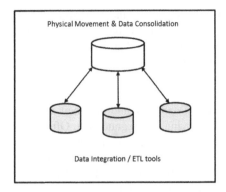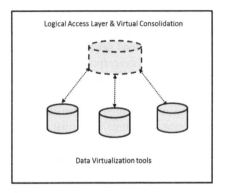

Figure 7.6 Comparing data integration and data virtualization approaches

From a technology perspective, data virtualization provides an integrated-development environment (IDE) for development teams to define and implement the appropriate virtual views. Data virtualization tools dynamically gather information from various types of data storage (relational databases, files, text data, unstructured data, etc.). The tools leverage these data to deliver a particular view to authorized users without the need for permanently storing data. Another key benefit of having a data virtualization platform from an infrastructure-management perspective is that it allows large organizations with diverse IT platforms to consolidate their physical infrastructure and the various software licenses (data caching, integration, ETL) and application-programming interfaces (APIs) around data that would otherwise require separate webservers and application servers (Figure 7.7).

As mentioned, having a middleware tool is not always a mandatory feature of the enterprise data services solution, but a data virtualization tool can certainly enhance development and delivery of an integrated-information view. However, virtualization tools become essential in a complex data integration environment with disparate types of source data feeds or data intense environments (such as real-time analytics or big data applications) to improve performance and scalability issues. With the assistance of data virtualization tools, consuming applications or users accessing enterprise data services are able to receive information in a quicker, more flexible, and dynamic manner. Moreover, most of these data virtualization tools also allow an organization to consolidate structured, unstructured, and semi-structured data under a single platform, making this a very attractive and popular solution among companies. Often, it is the flexibility of accommodating additional legacy systems, usually on disparate platforms, which makes data virtualization attractive to many organizations.

High-performance caching, sophisticated query algorithms, and other performance-optimization techniques also ensure quicker data delivery when multiple data services send requests to data virtualization tools. The primary objects created and used in data virtualization are usually a set of user-specified views and basic data services. These basic services are fine-grained and certainly not defined at the enterprise level for most virtualization tools that are currently available on

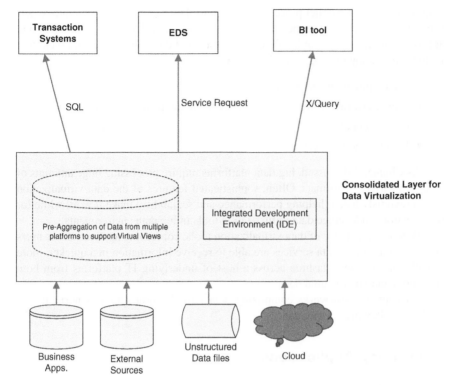

Figure 7.7   Conceptual framework for data virtualization

the market, although they provide a good foundation for aggregated views and base services (Tran, 2012).

Most companies who have used data virtualization tools so far recommend these tools as suitable for enterprise-wide use to access data across disparate platforms. This is largely because of growing realization among these "early adaptors" of data virtualization products that current vendor platforms can only provide an accurate and reliable view of data to consumers when an organization has an underlying data model and a common canonical message format defined for data information exchange. As shared, a critical success factor for any corporate data virtualization initiative (or data integration initiative) is that the underlying data has to be compatible and able to be integrated across enterprise source systems at a fundamental level. While the leading data virtualization vendor tools currently provide a highly effective mechanism to deliver integrated views quickly to bring together disparate data from multiple sources within an organization, these tools alone cannot be treated as a silver bullet or solution to many data quality and integration problems seen in large organizations.

However, a data virtualization tool can certainly aid in the development and delivery of an integrated-information view, especially in data intense environments (such as real-time analytics or big data applications) with advanced data architecture features to support parallel processing and controlled redundancies to improve performance and scalability issues. Data virtualization provides faster turnaround and agility by implementing an intelligent, sophisticated development environment that includes the following features (Figure 7.6):

- Data replication and partitioning
- Limited storage component for pre-defined, aggregated views
- Cache support
- Backup and recovery.

As Chapter 3 discussed, big data platforms require processing huge amounts of data in a variety of formats. Often, sophisticated features of the data virtualization tools previously listed (helping performance and scalability) make it worthwhile for organizations to leverage data virtualization tools in big data environments.

With the assistance of data virtualization tools, consuming applications or users accessing enterprise data services are able to receive information in a quicker, more flexible, and dynamic fashion across a host of underlying IT platforms from both structured and unstructured data.

Conceptual frameworks comprising data virtualization solutions normally include the following components.

Consuming Applications

In a typical data virtualization environment, runtime activities are usually initiated by queries or requests for data from a consuming application. Consuming applications often comprise customer self-service applications and new technologies such as the Cloud, social media, and mobility as well as analytic platforms that require information to support their applications. The key benefit for new or future consuming applications that use a data virtualization layer is that it often becomes possible for organizations to avoid time-consuming data integration activities that are typically seen in organizations when onboarding a new application. However, organizations introducing data virtualization technologies also need to incorporate a limited time for development and testing with highly skilled resources during the initial phase of implementation.

Data Sources

Within an organization, several existing legacy systems can act as data sources for user queries from the consuming application. These data sources are often hosted on various physical platforms. They can also include the following various types of source data.

- Transaction data that include all the detailed transaction information residing in operational applications (e.g. ERP, CRM).

- Master data that include all the detailed master and reference data.
- Analytical data that include all of the detailed reporting data stored in data warehouses and that are required by users for business intelligence (BI) and reporting purposes, as well as the data stored in "big data" analytic platforms.
- Unstructured data that can include human-generated content from various social media sites as well as machine-generated data from RFID, log files, etc.

New Technology to Further Improve Data Integration

To make the DaaS strategy a success within any organization, there are several underlying technologies that play a crucial role in the delivery of real-time data to DaaS subscribers. Let us now look at the major options available to organizations for data delivery to their consumers.

Message-oriented Middleware

The message-oriented movement (MOM) approach enables sending and receiving messages across heterogeneous platforms. The approach is very popular in organizations using SOA, as it reduces the complexity of developing applications that span multiple operating systems and network protocols. The middleware associated with MOM creates a distributed communications layer that insulates users from inconsistencies across various operating systems and network interfaces so consumer applications can read and exchange data in real time. This approach is often found most useful in environments comprising multiple systems on heterogeneous platforms with high availability requirements (Curry, 2004). This capability makes it very suitable for the DaaS environment.

Data Federation

This approach supports user access requirements against multiple data sources with high performance and is also suitable for the DaaS environment. Data virtualization tools execute queries against multiple data sources to create virtual integrated views of data in memory (rather than physically moving the data). Federated views require adaptation to various data sources along with a distributed query engine that can provide varied (for example, as an SQL row set, XML, or a web services interface).

Batch Computing

This is the traditional approach to data integration in batch mode and involves bulk-volume data extraction and delivery. ETL tools are used to consolidate data from primary databases and load them in various formats as dictated by a target system. However, since this approach cannot provide data in real time across systems, it is not the preferred mode of data integration in the DaaS environment.

Stream Computing

Several vendors now offer high-performance computing platforms that leverage real-time stream processing concepts as an alternative to replicating data. The stream computing platform can handle high volumes of data with speedy throughput of processing real-time messages. This approach of data delivery suits high-volume and mission-critical environments in keeping operational data current in multiple systems. It is also a very suitable technology component that can be added for implementing DaaS in a large organization dealing with huge volumes. Streaming technology is especially useful in a big data arena where it can handle high data throughputs necessary for the acquisition of large volumes of transaction data. The following section discusses this topic.

Stream Computing in a Big Data Environment

Some of the fundamental assumptions when designing real-time data services for big data analytics is very different from those required in traditional data. For example, the anti-terrorist department in a large federal agency can analyze terabytes of data from confiscated hard drives, cell phones, and USB drives to perform text analytics. They can also identify the most common words used in emails/chats, social media etc. To prevent criminal behavior, their big data analysis systems not only have to predict attacks after filtering all the data but they have to alert local enforcement officials with real-time data services. Local enforcement officials can then act swiftly against criminals and prevent attacks before it is too late. This form of predictive analytics often requires the use of data mining techniques on huge amounts of data (and is no less challenging than those techniques used in commercial sectors). Moreover, the prediction of criminal behavior in big data systems has to rely more on probabilistic models and less on deterministic modeling found in traditional analytics.

The majority of data integration efforts in big data implementations currently depend on high-performance batch computing platforms (such as Hadoop). This is often due to the sheer volume and complexity of data involved in a big data environment. However, batch computing is not suitable in some real-time application scenarios, especially when there are multiple data stream formats being processed. This is primarily because some of the fundamental assumptions when designing real-time data services for big data is very different from those required for traditional data. For example, the prediction of consumer behavior (such as in the stock market) in big data systems has to be designed based on probabilistic models and can rely less on deterministic modeling. This form of predictive analytics typically requires the use of data mining techniques from a complex range of structured and unstructured data feeds involving huge amounts of data. There is also a growing need for users to integrate the analysis of Hadoop and relational data after validating multiple data stream formats in real-time.

Stream computing is a new technology that can address the need to eliminate bottlenecks of real-time data acquisition in big data areas. While most batch computing tools follow a sequential model of storing then computing, stream computing follows a model of straight through (or non-sequential) computing in real-time.

In the stream computing environment all the incoming data is received as streaming data in real-time. Big data stream computing tools can then process and consolidate data generated from various applications such as log records or click-streams analysis of user browsing company websites. These include information from blogging, twitter posts, relational data, etc. Input streams incur multi-staged computing at low latency to produce newly generated results in output streams, within a matter of seconds.

Stream computing is particularly useful in a big data environment because it allows organizations to react quickly when incoming data feeds trigger certain events or generate alerts. Analytic systems can also detect new data trends that can help to create new opportunities in real-time.

Some of the established stream computing products currently available are IBM Stream Computing, Twitter Storm, Microsoft TimeStream, and Yahoo! S4.

CONSOLIDATED DATA INFRASTRUCTURE PLATFORM

Enterprise data services allow an organization to present an integrated view of data brought together from various sources to their data consumers in real time. The real-time integrated view of data is usually brought together from various platforms and transformed into the canonical format adopted for enterprise-wide exchange of data. To support these objectives, an organization needs to provide a consolidated infrastructure platform for data delivery to end consumers in a timely and cost-effective manner. This book avoids making any specific tool recommendations for setting up a DaaS environment. This is largely because technology components in the market's data integration segment are constantly evolving. That said, Figure 7.8 includes a representative list of IT tools that may be useful to readers when they try to engineer a DaaS-based solution in their own organization.

Overall, because such huge data volumes are being seen in many large organizations, the DaaS infrastructure should be viewed more as a shared infrastructure service.

The major benefit of introducing a DaaS layer is that it abstracts both physical implementation and underlying data repositories. If the DaaS solution is combined with data virtualization capabilities, then an organization can provide access to users with dynamic views instead of cumbersome data integration solutions (batch or ETL). DaaS-based virtualization solutions can make it easier to onboard new sources of data. It is also expected to simplify overall IT maintenance efforts over the long term. This is because the separation of logical and physical data layers allows the IT department to make quicker application enhancements via backend systems without affecting the view provided to the end users of various enterprise data services.

DaaS-based virtualization solutions typically include a physical data virtualization server that includes a sophisticated query engine that is specifically designed to process federated queries from multiple source systems. The server can also execute queries across one or more source systems with the aid of features such as parallel processing, cache storage, scan multiplexing, and constraint propagation techniques

---

Representative IT Tools Required for Publication of Enterprise Data Services

Hosting and Publishing Data Services
- Web server for hosting/publishing data services
- Service catalog
    - Design time repository for data services
    - Run-time repository for implemented services

- **Message Broker**
    - ▶ Transformation between formats
    - ▶ Entry point for requests from mainframe batch programs
    - ▶ Versioned at service level
- **Enterprise Service Bus (ESB)**
    - ▶ Used for enterprise and local service bus.
- **Data Integration and Virtualization**
    - ▶ Enterprise Application Integration
    - ▶ Message queues
    - ▶ Data virtualization tools
- **Data storage**
    - ▶ RDBMS.
    - ▶ Data modeling and model management
    - ▶ Metadata glossary
    - ▶ Database utilities
- **Data security**
    - ▶ Encryption tools
    - ▶ Data security tools
    - ▶ Access and identity management
    - ▶ Security tools for mobile devices

Figure 7.8 Representative technology for hosting data services

to optimize performance and provide end-user enterprise data services access in near real time. To aid performance and scalability, the data virtualization layer can also include a data storage component. This layer can be used to store incoming source data into a raw data table within the data storage device as well as to create data aggregates. Storing this data is usually based on pre-defined user views and, commonly, on user queries.

When an incoming query is received from a consumer, it uses the pre-defined format specified for a virtual view. Consequently, upon receiving the query, the DaaS-virtualization layer knows whether the data has been staged in the data storage component (cache). If the data is already available in the cache, queries can retrieve data faster by accessing the cache component provided by the virtualization layer, instead of trying to access the underlying systems that store the data in the operational environment. In addition to this, data validation and security controls can also be implemented as an individual object definition under the data virtualization layers. Proper authentication and authorization of usage is a crucial pre-cursor to data virtualization.

Finally, it is often the cache storage and pre-calculated aggregates stored by these data virtualization tools that can address query access and performance issues while implementing complicated data services. Combining data virtualization capabilities with data service components provides organizations with a comprehensive framework for accessing big data and analytical applications, especially when an organization needs to process huge amounts of data. With the assistance of data virtualization tools, consuming applications or users accessing data services would be able to receive information in a quicker, more flexible, and dynamic way across a host of underlying IT platforms, often from both structured and unstructured data.

SUMMARY

This chapter provided a detailed overview of service-oriented architecture. It explained the SOA based patterns that can be leveraged to make data services reusable across multiple projects in an enterprise. Overall, having an SOA-based strategy to enterprise data services can promote a greater sharing and reuse of data.

In addition to discussing SOA architecture components, this chapter also analyzed the recent surge of interest among a few pioneering organizations to share their corporate data resources with customers using data virtualization tools. By offering faster and convenient data access to business users through a logical data access layer, these tools significantly enhance a data provider's capabilities.

In contrast to traditional data integration approaches, data virtualization is also preferred in some traditional organizations because it does not require that data be physically copied and moved from existing sources. As data virtualization products in the market become more mature in terms of functionality, they can make the implementation of DaaS even more widespread among organizations.

Chapter 8

Data Quality and Standards

TOPICS COVERED IN THIS CHAPTER

- This chapter explains the role of data standards for the success of any DaaS program and provides an overview of how to ensure that the quality of data published by enterprise data services is suitable and fit for public consumption.

- The significance of data profiling as a foundational process for successful DaaS quality programs are explained. As such, this chapter provides details on how use of data discovery and profiling tools can be useful for organizations in assessing the quality of data received from incoming data sources.

- The significance of data standards is also discussed as well as how these standards can be practically implemented by a data provider in real life.

- Finally, the benefits of using a metrics-driven approach to improve the quality of a data service are explained.

"It is a capital mistake to theorize before one has all the data."

—Sherlock Holmes (Sir Arthur Conan Doyle)

As discussed, introducing Data as a Service (DaaS) can act as a key enabler for sharing and reusing information across an organization by providing a consistent set of enterprise data services both to external consumers and internal service subscribers. This requires adopting data standards that can support the secure exchange of data across diverse platforms, databases, files, and other unstructured data formats.

Effective data sharing and reuse can be achieved in organizations by combining reusable data services with effective measures on improving data quality on a regular basis. Organizations need to distinguish between good and bad data before deciding if the data for a particular domain is suitable for publication as a data service.

Automated data discovery and profiling tools can regularly monitor the quality of data against a set of predefined business rules and discover data discrepancies

Data as a Service: A Framework for Providing Reusable Enterprise Data Services,
First Edition. Pushpak Sarkar.
© 2015 the IEEE Computer Society. Published 2015 by John Wiley & Sons, Inc.

or noncompliance of these rules. Organizations can subsequently use data profiling results to proactively cleanse and improve data quality at the underlying source.

Achieving Data Sharing and Interoperability Adopting Data Standards

Before proceeding any further, you may have a few questions. For example, why do quality standards really matter when implementing data services? This can be best explained using a real-life scenario from the U.S. healthcare sector.

Imagine that a hospital or lab facility provider in the healthcare sector needs to work closely with the insurance company of their patients to settle claim payments and other related matters that are interdependent on each other to support patients. If these organizations do not use a set of common data standards, then the whole electronic data interchange (EDI) system can potentially break down due to a lack of sufficient interoperability standards. Without any data standards, none of these organizations can exchange data electronically across the U.S. healthcare system.

In addition to data quality, standards for semantic interoperability, the ability to exchange data with meaning, are also critical for data services. This is essential as data can be transported across multiple systems and published for a broad range of users. Problems arise when one term has multiple meanings or when two or more terms refer to the same concept but are not easily recognized as synonyms. In short, harmonizing disparate information systems requires data standards that are formally enacted as part of an overall governance mechanism and a quality framework that promotes their use.

To be truly effective, there has to be a trade-off among the competing priorities affecting a business organization while implementing data standards on its data service offerings. In essence, data standards should be judiciously introduced by a data provider to improve the overall quality of its published data without restricting any government regulations.

One of the key benefits of following the standards-driven approach suggested in this book is that it enables organizations to share data across multiple systems. Using standardized formats also allows data to be reused across businesses over the long term. For example, in the U.S. healthcare industry, common data formats for exchanging data across healthcare providers, insurance using ANSI EDI X12 standards has been established for several years. Several organizations are attempting to address the standardization of data exchange across the newly formed U.S. state and federal healthcare information exchanges, by using common standards and architecture patterns.

Within finance, insurance, and healthcare industries, there have been several organizations that have attempted to deal with data exchange standards by converting the XML or legacy formats into relational formats based on well-defined enterprise modeling standards. The use of several industry-wide reference data standards across organizations along with employing standardized XML messaging formats (see the

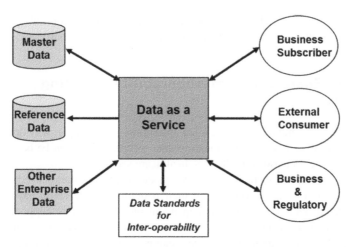

Figure 8.1   Achieving data interoperability in a real-life environment

box entitled "Common Data Standards") is helping organizations to improve data interoperability, exchange, and security.

By using data standards and canonical XML formats, the quality of data services provided to the end customer are significantly enhanced. In several sectors, use of standardized formats is an extremely powerful enhancement that can change the landscape of many industries requiring closer collaboration among partners (Figure 8.1, also see the healthcare exchange case study discussed earlier in Chapter 5).

Moreover, using enterprise service-oriented architecture (SOA) principles enables the organization to remain flexible and reuse their enterprise data most effectively. In fact, to enable proper and efficient data exchange from every legacy system to the data services layer, the need for components that are responsible for publishing messages to the enterprise service bus is essential. Standardized canonical messages provide an application–independent enterprise-messaging format that is critical for successful data exchange and timely data synchronization across different applications. The implemented XML-based messages for a data service should follow standards defined in the enterprise canonical model (ECM). This helps in making the exchange of data using enterprise data services across different systems seamless, timely, and efficient.

Sharing information among people in any organization cannot be fostered only with new technology or related processes. This is due to a whole range of reasons, from varied organizational cultures to personality and ego issues. In fact, even if you observe young children in any kindergarten class, it is interesting and amusing to see how the children get into fights over sharing their toys, storybooks, and even pencils with each other until a teacher or adult intervenes. Often, they argue on seemingly trivial issues. Our experience in the corporate world is no different. More often than not, when we investigate the root causes of the insufficient or ineffective sharing of data, it happens because of organizational reasons and is not due to any technology-driven challenges.

Current Data Standards Used Across Industry Sectors

The use of common data standards for messaging and data exchange predates the internet. A prime example of this is the usage of electronic data interchange (EDI). EDI represents a set of standard messaging formats for business documents to formalize electronic commerce between companies. Some of the common examples of data exchange standards widely used across industries include the following.

Accredited Standards Committee X12 (also known as ASC X12) comprises electronic data interchange (EDI) and context inspired component architecture (CICA) standards along with XML schemas that drive business processes globally. ASC X12 standards encompass health care, insurance, transportation, supply chain, and other industries.

Health Level Seven (HL7) and its members provide a framework (and related standards) for the exchange, integration, sharing, and retrieval of electronic health information. These standards define how information is packaged and communicated from one party to another, setting the language, structure, and data types required for seamless integration between clinical systems. HL7 standards support clinical practice and the management, delivery, and evaluation of health services, and are recognized as the most commonly used in the world. They provide standards for interoperability that improve healthcare delivery, optimize workflow, reduce ambiguity, and enhance knowledge transfer among healthcare organizations.

Society for Worldwide Interbank Financial Telecommunication (SWIFT) enables its clients in the banking industry to automate and standardize their financial transactions. This benefits the banks to help them make their business operations more efficient, lowering cost and reducing their overall risks.

Association for Cooperative Operations Research and Development (ACORD) standards have gained significant acceptance and usage in the insurance sector for exchange of data across insurance companies, their agents, and third parties.

For many years now, the financial services industry and regulators have also employed data standards for financial and market reference data. There are common identifiers for registered securities, regulated legal entities, and certain financial transactions. Financial data providers also use several standardized identifiers for their products (e.g., CUSIP has become a de facto standard across the financial industry standard to represent stocks, bonds, and other financial instruments. Similarly, the use of standard clinical diagnosis codes (from ICD) by insurers in the healthcare industry for making claim payments to healthcare providers has been prevalent for several decades.

Note: A few of the major data standards impacting organizations implementing DaaS, are listed in Appendix A for readers' benefit.

WHERE TO BEGIN DATA STANDARDIZATION EFFORTS IN YOUR ORGANIZATION

The consistent representation of information, based on common rules for structuring information, is fundamental to the efficient exchange of information. Data standards help organizations conduct business more efficiently by improving the data flow and facilitating the development, sharing, and reuse of data on projects across a particular industry, organization, or community of users.

Data standards also help in greatly reducing errors when data gets distributed to downstream applications. Data standards can help achieve reduction in quality errors across organizations by providing a consistent format or representation of data values, which can be derived from a set of business rules. Therefore, data standards, when implemented appropriately, will promote data transparency, consistency, and credibility among end users for the data published by a data provider. Using data standards also help protect the long-term value of data, as data assets become widely available for reuse.

If a data provider frequently faces quality-related problems with data they publish by a data service, it should identify and eliminate the problems' root causes. A detailed root-cause analysis using the Fishbone diagram (also called the Ishikawa diagram) can help in this situation, by analyzing real causes of the underlying quality problem. Root-cause analysis can also help organizations in identifying potential downstream impacts from quality-based challenges in the environment. Figure 8.2 illustrates the Fishbone Diagram.

The costs and risks associated with not addressing each of these root causes of low data quality need to be analyzed in detail and presented to the leadership team responsible for daily operations as well as your enterprise's data governance council.

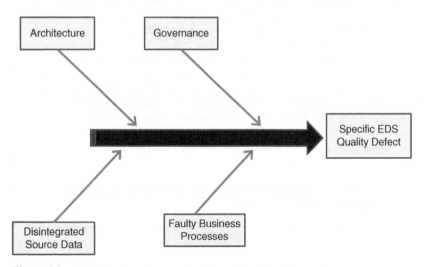

Figure 8.2   Identifying the root cause of quality problems for a data service

Frequent occurrences of data service interruptions, a drop in employee productivity, or lower volumes of transactions processed are evidence of the economic impact arising out of low-quality data. The use of statistical process control can be very helpful to address these situations. Statistical process control makes use of data gathered over time to understand common variations seen in a process as opposed to special root causes resulting in measurements outside control limits.

The benefits of introducing new data quality standards and significant productivity benefits and cost savings need to be communicated across the organization regularly. In fact, the benefits expected by following a standards-driven approach to enhance the quality of data service have to be clearly understood by the organization's business sponsors and key stakeholders.

Data Lineage and Analysis

The ability to track and view *data lineage* is a strong capability that is popular and necessary for IT architects to discover existing data stored across the application landscape, to analyze potential discrepancies, and then to recommend solutions. Often, the original designer has long left the company. It is difficult to know the origin of a particular data element or to design new systems in these situations with no documentation on data lineage. Thus, you need to understand where a particular data element is sourced from and how it impacts downstream systems. Without having answers to these data lineage questions, system designers in an organization cannot assess the true impact of any changes they make on data that are dependent on other systems.

Data profiling tools help to conduct a physical assessment at the outset of publishing a new data service. They can assess the quality of data received from legacy sources of data for publishing individual data services. This ensures that the quality of data published for consumption by DaaS subscribers exceeds their expectations.

Most of the data profiling tools provide organizations with an automated mechanism to gain a quick understanding of the data sources (lineage) feeding data to a specific system and all its relationships with other downstream system components. These solutions become very critical in large–scale re-architecture and subsequent system-development efforts. This is largely because companies often have a plethora of databases across the organization that have evolved into different parts over time. The following are common scenarios when viewing data lineage, which are typically valuable when using automated data profiling tools.

- Business users need to review the data on a report for business-analysis purposes.
- Business users need to look at the result of any type of search using a data service.
- Technical users cannot determine the location of a particular "column" in a database.

ROLE OF DATA DISCOVERY/PROFILING TO IDENTIFY DaaS QUALITY ISSUES

Data profiling is the process of developing an understanding of content, structure, and baseline quality of an existing data repository. Most organizations use data profiling tools to assess in detail how good the quality of data is in various legacy systems storing pieces of current enterprise data.

While earlier chapters briefly covered topics about data profiling, data quality in the context of data profiling is also important. The use of data discovery and profiling capabilities as a foundational step play a major role when establishing a data quality program. Data profiling is especially significant for the DaaS environment. This is because most of the data elements published by an enterprise data service are not stored but managed and modified by legacy sources. Therefore, automated data profiling tools not only help to assess quality of data received from legacy data sources, but they also play a major role in ensuring quality of the data published through data services.

As part of the data quality program, these sophisticated data profiling tools can also be used to compare the quality of data in a particular domain or entity over a period to monitor long-term improvements. Figure 8.3 provides an illustration of how a data profiling tool can be used to assess the quality of a legal entity-related reference data received from an existing data repository.

Data profiling tools typically utilize a set of algorithms that employ statistical and probabilistic technologies to analyze and explore the quality of data across multiple data sources. These automated tools can also analyze the different values

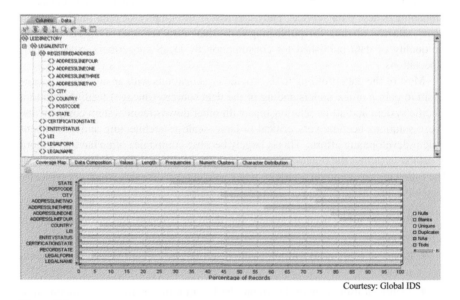

Courtesy: Global IDS

Figure 8.3   Data profiling results on reference data

received from data sources for a column. For example, the values in the wrong column for a phone number or address field can be easily detected by a data profiling tool.

Comparing these values with a baseline (or standardized) set of values, defined for that column by business SMEs, can help determine the overall quality of data received from a particular source of data. Profiling tools can also infer the underlying relationship that exists across multiple datasets. By using a variety of pattern-matching techniques, they can provide business insight from the underlying data, which is very difficult to perform manually without these tools.

In the context of metadata definitions, data profiling tools can help uncover semantic differences associated with key entities and attributes across different parts of an organization. This data discovery process can be followed by subsequent activities for standardizing semantic definitions and for data cleansing. In addition to this, the data lineage of data elements published on data services can be established and stored for future project use by IT application teams.

By profiling data, an IT organization can quickly evaluate the content, quality, and structure of underlying databases, files, etc. It can also discover the underlying quality problems in source systems with minimal effort (Figure 8.4). Data profiling can therefore help to identify actual problems with the data as they relate to business needs. For example, if the marketing group in an organization wants to increase the impact of an online ad campaign, data profiling tools can easily help to identify anomalies such as empty or missing address or phone records, incorrect reference-data entries, duplicate entries for the same contact, and problems with data uniformity.

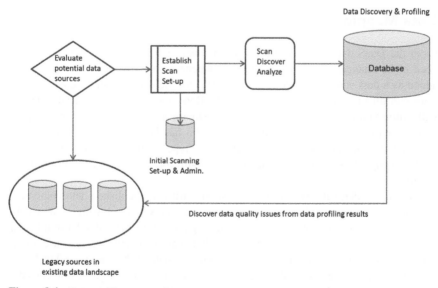

Figure 8.4   Data profiling process flow

The following are some major features of data profiling tools.

- Data discovery functionality in automated-profiling tools can uncover a data dictionary as described by the system catalog and make it accessible.
- An inexpensive way to identify low-hanging fruit when it comes to underlying data issues. It can uncover outliers such as data fill percentage, patterns, frequencies, structure violations, and valid values, which can flag data inaccuracies to a data steward/subject-matter expert (SME).
- Identify data redundancy by discovering data duplication between databases.
- Provide an inferred data model in addition to a documented model from the system catalog.
- Track down the distribution of compliance-sensitive data (e.g., social security number [SSN], clinical diagnosis codes under ICD across networks, Share-Point locations, and databases).
- A slew of complementing features to help with data management tasks.

The data lineage can be gathered from different types of sources across the organization, including:

- Data models
- Databases
- Files/XML schemas
- COBOL copybooks
- BI/ETL tools.

Data Mappings

From the DaaS data delivery and release-management perspective, data mappings need to be changed by technical analysts whenever new applications need to be added as a data source (source of truth [SOT]) for the data service. Metadata solutions can fill this gap felt by storing Create–Read–Update–Delete (CRUD) details with information such as which user or upstream application has created a particular data element, which downstream system has been using the element, and the time the element was changed, etc. This type of information can be gathered in many cases by using automated tools built for data discovery and profiling information.

To ensure that subscribers of a data service trust the published data content, it is important to conduct physical assessments at the outset of publishing a new data service on the quality of data received from the legacy sources of master data published by DaaS. Typically, in a large organization, there can be several legacy sources that need to be mapped to the data elements to publish data at the enterprise level. For example, to populate a new data service in an organization (e.g., customer), one may need to evaluate the quality of information feeds from multiple areas: customer relationship management (CRM), external data sources such as Dun & Bradstreet, and internal legacy systems. Only after assessing the quality of underlying data can the DaaS design team formally identify a particular legacy application as its authoritative source. However, it is usually very time consuming to do this in a large organizations where they may have numerous legacy applications to evaluate for sourcing their data.

Periodic Data Audits

Even after the data service has been deployed, the DaaS governance team has to conduct data quality assessments periodically on the quality of data received from source systems deployed in the production environment.

Automated data profiling tools can be especially useful for periodic data assessments and automated data cleansing purposes (Figure 8.5). For instance, during a Sarbanes–Oxley (SOX) compliance-related audit, IT auditors in organizations often have to analyze underlying financial data and identify any reporting anomalies for auditing purposes. This is where the use of a data profiling tool can be indispensable

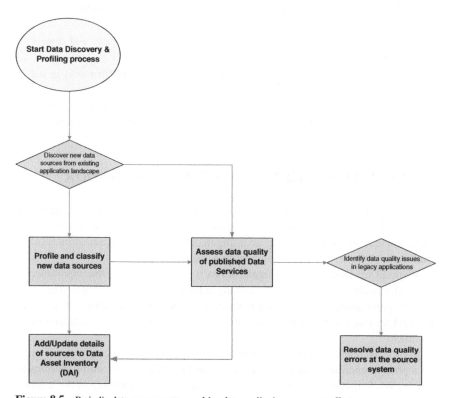

Figure 8.5   Periodic data assessments can drive data quality improvement efforts

to an organization. Essentially, data profiling software uses several sophisticated processes to perform core analysis on data that are found inside an organization's databases. Data profiling tools conduct the necessary data discovery and analysis within an organization's IT environment by:

- Connecting to its existing databases.
- Scanning the existing IT environment to discover important tables.
- Reading through the data to find out in-depth information about data objects.
- Classifying columns under different groups based on the type of data.
- Displaying how different tables are related.

All this requires the tool to run multiple interdependent tasks using a number of applications. To simplify this process, a number of workflows can be introduced to run all the required processes automatically with minimum manual intervention.

How to Conduct Data Discovery and Profiling Using a Leading Vendor Tool

- Data discovery: The software scans repositories of data in the systems environment.
- Data profiling: The software analyzes the data in both databases and content repositories.
- Data classification: The software determines all the patterns that exist in the environment and categorizes the data.
- Data semantics: The software connects all similar data objects together, creating enterprise maps of business objects (e.g., customer, product, employee, vendor).

DATA QUALITY AND THE INVESTMENT PARADOX

The internationally renowned quality expert Ed Deming has famously been quoted as saying, "reliable service reduces cost." I agree with Deming's remarks in the context of data services and suggest that by investing in data quality, an organization is likely to reduce the long-term cost of maintaining a data service.

While IT leadership in most organizations is usually aware of the importance of having a foundation of good data and usually supports the overall mission to improve access to good quality data, it often faces difficulties in raising funding to enhance data services that can be used enterprise-wide (especially when the company faces lean times).

In fact, the reality is that investments for data quality in most corporations today face a phenomenon that can be compared to an IT black hole or an IT investment paradox. While investments in IT quality have been steadily growing in the last two decades, sponsors responsible for project funding often have a simple question: Are the benefits/returns from IT investments as high as initially expected?

As a business enabler, DaaS and its underlying data has become crucial to most organizations for achieving their business goals as well as for differentiating the company from its competition. Achieving market leadership is increasingly a function of getting the right data inputs from the field, interpreting raw data, and passing this value-added information to strategic decision-makers. The quality of business decisions and underlying data supporting these decisions ultimately decide the fate of many organizations.

To support DaaS, the quality of underlying data received from various application sources is also critical. Fixing quality problems in underlying legacy sources after the fact can be costly for organizations running an online retail-service-like business. This is largely because subscribers who have encountered data trust issues with a particular data service may never return to use it, even if the data quality problem had originated in one of the external data sources feeding the data service. There are also other additional costs that can be seen when companies do not prevent major quality defects from affecting daily business. Some of these costs include scrap/rework costs, assessment or inspection costs, process failure costs, as well as lost and missed opportunity costs.

Therefore, service-implementation teams have to take a preventive approach to data quality issues while ensuring service to consumers is reliable, timely, and trustworthy if they want subscribers of a data service to depend on it over the long term. Let us now look at the detailed quality measures for supporting an enterprise data service published by a DaaS-enabled organization.

QUALITY OF A DATA SERVICE

As mentioned, one of the core principles of this book is the belief that data is a corporate asset that needs to be shared with internal and external data consumers. Data services in an enterprise can therefore be viewed as similar to a service utility such as water or electricity that are obtained from a local electricity or water agency.

Recently, XML has been used for exchanging data, usually point-to-point across systems. However, a lack of any common XML schema standards has made it challenging to integrate disparate systems. Even tool vendors who provide XML interfaces to customers maintain their proprietary XML schema and document-type definitions (DTDs), which makes data integration and exchange rather challenging. To avoid this, DaaS service providers have to ensure that common data and XML standards are used to make it easier for their data consumers. The introduction of these standards can also enable easier data integration with subscribing DaaS applications on different platforms. Consequently, data interoperability, or the ability to make systems and organizations in a regulated industry work together, then becomes a reality. In order to meet these data interoperability needs, as well as ensure the quality of published data, appropriate service-quality and underlying data standards need to be set up. These should ensure the value of data service to key DaaS users and other stakeholders. The quality of overall customer experience must be considered as a critical yardstick for measuring service success.

The following are some keys considerations for assessing the quality of the overall DaaS delivery to subscribers.

- The DaaS system must supply data to all consumers or subscribers of the data service within the SLA and timelines that are predefined and agreed upon by key stakeholders and consumers.

- The DaaS service provider should ensure that data provided by the service have data integrity and follow consistent data definitions.

- The DaaS delivery infrastructure must be robust and enable data interoperability by fostering data exchange between various kinds of applications hosted on varied system platforms.

- The DaaS delivery mechanism of the service provider should ensure that the information published by the service meets data and messaging/XML standards to ensure system interoperability.

- The DaaS delivery mechanism must be scalable as the number of DaaS subscribers increases.

- The information published via the data services component has to be delivered in a secure manner to subscribers authorized to access, based on enterprise-data security and privacy policies.

To summarize, when evaluating the quality of an enterprise-level data service, you need to look at assessing not only the quality of the data provided by the service but also ensure that the service delivery mechanism used for data delivery meets DaaS subscribers' expectations.

Assessing the quality of a DaaS program involves evaluating a diverse range of data and service-quality metrics (Figure 8.6). The following are three broad yet major categories for assessing a data service.

- The quality of data architecture and its related components (e.g., completeness of the canonical model, consistency in metadata).

- The quality of service delivery to data subscribers and external parties (e.g., SLAs for service delivery, response time of published data service).

- The quality of service governance (e.g., data retention standards, change-management processes).

SETTING UP STANDARDS IN A DaaS ENVIRONMENT

After the initial setup phase, the DaaS-development support team must ensure that their ongoing efforts to improve service quality are aligned with the enterprise's

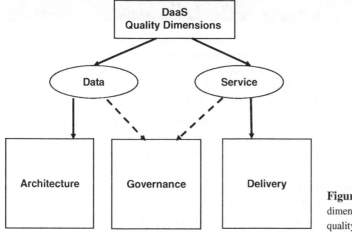

Figure 8.6 Major dimensions of DaaS quality assessment

data governance process. This section discusses how to review the organization's existing data and suggests a few ways in which to implement quality controls on data distributed to consumers using enterprise data services.

Before proceeding any further, let us address an important question. Why do quality standards really matter when implementing data services? The best way to explain this is using a real-life scenario from the healthcare sector in the United States. If these organizations do not use a set of common data standards, then the entire electronic data interchange (EDI) system could break down due to a lack of sufficient interoperability standards. Without any data standards, none of these organizations can exchange data electronically across the U.S. healthcare system.

In addition to data quality, standards for semantic interoperability—the ability to exchange data with meaning—are also critical for data services. This is essential as data can get transported across multiple systems and be published for a broad range of users. Problems arise when one term has multiple meanings or when two or more terms refer to the same concept but are not easily recognized as synonyms. In short, harmonizing disparate information systems require data standards that are formally enacted as part of an overall governance mechanism and a quality framework that promotes their use.

To ensure conformance to enacted governance policies, it is important to specify some steps to regularly audit the implementation of data governance policies as well any related processes. Apart from laying down data standards and policies, the data governance steering committee has to ensure that its directions are actually being implemented in day-to-day operations in a way that is effective and generates value for the organization. To do this, the technical leadership responsible for execution has to implement a series of data controls across the DaaS lifecycle processes. These controls are typically derived out of underlying data standards that are applicable to a particular organization, industry, or country where it operates.

Building the Roadmap for Data Quality and Standards

The roadmap for building data quality and standards needs to start by assessing where an organization is currently on the overall maturity curve and then define what steps are needed to create a streamlined path to an actively controlled, data-driven enterprise that leverages its data as a strategic asset. At minimum, the roadmap to improving organization-wide DaaS capabilities needs to include the following:

- Building a future state vision for information management and sharing within the entire organization.
- Understanding data assets (e.g., data sources) the organization already has in the form of a data asset inventory.
- Assessing the current state of data assets and quantifying the impact to transform them as authoritative sources of truth.
- Classifying data and understanding its relationships in existing legacy systems and relevance to the business.
- Upgrading business processes with relevant data to solve problems dynamically.
- Implementing enterprise information management policies (e.g., data quality, data privacy, or security) to enforce regulatory or corporate mandates.
- Proactively identifying issues based on quality and performance metric to help make improvements continually.

It is therefore important to inspect the "real" data in an organization's major existing applications to ensure that information policies introduced by the data governance steering committee are being complied with by various IT project teams as well as by the teams responsible for day-to-day operations. For example, if the enterprise data governance team wants all application projects to reuse enterprise data artifacts on all future initiatives, there needs to be a rule or control in place specifying that the leadership should not certify the project moving forward to development activities during the architecture/design-review phase. The leadership should also not provide any further project budgets to any project that has not engaged the EIM architects to reuse artifacts related the enterprise data model (EDM) or to the metadata glossary. Similarly, database administrators (DBAs) should not be allowed to create yet another redundant database request from a project team until the request has been reviewed by data standards teams. This ensures that the new database that has been requested contains information that is non-redundant or required following some clear business need agreed upon by the data governance committee and IT stakeholders. Figure 8.7 shares some major categories of data standards in a DaaS environment.

Having these types of "credible" data controls in place prevents the possibility of company leadership being exposed to risk when it is too late. A similar situation was witnessed when several chief financial officers (CFOs) at large U.S. organizations had to face severe penalties due to noncompliance of SOX Act provisions by IT teams (e.g., not implementing data controls and DB security issues).

	Control	Description
1	Data definition standards	Ensures alignment of new projects being developed with enterprise data modeling standards and common metadata.
2	Data exchange and interoperability standards	Ensures the viability of data exchange and interoperability across systems with common exchange standards. This includes semantic interoperability, i.e., the ability to exchange data with meaning across different systems and users.
3	Database standards	Standards for the creation of new databases as a way to restrict the proliferation of redundant databases.
4	Data access and security standards	Standards on how data flows between applications, user access rights, and security entitlements.
5	Data sourcing standards	Identifies authoritative systems where data should be sourced for publication to DaaS consumers.
6	Data retention and archival standards	Dictates what data need to be retained and archived. Also determines the period of retention necessary to comply with legal/audit requirements.

Figure 8.7   Major categories of data standards

However, one needs to distinguish between these data controls (in the context of data governance and its related processes) in contrast to data quality validation checks used to improve data quality of IT systems. Data control needs to be viewed more as a governance mechanism to communicate to the company leadership that the data assets they own possess data integrity and are reliable to use. In contrast to this, data quality-related validation checks address specific system-related errors as well as their root causes.

Use of a Metrics-Driven Approach to Improve the Quality of a Data Service

Having examined various types of data standards and quality controls, let us now look at the use of metrics for data service quality monitoring and improvement.

While it might not sound very appealing at first, it is frequently seen that timely access to quality data can be the difference between a successful data service implementation or one that falls short. Unfortunately, bad, incomplete, or missing data can burden and even cripple a company. This makes periodic measurement of performance on data and service quality improvements a cornerstone of success. Figure 8.8 illustrates how to use KPIs for data service quality monitoring and improvement.

For sustainable data service, quality improvements using a metrics-based approach are very crucial. These metrics are usually internally defined performance

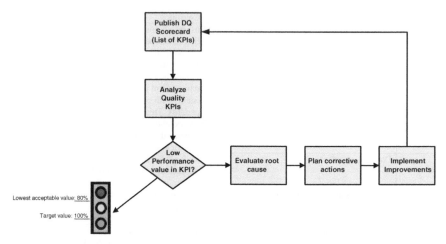

Figure 8.8 Usage of KPIs for data service quality monitoring and improvement

targets, which are clearly measurable and important for the organization over the medium or long-term.

Example of Common Data Service Quality Improvement Metrics

- Average response time from request to completion for a new data service request.
- Number of Services where the agreed service levels are fulfilled (based on SLA).
- Number of Service interruptions occurring because of insufficient service or capacity shortage.
- Duration from the identification of service interruption to the implementation of a suitable mechanism to address.
- Number of identified security incidents, classified by severity category.
- Number of products in the catalog with a non-unique description.
- Number of duplicate customer records detected every month.

By setting up a comprehensive set of quality metrics for a data service (based on key performance indicators), an organization can objectively use the system as a mechanism to assess service delivery quality. They should also ask determining questions such as the following:

- What level of quality needs to be maintained for different data services in our organization?
- Do all quality characteristics get afforded the same priority by stakeholders our organization?
- How do we measure success on these quality dimensions?

If data and service quality metrics haven been properly implemented, then the neutral and objective results from metrics can be very effective for getting sponsor funding on data quality initiatives. It is also very useful for holding discussions with the data governance steering committee on upcoming areas that need improvements related to data quality or service delivery improvement.

To control variations of service quality defects, the use of control charts and other statistical process control techniques to detect quality defect occurrences and related trends are quite commonplace. These are control limits placed by the data stewards supporting the customer team. If the quality performance falls below the acceptable range of values defined in the control chart, then it can be concluded that the quality of data service does not meet business stakeholders and service subscribers' necessary expectations.

Let us look an example to make this point clear. In many situations, access time and the number of users of a data service are two separate measures that can be calculated to produce a combined metric for measuring DaaS scalability performance. Through successive iterations that become more precise with greater adoption, this measure can lead to achieving the KPI (e.g., establish a one-second service response time for a specific set of external or internal users of the DaaS) on the scalability of a data service over the long run.

For most individual KPI metrics, there should be a few key threshold values (e.g., lowest acceptable value, highest acceptable value, target value) for quality metrics that need to be established at the outset of the data service performance measurement process.

Any outlier that does not fall within these threshold needs to be investigated further in order to identify root causes and eliminate them from your environment, as considered necessary. However, it should be clarified here that defining appropriate thresholds can be extremely difficult in many IT environments.

In the DaaS environment, organizations have to track the overall quality of tdata service as well as provide an actionable set of data controls for the QA and governance teams when service performance does not meet the service level agreement as well as consumer expectation of any enterprise-level data service.

Lastly, the benefits of introducing new data service quality standards and their significant productivity benefits and cost savings need to be regularly communicated across the organization. The benefit expected by following a standards-driven approach to enhance the quality of data service has to be clearly understood by the organization's business sponsors as well as key stakeholders.

SUMMARY

The quality of data published by a data service for DaaS subscribers is critical to its success. When a business organization publishes bad quality data to its consumers, the effect can be disastrous. Therefore, it is critical for any data provider publishing data to subscribers to regularly assess and ensure they receive quality data from their data sources.

This chapter explained how data profiling capabilities can help to conduct physical assessment of the quality of data received from any source application source published as data services. These assessments need to be done periodically to ensure the quality of data received from legacy sources meets the DaaS stakeholders' expectations. Moreover, the need to comply with data quality and interoperability standards is also crucial for success of any organization implementing data services. Semantic interoperability, i.e., the ability to exchange data with meaning across different users is a critical factor for the success of data being reused successfully across an enterprise.

Finally, we looked at various factors affecting the quality of data services on real-life projects, including timely and secure service delivery, using consistent sets of data definition, and compliance with data standards and regulations.

Part Three

DaaS Solution Blueprints

Chapter 9

Reference Data Services

TOPICS COVERED IN THIS CHAPTER

- This chapter presents a detailed overview of how Data as a Service (DaaS) can be successfully deployed in organizations for disseminating shared reference data to downstream data subscribers and consumers.

- A detailed solution blueprint is provided for designing and developing reference data services (RDS) that can be reused across the enterprise by using common design components and standards.

- Several illustrative case studies are also discussed on reference data services from the financial and healthcare sectors.

"Data that is loved tends to survive."

—Kurt Bollacker, Data Scientist

The DaaS framework helps organizations promote overall quality of data. It also can reduce deployment costs by using reusable architectural patterns, which serve as an enabler to accelerate service deployment within organizations.

As discussed in Chapter 2, IT reference architecture patterns also help provide a proven solution to a repeating problem in a given context. This chapter, along with Chapters 10 and 11, propose solution blueprints that define the most efficient ways that an organization's users can access key categories of an organization's enterprise data such as reference data, master data, and big data. Solution blueprints on how each category of data can be deployed as reusable data services are also discussed. The blueprint is based on the composition of underlying architectural patterns and relevant architectural building blocks.

Data as a Service: A Framework for Providing Reusable Enterprise Data Services,
First Edition. Pushpak Sarkar.
© 2015 the IEEE Computer Society. Published 2015 by John Wiley & Sons, Inc.

Defining Reference Data

Reference data have been used extensively to support applications within organizations. Reference data are used to hold information about entities that the enterprise manages in its business (e.g., countries and currencies) or to hold information that categorizes the enterprise's data. The management of reference data takes place in multiple applications. Often different applications in the organization can store the same reference table with different values. This makes it virtually impossible to reuse reference data values across systems without an effective way to translate the values. A reference data service can be a good pattern to address this business need. This chapter explains the solution blueprint to this commonly occurring data service pattern. It also includes several illustrative examples and case studies across multiple industries.

Reference data are commonly known as code tables or lookup tables. These tables are typically structured as rather simple database tables with just two columns: one for a primary key code and another for a description. Some of the common reference tables seen in business organizations include state codes, country codes, currency codes, and product codes.

There are also other examples of reference tables that are used frequently across specific industries. For example, in the airline industry, the 3-character airport code is a reference code that is used by all airlines for booking flights (Figure 9.1). Similarly, the international standard book number (ISBN) is a reference code that uniquely identifies books that are sold commercially.

Unfortunately, it is also easy to observe that senior IT professionals are often less than enthusiastic about the importance and priority accorded to reference data, and some have even considered this area somewhat outdated. This happens largely due to the perception that reference data have limited strategic value to an IT organization.

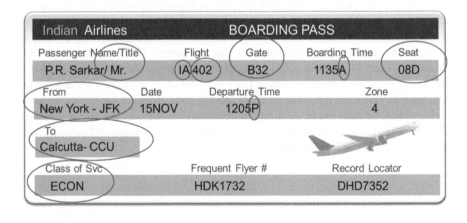

⊂⊃ indicates **Reference Data**

Figure 9.1   An example of reference data from the airline sector

Essentially, people often link reference data to the mundane world of lookup values, codes, code mappings, and hierarchies. However, this chapter discusses an area of reference data that is far more than this, and is critical for running day-to-day operations of a company. Moreover, reference data are usually provided to operational and analytical systems as read-only data services.

Due to this criticality, some areas of reference data are regulated by standards organizations. For example, ISO 4217 is a standard published by the International Organization for Standardization. Although it is not exactly an acronym, it provides a standard updated list of currency details by country code. The ISO 4217 code list is used globally in banking and business for real-time trading as a standard for currency and exchange rates.

DELIVERING MARKET AND REFERENCE DATA USING REAL-TIME DATA SERVICES

In the financial sector, market and reference data allow traders and investors to know the latest prices and trades for financial instruments such as equities, fixed income products, derivatives, and currencies, as reported by stock exchanges across the world. The real-time exchange of market and related reference data to trading applications has long been an illustrative application of data services (Figure 9.2).

The market data for a particular financial instrument could include the CUSIP identifier of the instrument (9-character alphanumeric code which identifies a North American financial security), where it was traded, the ticker symbol, exchange code, time of the last trade as well as latest bid and ask prices. It may also include other information such as volume traded, bid and offer sizes, and static data about the financial instrument that may have come from a variety of sources. There are a number of financial data vendors that specialize in consolidating and distributing market and reference data. This has become the most common way for traders and investors to access market data.

Market (or price) data are not only used in real time to make decisions about buying or selling securities, but historical market data can also be used to calculate market risk on portfolios of investments owned by institutional investors. Most companies in the financial sector therefore need to provide real-time updates on market reference data to their trading applications on a critical basis.

The speed at which market data are distributed can become critical when trading systems are based on analyzing data before others are able to, such as in high frequency trading. Delivery of price data from exchanges to users such as traders is very time sensitive. Specialized technologies are needed to handle collection and throughput of massive data streams while simultaneously distributing information to thousands of traders and investors.

Similarly, as discussed in Chapter 9, the recent mandate by financial regulators has made adoption of the legal identity identifier (LEI) mandatory. The ISO standard (ISO 17442:2012) clearly specifies elements of the LEI scheme to identify legal entities relevant to any financial transaction. It is clear from the LEI effort that

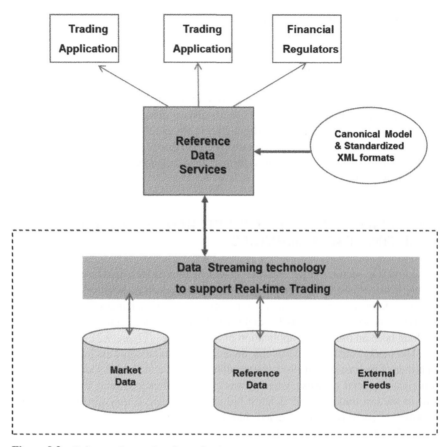

Figure 9.2 Reference data services for market data

the discipline of reference data management (RDM) is already becoming increasingly critical for regulators in some industry sectors due to major events such as the global financial crisis. Some areas within reference data are also being made available commercially to organizations from external data vendors (e.g., Dun and Bradstreet [D&B]). Use of standardized reference data provided by vendors often helps organizations quickly address growing business demands for information quality and consistency. However, barring these few isolated areas that involve using reference data from external vendors, the major portion of reference data is maintained internally by organizations. More often than not, reference data that are maintained internally become a cause for concern. In my experience, IT application development projects usually follow no standards or consistency when it comes to internal usage of reference data. They pull reference data indiscriminately from various application teams or even create their local copy to support business operations. This often leads to a nightmare for leadership responsible for overall governance of reference data across the organization.

COMPARING USAGE OF REFERENCE DATA AGAINST MASTER DATA

While reference data management is often seen as closely associated to master data management (MDM), they also have some distinct differences in several key areas of usage.

The first misperception about RDM is that many IT practitioners consider it as a subset of MDM, even though reference data have several unique attributes, business requirements, and workflows involved. For example, unlike master data, a significant amount of reference data is made available for use from outside an organization (often from industry standards' organizations). Examples could be country codes (covered by the global standard ISO 3166-1), currency codes (ISO 4217), industry codes across North America (NAICS), and market data.

In fact, reference tables are also traditionally less volatile (or more static) in nature, as their values change less frequently. For example, currency codes for any country hardly change each year. In contrast, most of the master data elements usually comprise a smaller set of data entities (customer, product, etc.), which are critical to running business operations within an organization. Often, such entities need to be shared enterprise-wide in order to drive consistency in operational data use, to support analytical reports, or to support regulatory compliance needs (e.g., KYC in the financial sector). Since master data usually originate from various operational sources within the organization (e.g., customer relationship management [CRM] systems, account opening systems), the values of master data can frequently change. For example, the customer identifier in a typical MDM implementation for an airline can change with far greater frequency compared to the currency or country codes stored in reference tables for airline billing.

It is often more effective to implement reference data (commonly used for looking up values) in combination with a business rules engine (BRE). There are several BRE products in the market that can actively manage the workflow of reference data over their lifecycle.

However, companies that depend heavily on external reference data (in the financial sector, for example) can treat RDM as a separate function due to the specialized set of business rules and governance required to support industry regulations across the world (KYC, AML, Basel, etc.).

As discussed, the maintenance and ongoing use of reference data also have a huge dependency on underlying business events (such as organizational changes) and impact on how the data will be used within a particular organization. Therefore, when managing reference data, one needs to deal especially with the underlying business rules, as well as the semantic meaning and consistency in terms of data definitions and metadata. It is helpful to note that reference data items usually have very specific definitions, and perhaps, for many attributes, there are domain values explicitly associated to standardized industry codes. For instance, definitions of currency codes or country codes do not change all that often and are less volatile. In contrast to the relatively stable definitions seen in reference data, the definition of master data (e.g., customer) is often very subjective and can mean different things to different divisions within the enterprise (and their respective business users) (Chisholm, 2006).

Therefore, these types of semantic issues highlight how there are significant differences between master data and reference data. The problem of storing and making available reference data code values, domains, and definitions for individual rows of reference data makes it critical to emphasize the need to understand contexts and related definitions at a more granular level and in a more detailed manner. These diverse challenges require very different solutions.

Moreover, there is need for high quality reference data to support industry compliance efforts, as well as to support their downstream analytical and business intelligence (BI) applications without investing in MDM processes. For example, the drivers for adopting high quality reference data in many healthcare organizations involve adapting to regulations on the conversion of industry codes from the International Classification of Diseases (ICD) 9 to ICD 10, and enabling real-time data exchange with providers and billing organizations.

Recent Study on Big Health Data in the United Kingdom and United States

A recent study on the National Health Service (NHS) in the United Kingdom cites a clear lack of governance rules on how NHS data is published and in what sort of format (Keen, 2013). While some progress has been made in the United States recently with the development of data standards, there is still a lack of standards' compliance in some services (especially clinical reference data, e.g., diagnosis codes, provider).

The lack of interoperability seriously limits possibilities for automating healthcare exchanges that have been set up recently across the United States and federal systems to provide affordable health care in the country. The lack of data governance policies, standards, and intelligent use of metadata to support important trends in health services is causing healthcare costs to increase rapidly.

A move to a DaaS-centric model with governance processes and underlying technology-platform enablers could help in re-architecting the healthcare sector while bringing down overall costs with improved credibility among consumers. Please refer to the case study titled "Using Standardized Clinical Reference Data in U.S. Healthcare Sector" later in this chapter.

Due to these factors, reference data services are treated as a separate category of services that are distinct from master data services. Having a reference data strategy that is tightly coupled with data governance facilitates easier compliance to the use of standardized reference data elements across an enterprise's projects. Given their varied use, complexity factors, and distinct audience from the DaaS perspective, it helps to treat reference data consistently across the company. Consistent use of reference data standards also helps companies comply with international, government, and industry standards (e.g., global reference data on CUSIP, currency codes, industry codes in the financial sector or reference data codes in the U.S. healthcare sector for complying with the International Classification of Diseases (ICD) diagnosis codes (as specified by the World Health Organization).

In the larger context, however, there are also some important linkages between reference data management and master data management. Organizations should not treat MDM- and RDM-related services as completely separate components, as there are still some areas where they overlap significantly.

UNDERSTANDING CHALLENGES OF REFERENCE DATA MANAGEMENT

Organizations that have no formal governance of reference data can face numerous challenges. Some of the commonly faced challenges can be classified into the following major categories:

- **Manual changes**
  - Lack of a standard process for managing changes
  - No audit trail, no review or approval
  - Difficult to implement a security policy
  - Sarbanes–Oxley Act implications
- **No clear ownership**
  - Limited business involvement
  - IT ownership and involvement in application specific code table maintenance
  - Often no agreed internal standard
- **Managed in multiple places**
  - Leads to duplication and introducing errors
  - No way to manage reference data at the enterprise level
  - No process for agreeing on changes to reference data across the business

Historically, firms in many sectors (e.g., financial services, healthcare, or insurance) have built and maintained their own security and client facing databases in isolation without following any common industry data standards. This made data interoperability and sharing information with other market participants a challenge. To add to this situation, as these organizations expanded through mergers and acquisitions, each line of business spawned their own data silos. It is not uncommon for these data platforms to reside on aging infrastructure that depend on disparate data stores sharing no common standards or quality. The probability of data quality errors is especially high when prevailing disparities in data formats are being used to exchange reference data across financial institutions. These errors can often occur at the original data source, during any number of in-house operational processes, or with third parties and vendors supplying the reference data (e.g., D&B from Chapter 1).

Most industries have faced concerns around data quality. Increasing international scope of many businesses such as mergers among several banks also raised further data quality concerns. Many of these banks face issues of global complexity, e.g., country based regulations and currencies that introduce new data elements, as well as variations in existing data.

Faulty reference data also affect a firm's ability to implement its data interchange capability fully, especially in real time. In such scenarios, inaccurate data will delay the processing of a financial market or a healthcare EDI transaction. Although reference data comprise a minority of data elements in trading applications or in the healthcare transactions with a patient, they often need to be reused by multiple applications. This leads to a disproportionate number of problems when there are inconsistent or inaccurate reference data. Similarly, trades may be rejected from automated processing routines due to non-standardized or inaccurate reference data. Even within analytical systems, reference data of poor quality can create a major problem. To address these data quality concerns within large organizations, further improvement is needed around governance and administration of reference data (IBM Reference Data Management paper, 2012).

The fragmented acquisition and maintenance of reference data causes low and inconsistent data quality, difficulty in distributing data on a timely basis, and problems in governance of the data resource, all leading to higher costs and risks. It may be possible in some organizations to implement a centralized data repository that provides data stewards to maintain all of the reference data tables. However, if this cannot be achieved, the alternative is to follow a distributed model of reference data governance. In this setup, the reference data are broken down into individual data domains by business area. The business data stewards are responsible for maintaining the reference data in each data domain. The process for acquiring, consolidating, and cleansing data must be rationalized, leading the way to a single or distributed "golden" centralized store of reference data that can be accessed by any authorized application or user.

OTHER REFERENCE DATA MANAGEMENT CHALLENGES

Teams responsible for an organization's reference data management need to begin by identifying the various areas where common sets of reference data can be deployed across multiple projects (Figure 9.3). Subsequently, they need to support these projects to construct and edit reference data hierarchies to view and navigate through records quickly via a parent–child relation. They also need to develop functionality and process workflows to collaborate, synchronize, update, and monitor reference data across the entire organization. Using data services can allow for quick and timely access to reference data by users across the organization. However, it is understood that the IT security administrator needs to assign and manage user access rights to key tables with clear data entitlement policies before data services publish the reference data.

In many organizations, issues related to history, maintenance, and governance of reference data code values stored in an organization's data repositories, as well as their definitions, can be a common cause for concern. In my view, some of the issues related to reference data updates or mapping-related anomalies can become a major obstacle to the success of any RDM initiative, unless carefully addressed in the project's early phases.

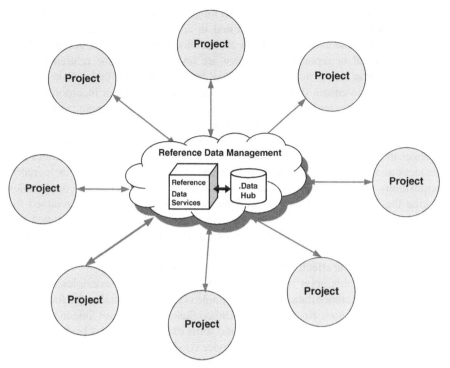

Figure 9.3   Overview of reference data management

Guiding Principles on Reference Data Use

- Reference data belong to the entire organization, not to any individual department.
- Reference data need to be shared across the organization unless there are data privacy concerns.
- Reference data values that represent the most accurate, current, and relevant version should be stored in authoritative golden sources.
- Business stewards or data owners are responsible for maintaining the reference data in their individual data domain.
- There should be clearly defined data governance policies that specify how changes to reference data values are approved, who makes the changes, service level agreements (SLAs), etc.
- The quality of the reference data published to data consumers should be continually monitored.
- Suitable change-notification alerts should be provided to all data stewards when reference data changes are made.

One of the major impacts arising from long-term maintenance of reference data codes is when a specific data value stored in an existing table (e.g., an industry code) changes in the existing setup. In all likelihood, this change is going to affect other operational or reporting tables that are linked to the same reference table. The organization has to maintain referential integrity in other tables linked to the reference table to ensure that existing queries and/or reports can incorporate these changes without any major impact. Within the reference data community, this entire chain of impacts is typically called recasting.

The most common occurrence of business events driving major reference data changes in real life can be seen when there are internal organizational changes in a business as it evolves over time or with external business events such as mergers, acquisitions, or losses. These business events subsequently affect the reference tables storing the organizational data as well the organizational hierarchies retained for reporting purposes over time. From one year to the next, a given organization can take on a completely different set of organizational hierarchies. With new changes in organizational structure, the use of reference data specialists is how the history of these changes can be effectively captured and reported.

To illustrate this point more clearly, let us turn to a few examples involving real-life use of reference data. The first example is related to postal codes for mailing addresses. As we know, zip codes in the United States change from time to time with entirely new postal codes being added, and some existing zip codes being split. For example, let us say that the U.S. Postal Service (USPS) merges its USPS designation of a town called "East Brunswick, NJ" with the adjoining town of "Monroe, NJ." From a RDM perspective, this move would affect all the existing addresses for "East Brunswick, NJ" in an organization, as stored in the reference table storing customer addresses. It would also cause certain existing customer mailing addresses that were previously valid to become invalid.

The possibility of having invalid customer addresses that were once valid becomes a real risk for the customer facing systems using reference tables, unless these errors are discovered and corrected by appropriate teams managing reference data. Additionally, it also might appear that customer records containing Monroe Township have doubled in size. Therefore, if any demographic or CRM-related reports in an organization were based on zip codes, these may suddenly give misleading results to decision makers.

As a final example, let us consider a reference table storing the credit rating category of bank customers. The bank may originally have individual code values for platinum, gold, silver, and bronze ratings. Suppose in a couple of years that the company's leadership decides to include a new rating of titanium for their highest rated customers. To support this new business requirement, the records containing the code value of platinum may need modification. A new business rule to split existing platinum consumers into the existing platinum or the newly introduced titanium rating also has to be introduced. In this situation, all the client records containing platinum value will need to be reassigned to either of these two values based on business rules (platinum and titanium). In this complex situation, the interrelationships among these values and their proper sequence must also be added to related tables storing the code value sequence and relationship tables.

In all the complex situations previously described, not only must reference data values be added to the underlying code value tables storing reference data codes, but also the interrelationships among these values and their proper sequence must be added to other related tables storing the code value sequence and code relationship tables. Additionally, with these events, the organization also needs to come up with new business rules that enable them to modify all the reference data values stored in transactional tables across the organization. Only this level of end-to-end consistency can ensure that reference data changes in the organization do not pose the serious risk of losing information integrity.

In addition to these issues, there can be interfaces to external systems that are impacted so these also need to be mapped to the latest changes in reference data values. These interfaces can use integration techniques (e.g., ETL, Message Queue, data services) to transfer reference data from multiple existing applications that are often hosted on diverse platforms. While importing data from these disparate applications to the reference data hub (or database), there has to be a clear set of code value mappings defined for reference data elements similar to when they are imported (or exported) from various external systems to the reference data hub.

ROLE OF REFERENCE DATA STANDARDS AND VOCABULARY MANAGEMENT

By using reference data standards and a common data vocabulary, IT departments can resolve challenges faced in managing reference data across applications. As discussed, by using the DaaS approach, organizations can quickly provide a publish-subscribe model to share critical reference data across the enterprise in a timely and efficient manner using a host of data services. This approach is based on reusable data services can can also provide a well-established governance process, security, and audit control around reference data mastering. Architecture components should also include a semantic data model for RDM (this should be vendor/technology agnostic) along with a shared business vocabulary and taxonomy for use of consistent definitions of reference data at the enterprise level. It should also be a key priority to use a metadata repository to store a business glossary based on a common vocabulary to classify, manage, organize, and integrate the reference data.

The primary purpose of a business glossary is to achieve consistency in the description of various types of reference data stored in the DaaS environment and to help facilitate users during information retrieval. Some major reference data attributes that are useful to retain as metadata are as follows:

- A list of all the reference tables required by the DaaS environment.
- The data definition and business definition of each code value stored in all reference tables.
- The meaning and purpose of each value domain.
- A list of business rules associated with each code value. For example, if some codes are subject to data security or privacy restrictions, then the security and

Code Value	Description	Parent Code	Parent Code Description
NJ	New Jersey	US	United States of America
MA	Massachusetts	US	United States of America
PA	Pennsylvania	US	United States of America
AB	Alberta	CA	Canada
ON	Ontario	CA	Canada
QC	Quebec	CA	Canada

Figure 9.4   Example of hierarchies associated with reference data for ISO country codes and state codes

visibility rules should be stored in the business glossary for ready reference by users.

- Identify which business steward is accountable for maintaining changes to reference data and the quality of the data.

- Identify which IT team is responsible for actually making changes to code values in reference tables.

- Data validation and quality rules.

- Data mappings to sources for individual reference tables.

- Hierarchies associated within different reference data sets. Figure 9.4 gives an example of a State/Country Code hierarchy.

Some reference data sets can also require hierarchal relationships to be stored between codes where each level in the hierarchy has a different business significance. For example, a product code set could have reference data values that are at multiple hierarchical levels.

The metadata glossary should also store service mappings and taxonomy details while designing data services for reference data. The taxonomy area has become especially significant in enterprises lately to support big data applications' unstructured and structured information needs of.

The following list are the key roles and benefits of having a metadata glossary in any organization supporting data services using reference data.

- Central repository of reference data information for the enterprise
- Use of reusable reference data services in real time
- Vocabulary management of reference data
- Common message formats for sharing reference data across the enterprise
- Manage and govern both internal and external code sets
- Possibility to publish big data services through the Cloud

- Provide governance, process, security, and audit control around mastering reference data

- Manage complex mappings between different reference data representations across the enterprise
- Efficiently manage the use of external reference data standards within the enterprise

Finally, in cases where the organization uses reference data codes that are externally defined, for example, ICD codes that are maintained by the World Health Organization (WHO) or ISO currency codes, updates from the external agency need to be monitored by business data stewards and reconciled with the organization's stored internal reference data records. Similarly, the exchange of reference data has become critical in the U.S. financial sector with Legal Entity Identifier (LEI) provisions mandated by regulators within Dodd–Frank legislation (see the following related LEI case study).

Legal Entity Identifiers (LEI) for Financial Counterparties

The implementation of timely and free exchange of LEI reference data is currently underway across many financial institutions globally. With the recently passage of Dodd–Frank legislation in the United States, it is now mandatory for financial institutions to exchange reference data information on counterparty transactions with regulators while conducting any transaction with other institutions.

LEI regulation is necessary to fulfill systemic-risk monitoring, transparency, and market-abuse prevention provisions of the Dodd–Frank legislation. Moreover, it is expected to help a company (as well as regulators) monitor potential risks of any counterparty defaults, so that a financial institution can take action before any major catastrophic event is triggered.

The LEI regulation requires all financial institutions to use an ISO-specified LEI for all counterparty transactions against other firms. This connects counterparty records from multiple systems in different divisions and regions. In result, the use of enterprise data services is becoming very popular among financial companies.

Enterprise data services help identify providers who can deliver this new LEI infrastructure and then the company solicits responses from potential solution providers who are interested in helping regulators to deliver LEI solutions. The need for consistent and reliable data services is part of the LEI-implementation strategy taken by most of these companies.

- LEI reference data should be freely available, without restrictions on reuse or redistribution, and they should be in line with any jurisdiction's regulations on privacy.
- Data elements for the LEI process should follow ISO standards and other financial regulations. Apart from LEI data, regulations include LEI-related reference data, e.g., corporate hierarchy information.
- Mechanisms should be in place to monitor LEI usage over time with active governance of parties.
- Timely notification and alert reporting should be built, in case there are any discrepancies reported.

Several vendors have started providing data services-based solutions that can publish quality LEI reference data for regulators to review (Figure 9.5). These new data services will also make data available to other partner organizations within the financial sector, as mandated during financial transactions with counterparties. These services are expected to be critical for successful data exchange and timely data reconciliation across different applications. More importantly, timely LEI data exchange using real-time services will help reduce overall risk to the global financial system and reduce the chance of a future global financial crisis.

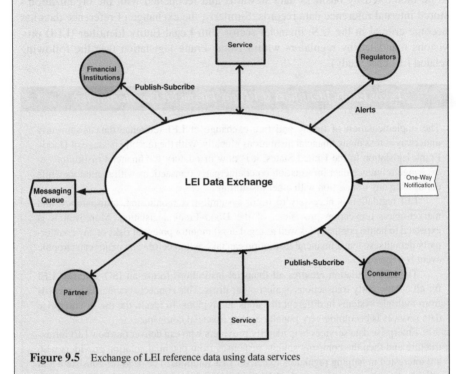

Figure 9.5 Exchange of LEI reference data using data services

COLLABORATIVE REFERENCE DATA MANAGEMENT IMPLEMENTATION USING BUSINESS PROCESS MANAGEMENT/WORKFLOW

One of the latest trends is that organizations want to execute workflow processes for reference data management utilizing tools with business process management (BPM) and workflow capabilities. From the enterprise perspective, this makes great sense, as a complete end-to-end solution requires both business rules and reference data to be applied across domains. Most vendors will have to look at innovative ways through which to consolidate enterprise BPM and RDM solutions into a unified

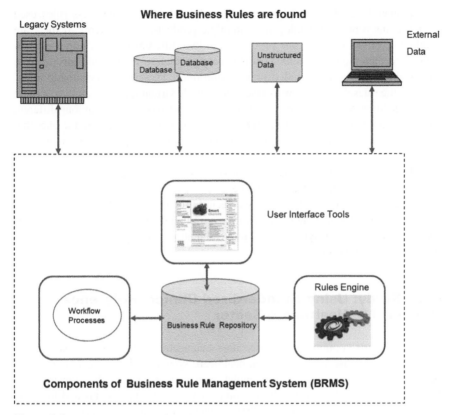

Figure 9.6   Leveraging BRMS reference data management

solution offering that can be useful for data stewards to execute as part of their governance efforts and vice versa. In short, reference data hubs need to be viewed more as value-enabled, business process hubs instead of merely data hubs.

To achieve the integration between RDM and BPM, it is best to consider an implementation style that involves using a business rule management system (BRMS). This includes a business rule repository that stores an organization's defined business rules and policies. The business rule engine is a system that is designed to ensure that business rules are managed based on a specific event (Figure 9.6).

A business rule engine can improve the effectiveness and credibility of the RDM solution among end users by providing the following functionalities:

- Helping to automate and test business policies using business rules, decision trees, and tables.
- Storing, organizing, and reporting on harvested business policies.
- Deploying and monitoring automated business policies as they execute.

Another type of event trigger is seen while storing the business rules used for retrieving a product catalog from multiple product-based systems. If there are conflicting values for the same product from two different systems doing product data entry, then the business area should specify which of the records survive from among the two. These are called survivorship rules. The term "survivorship rules" refers to the rules defining how to assemble a single virtual record from two or more records in different applications. A business often has to specify from among different data entry applications supporting RDM, recording which received are the ones that should survive in enterprise view, and then these survivors are passed back to the data services user.

However, it is easier to have business rules driven implementation when one data entry system can be used for data entry or when it dominates the bulk of data maintenance. The virtual approach is especially recommended for an organization that starts their reference data efforts within a limited time span. With business rules added for workflow, this type of RDM implementation can be good for synchronizing reference data across the organization.

Case Study: Using Standardized Clinical Reference Data in U.S. Healthcare Sector

In many experts' opinions, reference data management systems are expected to significantly increase within the U.S. healthcare system. This is largely because in sectors such as healthcare, recent regulatory mandates such as the conversion to ICD 10 codes have forced healthcare companies to revise their plans and focus on providing a reliable set of clinical reference data to their business users.

As per the Center for Disease Control and Prevention (CDC), there are two related classifications of diseases with similar titles, and a third classification on functioning and disability. However, this book's purposes, we concentrate on the ICD (clinical modification).

The CDC's web site shares, "The International Classification of Diseases (Clinical Modification) is used to code and classify morbidity data from the inpatient and outpatient records, physician offices, and most National Center for Health Statistics (NCHS) surveys." As new disease classification codes evolve over time, the NCHS is expected to keep these lists of reference codes up to date. After NHCS come up with new or revised clinical diagnosis and procedure codes (ICD 10 from ICD 9), the Department of Health and Human Services issues guidelines to all healthcare organizations to comply with the revised diagnosis and procedure codes.

For example, the U.S. Department of Health and Human Services issues a compliance date for use of the new ICD diagnosis and procedure codes released every few years. Most of the organizations in the healthcare value chain (e.g., providers, payers, insurance companies) need to comply by using these reference data (the latest compliance dates for ICD 10 released by the U.S. Health and Human Services Department is October 1, 2014) and by ensuring that electronic data interchange can in fact take place seamlessly across partner organizations.

However, instead of taking a tactical approach to resort to large-scale data conversion from the prior 9 digit ICD 9 diagnosis codes to the newly introduced 10-digit codes, many organizations may be better off employing a well thought out reference data strategy. Thus, if in the future, the government issues major changes in the diagnosis and procedure codes, the company can manage changes in a streamlined manner that also poses less risk of data quality issues (Figure 9.7).

Within ICD clinical modification, ICD diagnosis codes are used by inpatient and outpatient providers for billing and reimbursement, while ICD procedure codes are used only by inpatient providers for billing and reimbursement.

The ICD 10 codes also need to be used by healthcare organizations engaged in Health Insurance Portability and Accountability Act (HIPAA) approved electronic transactions. Thus, for example, in the X12 EDI transaction number 837 that establishes standards for submitting healthcare claims, authorized healthcare providers (physicians or hospitals) can use the Reference Data Services (from the insurance/payor company's web portal) to access the appropriate ICD 10 diagnosis and procedure codes for reviewing claim eligibility for a medical procedure by the provider. (Please refer to Figure 9.8 providing an overview on the claims payment process.) Similarly, the insurance company can use EDI transaction number 835 to provide an explanation of benefits (EOB) remittance advice to providers as well as to make claim payments to the provider electronically.

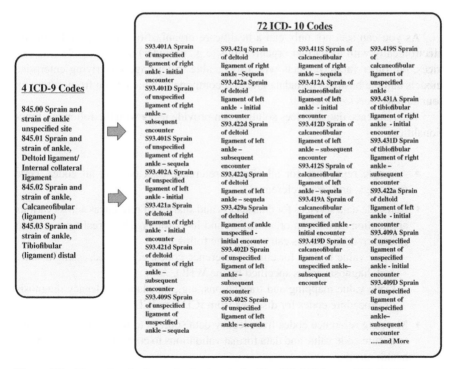

Figure 9.7   Diagnosis codes for sprained and strained ankles: ICD-9 CM versus ICD-10 CM

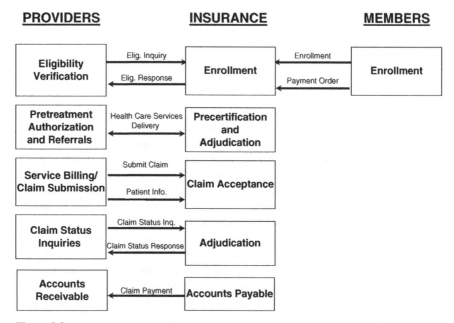

Figure 9.8   Healthcare claim submission and payment exchanges

As you can see, not only can a healthcare organization exchange information electronically with its partner organizations (e.g., provider) using reusable data services, but other future projects will also be able to leverage underlying enterprise models and the business metadata glossary component, which come from setting up foundational service layers.

The reference data services solution can provide users with the following functionalities:

- A single repository for all clinical reference data (storing all codes, code mappings, and cross references).
- Reusable data services for data access and sharing of references across various applications within an organization and its partners. These real-time clinical reference data services can support the following:
    - Code value lookup for clinical reference codes, e.g., for accessing disease and diagnosis codes specified by the WHO.
    - Code value mapping and translations, e.g., translation of legacy diagnosis or procedure codes for diseases from ICD 9 to ICD 10.
- Mapping reference codes from legacy data sources to ICD. This is necessary to ensure code value and data format validations to come up with a customer's health profile.

From a technology standpoint, the proposed reference data services solution includes the following major technology components.

- User Interface (UI) validation: In an ideal world, it is important to bring data validation tasks upstream and as close as possible to the point of data entry. An organization should introduce a UI validation component to serve as the first line of defense to prevent bad data entering from legacy stems storing reference data.

- Rules-based engine: This component is needed to determine workflow and data synchronization from/to impacted legacy systems.

- Enterprise service bus (ESB): This server supports real-time or near real-time messaging and data synchronization requirements with various upstream and downstream systems consuming the output from published data services.

- Database server: The database server supports hosting the reference data hub to store various reference data codes and definitions. The reconciliation of data changes was done in the reference data hub.

- Webservers to support the publishing of reusable data services for downstream applications.

- ETL server for supporting batch data load processing.

- Test management server for testing change management and quality assurance prior to deployment in the production environment.

Most real-time reference data services are related to clinical data and are critical to healthcare companies. Consequently, these data services were designed after a detailed review of the following considerations: delivery method, frequency, format, reliability, etc. These data services can also be very useful to healthcare organizations to maintain their electronic health records (EHRs) and support online medical users, clients, and partner organizations. Using these foundational components, IT integration architects can reconcile complex mappings between different reference data representations across the enterprise in a systematic manner over a short period of time. However, IT will need continued support from business teams in maintaining the data definitions of these reference data sets.

SUMMARY

This chapter presented a detailed approach regarding how DaaS can be deployed successfully in any organization to distribute reference data using data services.

Unfortunately, in the past, many IT professionals have often been less than enthusiastic about the importance and priority of reference data, and some have even considered this area as somewhat outdated. This happens largely due to the perception that reference data have limited strategic value. Essentially, IT professionals have often linked reference data to the mundane world of lookup values, codes, code mappings, and hierarchies. However, as we learned in this chapter, this area of reference data is far more than this, and is critical for running day-to-day operations of a company. The centrality of reference data and their foundational nature make them a great place at which to start your DaaS enablement journey. Reference data services can be provided for operational and analytical systems as value-added services.

Many leading organizations in the financial and insurance sectors have already invested in the area of reference data management and market data-related services. Healthcare companies are also in a similar period of transition as they standardize clinical reference data to meet with ICD-related global compliance requirements mandated by the World Health Organization.

Chapter 10

Master Data Services

TOPICS COVERED IN THIS CHAPTER

- This chapter provides a detailed architectural pattern for designing and developing master data services (MDS) that can be reused across the enterprise by using common design components and standards.

- It also evaluates a virtual approach to implement master data management (MDM) across organizations. The benefits of decoupling business and technology dependencies by adopting a virtual approach to MDM are also covered in detail.

- Next, it looks at MDS as an effective alternative to existing styles of MDM implementation without physically consolidating master data in a single hub.

- Finally, this chapter has several illustrative examples and a detailed case study on an MDS implementation at a large financial institution.

"There's a lot of power in generating data and executing data."

—Ken Thompson

The use of service-oriented architecture (SOA) and data services can lend itself well to sharing master data across any enterprise. In fact, leveraging the DaaS framework can produce several benefits including achieving greater consistencies in master data and opportunities for effective reuse. In addition to this, the master data services (MDS) model proposed under the Data as a Service (DaaS) framework allows organizations to implement master data management (MDM) in a way that is independent of any specific implementation decision. This virtual, platform-independent approach to MDM has been termed by several industry experts as Master Data Services (Loshin, 2009).

The conventional method employed by most organizations for addressing MDM is to gather all their master data scattered across multiple applications and consolidate the data into one physical master data management platform. However, in most cases, the physical consolidation of master data from multiple data sources can be time

Data as a Service: A Framework for Providing Reusable Enterprise Data Services,
First Edition. Pushpak Sarkar.
© 2015 the IEEE Computer Society. Published 2015 by John Wiley & Sons, Inc.

consuming and risky. Consequently, this chapter proposes an alternative approach of providing virtual access to data for consumers by leveraging the foundational components of DaaS.

INTRODUCTION TO MASTER DATA SERVICES

Master data services are useful for the publication of master data and for sharing related identifiers to downstream applications that are hosted on a wide range of disparate, legacy platforms. Let us look at an example from a manfacturing organization to illustrate how MDS can make a difference as strategic enablers for business operations. Over the lifecycle of a new product line, there can be a need for the manufacturer to have frequent exchanges with suppliers to obtain parts' information. The process of requesting and exchanging product information with a supplier over the phone or through paper exchanges can be extremely time consuming and dissatifying for the end consumer. A recent IBM study found that retailers spend an average of 260 working hours a week obtaining product information from suppliers (Soares, 2011). Given these circumstances, if users are given the option to access the product details from a competing supplier's portal using standardized data services (i.e., using the DaaS framework), they would certainly prefer to do so.

Having said that, at a minimum, the reference architecture for a master data services solution should help an organization to share master data using reusable data services. It should be able to support multiple types of master data and any aggregates and relationships among them. It should also be able to support a range of functionality needed by users to define, use, and analyze master data.

Master Data Services

Master data services are data services published for clients to access the authoritative master data stored by the data provider. MDS are often considered business services and an organization can choose to expose these external business services for consumption by authorized users and applications. External client-facing data services often need to leverage the business rules associated with the data subject area.

For example, finding the nearest hospital or the nearest physician in a particular specialization (e.g., pediatrician, cardiologist, neurosurgeon) in your neighborhood can be classified in this category of MDS. The detailed hierarchy and relationships between hospitals, physicians associated with a hospital, as well as their specialization are also provided based on underlying business rules for healthcare providers, while providing this data as a service to the consumer.

One of the key differences between an MDS solution and a traditional MDM hub is that the MDS-based solutions can use a virtual DaaS platform hosting MDS instead of storing the data physically in a centralized MDM data hub. Lastly, organizations adopting MDS can easily adapt their canonical model as they discover new business requirements. This makes the MDS solution fast and agile to build as the world changes.

Next, let us turn to how to complement traditional MDM strategies with enterprise data services (EDSs), which can provide a unified view based on the enterprise data model (EDM). It is essential that all business segments agree to use an enterprise version of master data also known as the golden record.

For users to access the golden data record virtually using MDS, there should be a well-defined data access and distribution strategy to support the needs of key MDM stakeholders and consumers. This requires a clear plan by DaaS sponsors at the outset of the initiative.

- Identifying who the business consumers of the MDS are (e.g., internal and external consumers, regulatory agencies, vendors).

- How do the consumers want to use the master data published over the MDS delivery framework?

- Identifying the critical data elements (CDEs) that are necessary for building the virtual data layer and representing them in the EDM.

- Finalizing the canonical model to be used by MDS based on the EDM (Figure 10.1).

- Categorizing data sources that can populate the enterprise canonical model (ECM) and mapping these source elements to the CDEs.

Following the MDS approach, the virtual data layer built for data consumption can lower the complexity of delivering master data from multiple legacy systems storing

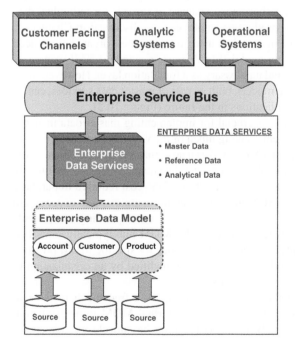

Figure 10.1   Role of the enterprise data model

different versions of the master data. The MDS approach is largely based on the concept of DaaS. Implementing this in organizations is relatively easy and quicker in comparison to implementing master data management hubs that need to consolidate data from multiple sources physically on a single platform.

Master data services can be implemented using XML messages that employ standardized data formats while exchanging master data. These data formats are derived largely from the organization's ECM.

As described in Chapter 7, data virtualization tools can be used for improving the performance and scalability of the master data services solution. Performance and scalability become especially critical while linking data from multiple sources, often on disparate platforms. Using data virtualization tools can make the virtual data access appear transparent to the data consumer (almost as if the data were co-located).

However, the DaaS-based implementation model works best when organizations already have an authoritative database of records for individual data subject areas that have been identified (e.g., customer or provider). Organizations that use the virtual-implementation style need to invest significantly in data governance (DG) efforts, as each subject area needs to have its own unique system of records formally defined from among existing operational systems. This is because an organization having multiple databases with no clear system of records for its master data can have a very challenging and complex data integration environment. As a single operational system becomes the system of record, access by an individual data service also becomes easier—with all data entry systems sending it periodic feeds and with no other sources making updates.

Therefore, the virtual MDM-style implementation using the DaaS model is ideal for organizations to achieve an authoritative database of records for individual data subject areas (e.g., customer or product or employee). As discussed in Chapters 4, 5, and 6, to get a single view of master data using data services, organizations need to build an enterprise-logical data model (ELDM), use a standard XML canonical format, data mappings, and a metadata glossary as a foundation layer. However, these foundation components (e.g., the model), built as part of master data services, can be leveraged by other enterprise applications in the future (Figure 10.2).

Consequently, the role of DG is crucial for implementing master data management in a virtual DaaS environment. Having much of the web infrastructure (e.g., an enterprise service bus [ESB]) in place also makes it advantageous for the organization to move quickly, because it is possible to get master data management started quickly by building the data services internally at a fraction of the cost required to purchase a master data management hub externally, pay system integrators, and expect them to deliver on promises (Dyche, 2011). In contrast, the corresponding components (e.g., vendor model, message) when using a vendor MDM hub typically cannot be reused, because they are usually designed by the vendor for specific MDM projects. Moreover, the vendor MDM model often cannot be modified by an organization to meet their organization-specific requirements.

On the other hand, often there is no such thing as a free lunch in the real world. Consequently, even as organizations opt for virtual MDM implementation, there is a risk of failure, especially if an organization has no clear roadmap for

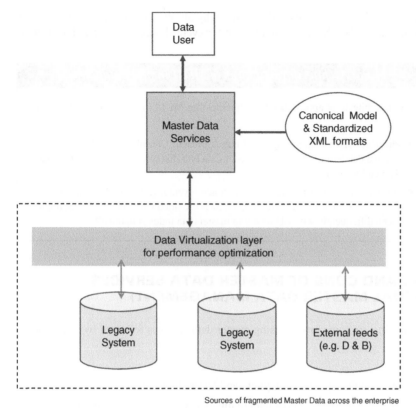

Sources of fragmented Master Data across the enterprise

Figure 10.2   Virtual master data management approach leveraging data services

MDM governance. For instance, a critical role is played when defining standardized exchange formats as a foundational step to deploying Master Data Services. This is largely due to the fact that in virtualized MDM implementation, there is no centralized MDM hub (or even registry) storing golden-copy records such as in the transaction-style MDM, so these standard formats become critical for successful transport to and from the MDM hub.

When a user makes a request for master data, the EDS has to invoke a service call to get a single virtualized view of the master data. These requests can be in the form of canonical XML message formats. The data service takes the data from the data source, transforms it to the standardized exchange format, and then makes it available to the data consumer using the ESB. The ESB software layer is used by the webservices' applications for message routing and event-driven invocation to validate and translate inbound and outbound electronic messages.

To build the view, canonical XML messages need to be mapped to the multiple data stores that actually store the data physically. If the message formats are not compatible, no exchange or sharing of data is possible. Even if there are physical sharing of the data, users would not get a consistent or reliable view of their data, or of what those data mean. This is the reason why all master data exchange messages should use a standard XML schema format for event-driven master data integration.

Major Architectural Patterns of MDM Implementation

The major architectural approaches for implementing MDM in any organization are as follows:

- Physical master data management hub approach: Consolidated hub with a centralized database. Consolidated master data hub that physically stores the master data entities in a database.
- Virtual master data management approach leveraging DaaS: Providing master DaaS to consumers. Access to master data is provided virtually with MDS, implemented frequently with EDSs (a thin master data index is optional).

PROS AND CONS OF MASTER DATA SERVICES (VIRTUAL MASTER DATA MANAGEMENT)

The following are some pros of using master data services followed by some cons.

Pros

- Low complexity, easy and quick, and less risky to implement.
- Replace multiple points of data maintenance and point-to-point interfaces.
- Master data elements from disparate systems can be assembled in real time with a data index to determine unique identifiers and cross-reference identifiers to map back to customer records in source systems.
- Another benefit of using MDM is that the cross-reference identifiers can be easily linked to unstructured document comments (spread out across different sources) in different ways (through tags) to make them accessible to users.
- The standardized canonical model, data mappings, and metadata glossary built as a foundation layer for an MDM can be reused by future projects trying to integrate data. For example, the MDM interface can be used for on-demand master data integration to applications, portals, business-intelligence (BI) tools, etc.

Cons

- Organizations need to invest significantly in DG efforts early on.
- Each subject area needs to identify its authoritative data source(s).
- Organizations need to build foundational-layer components: EDM, canonical models, data mappings, and metadata glossary.

- Operational systems still remain as the data entry systems and there are no source updates.
- Data quality can be an issue if sufficient efforts are not made to clean up the source data.
- Query performance may be a concern without a master data index in a large implementation
- Cannot support complex business rules without a business-rules engine.

LEVERAGING THE GOLDEN SOURCE TO RESOLVE DEEP-ROOTED SOURCE DIFFERENCES

It is not unusual to find that many organizations retain multiple, inconsistent copies of master data (e.g., customer, product, supplier information) for a host of reasons. For example, while responding to a particular customer-related inquiry, a business user may obtain different answers to the same enquiry.The risk of inconsistent and bad decision-making increases due to lack of reliable data being available to decision makers. Often, due to this lack of consistency at the enterprise level, individual user teams within divisions are usually found to maintain their own copies of customer and product master data to meet their immediate needs for their users in their division.

This is a messy scenario and a nightmare to both the IT and business divisions from a DG perspective. For example, if the data change in any of the legacy source systems supplying master data, all the downstream systems could go out of sync, as they will still be using the old copy until the relevant data are refreshed.

If it is not possible to identify a single source of truth (SoT) for master data in a domain, then the use of Master Data Services may be the only viable option. All underlying data quality issues have to be reconciled at the source of the data. In some organizations, this problem is addressed by purchasing a vendor-based MDM hub. The expectation is that the tool will magically resolve all the underlying data quality-related issues.

Therefore, it is essential for any master data services to utilize data from various legacy source applications to ensure that information that is published to customers via the DaaS framework has good data quality and standards.

Additionally, organizations could designate specific applications as the SoT for a particular information domain. For example, the customer relationship-management (CRM) system in the organization may be designated as the SoT for the customer domain. The DG council can designate a data steward for each of these SoT applications to ensure that the data from various divisional systems are updated to the SoT in a timely manner. If it is not possible to only use a single SoT, then the use of an operational data store (ODS) to reconcile deep-rooted differences may be the only remaining option (Figure 10.3).

Companies often build an ODS that acts as a staging and integration zone between MDM and the other downstream systems (e.g., sales data marts). Having data services also reduces effort in terms of integrating MDM with the other legacy

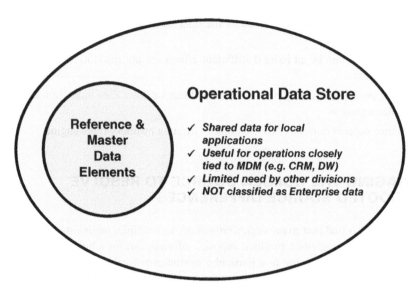

Figure 10.3 Role of ODS/staging area in master data services implementation

data applications that often act as the defacto SoT for master data in a particular domain.

FUTURE TRENDS IN MASTER DATA MANAGEMENT USING DaaS

In contrast to investing substantial time and effort in building MDM hub systems, organizations need to also examine if they can provide master data services (i.e., if they can provide DaaS) virtually to their users.

The trend toward virtualizing MDM has to be complemented by active and continual governance efforts from business stewards owning the data. Often, adopting a distributed governance model that empowers the stewardship of data by a person or organization closest to the "truth" can improve underlying processes affecting data quality in applications across the organization, instead of attempting a simplistic solution based on data reconciliation in a downstream MDM platform.

Moreover, using virtualized DaaS-style implementations also better suit the needs of large, global organizations spanning multiple continents. This is because business and government regulations on data privacy, security, etc., can be completely different across different regions of a global company. In fact, in some industry sectors such as banking, storing all data physically in a consolidated MDM hub can be unviable for legal reasons. For example, some European countries have mandated that no financial data can cross their geographic national boundaries. Moreover, even if the data are extracted into a centralized MDM hub, the different business rules used to process the data in various operational applications can be risky, complex, and unwieldy. Therefore, due to a host of business, political, or national security-driven concerns, we think that the trend for building virtual MDS is likely to grow in the future.

Having said that, consolidation of master data in a centralized MDM hub can still be useful for many organizations that want to address enterprise-wide MDM without having complex government or business regulations to support multiple regions. It is also going to be useful in organizations that operate in lesser countries or have a smaller range of distributed master data (e.g., two to three data sources) within the organization.

However, barring these situations, most problems can be addressed through organizations using MDM without any significant investment in data consolidation. In my view, MDM can be the central vehicle of communication, and all systems can directly communicate with it by using webservices, SOA, and Cloud platforms.

One of the other advantages of dynamically assembled records is that the virtualized DaaS solution can virtually maintain multiple views of the master data that are aligned to individual lines of business and their specific functional requirements, data visibility requirements, tolerance toward false positives and negatives, and latency requirements. Mature enterprises increasingly require multiple views for the golden record and the dynamic record assembly works better to support this need (Dreibelbeis, 2008).

One of the main reasons why some large corporations experience serious issues in the long run with MDM concerns the growth of their business over time through mergers or acquisitions. In these situations, two organizations that merge often store duplicate master data records (since each likely had at least one master database of its own prior to the merger) with completely different business rules. In most organizations, the IT architects who are responsible for the transition resolve this problem through re-duplication of the master data as part of the merger.

In practice, however, reconciling several master data systems into a single, persisted copy can pose several challenges because of dependencies that existing applications have on underlying business processes and the disparate rules in the two organizations. As a result, while the organization merges different business acquisitions, their IT support systems often cannot fully merge, but remain separate to meet individual business demands of each business division. Many IT organizations try to resolve these environmental differences by defining a set of reconciliation processes that ensure consistency between data stored in the two systems. Over time, however, as further mergers and acquisitions occur, the problem multiplies, more and more master databases appear, and data reconciliation processes become extremely complex, and consequently, unmanageable and unrealistic. It is in these situations that the traditional MDM systems need to be augmented by virtual approaches such as MDM services and rules-driven MDM.

Demerits of Master Data Services and Addressing Gaps

One of the major demerits of virtual MDS (as opposed to storing master data physically in a data hub) is its slow access time. Performance is expected to suffer for queries involving large data volumes. This is because the record is assembled dynamically each time during a request for master data retrieval. However, with master data services running on data virtualization engines, many of the performance-related concerns can be addressed by pre-built aggregates, cache storage, etc., as discussed in Chapter 7.

Performance metrics can be confirmed by organizations by evaluating benchmarks from data virtualization tool vendors. Several recent data virtualization implementations have shown that master data can be assembled "on the fly" and dynamically with practically no performance impact if the underlying model is properly in place and implemented. The risks and costs associated with integrating several systems with a data virtualization option can also reduce drastically when compared to the physical storage of master data in a MDM hub.

Most of the other problems that can occur with the MDS approach can be removed with a well laid out set of reusable components that are specified in the DaaS reference architecture (see Chapter 2). For example, by employing a common exchange model for messaging, architects can map data objects in different application sources to elements in the canonical data model (CDM) and to the corresponding term in the business glossary.

This book's proposed approach to MDS should be accompanied by continued DG efforts over the lifetime of these MDS. In fact, DG is critical in achieving sustainable and effective MDM irrespective of implementation style. Organizations that fail to execute DG significantly narrow their chances of success and their return-on-investment (ROI) for MDM programs in the end. Therefore, it is critical to have formal governance and oversight of MDM initiatives by a distributed team of data stewards.

COMPARING MASTER DATA SERVICES APPROACH (VIRTUAL) WITH MASTER DATA MANAGEMENT APPROACH INVOLVING PHYSICAL CONSOLIDATION

Having evaluated both MDM implementation styles that have been previously discussed in the financial, healthcare, and insurance sectors throughout this book, each implementation style has its own strengths. However, it is important to evaluate both options carefully and not to become caught up in myths that often accompany vendor-provided MDM hub solutions.

Moreover, in many real-life scenarios, an organization can find that the vendor has provided a MDM-product solution based on a generic design set of functionality or a generic data model (e.g., a party or product model) upon which MDS are built, without regard to each organization's finer differences between their business models.

The need for customization specific to an organization's unique needs makes MDS worth serious consideration by most organizations. Often in the corporate world, many organizations (if not all) evolve and change over time by reacting to major business events. Sometimes they grow or merge with other companies. If the companies used different platforms before the merger, it makes IT consolidation even more difficult when the virtual approach of master data services is not employed.

Sometimes there are new regulations that make it imperative for an organization to change direction. These business realities can often significantly affect the underlying business model. Consequently, any change to the underlying model could mean rewriting all of the data service components. However, many MDM vendors have so far been able to provide master data solutions successfully in a few domains such as the customer domain, where the underlying use of a standardized party model can generate conformance to some industry data standards.

From a technology perspective, at a minimum the choice of virtual MDM implementation styles should help enterprise architects and MDM system integrators to select the appropriate MDM pattern and implementation style for their organization. They can decide whether to choose the appropriate solution architecture after looking at comparative merits and suitability of a consolidated MDM hub versus a quick deployment of a virtual-style MDM with the MDS approach. However, the intention behind the MDS approach is not to undermine architectural merits of the traditional MDM approach with data physically consolidated in a hub.

If we look at future trends in the MDM market, one can see the emergence of a few Cloud-hosted solutions that can successfully operate complex data matching and consolidation processes. A Cloud-based MDM solution combined with the DaaS components explained throughout this book may eliminate an organization's need to build a physical MDM hub altogether.

Readers should come to their own conclusion given the underlying factors in their organization and industry trends.

CASE STUDY: MASTER DATA SERVICES FOR A PREMIER INVESTMENT BANK

Overview

As part of a major revamp, the global wealth management (GWM) division at a leading bank sponsored a customer data management improvement program focusing on improving master data across the organization. Since this financial institution had multiple lines of business, including investment banking, wealth management, private banking, etc., it needed the means with which to connect their customer records (referred to also as clients) from multiple systems generating master data across different divisions, countries, and regions.

From a data governance standpoint, the initial objective of this program was specifically to address a few compliance regulations recently introduced by the U.S. government for banking customers (e.g., anti-money laundering (AML), KYC, LEI).

To identify the customer master list across all divisions of the bank uniquely, the MDM task force recommended that the bank introduce the concept of the unique party identifier across divisions. This identifier was felt to be essential from a risk/compliance perspective for identifying duplicate clients across the organization.

Over time, this global bank had grown to become a financial supermarket owning multiple lines of business (corporate banking, wealth management, investment banking, etc.). Consequently, individual divisions had built multiple MDM platforms with their own versions of customer. Given the size, complexities, and risks involved in global data integration, the MDM task force did not recommend a physical consolidation of master data from multiple data sources into a single MDM hub. The task force instead recommended that individual divisional systems cross-reference their divisional identifiers utilizing the newly introduced master data services.

DETAILED SCOPE AND BENEFITS

The specific objectives of the master data services initiative in this organization included the following:

1. Transform their global wealth management business model and related data strategy from being account-centric to client-relationship centric. The shift to focus on customer needs meant that the organization had to have a 360-degree view of their customers, so the master data strategy had to be developed in close alignment with a company-wide CRM initiative that would run concurrently. The business leaders wanted to build a relationship-driven business model driven by client satisfaction. The other objective was to achieve improved efficiency in their CRM and retail brokerage operations.

2. Develop a comprehensive household-based global wealth management business model that to ensure that this organization would have a complete end-to-end understanding of their relationship with existing and prospective clients. They also wanted to be in a position to serve the needs of their international clientele by understanding the possible relationship of these clients with other high net-worth individuals. For example, a financial advisor would utilize their existing relationship to contact high net-worth clients to offer investment opportunities. The expectation was that these would help the company identify increased upselling and cross-selling opportunities and grow revenue over the long run.

3. From the corporate perspective, the initiative was expected to help the brokerage comply with several new financial regulatory guidelines and provisions introduced in the sector (e.g., KYC, AML, OFAC). There was also a need to exchange client information with other parts of the global bank to ensure that high-risk clients could be identified and divisions could alert the other parts of the bank quickly to take corrective action. The immediate need was felt across various divisions to introduce the single customer identifier, valid across more than 100 countries where the organization had client operations.

From the tactical perspective, major benefits to banking operations were the following:

- Screen new clients and prospects
- Discover new customer relationships
- Cross-sell/upsell to existing customers based on their investment objectives/ goals
- Improved customer service
- Better branch/FA efficiencies
- Fraud detection and alerts
- Compliance to corporate and regulatory standards.

Based on these strategic and tactical business objectives, business leadership engaged the IT architecture team and senior IT development leaders to develop a master data strategy that could bring this transformation to the organization. Figure 10.4 shows a proposed solution architecture for master data services.

PROPOSED SOLUTION ARCHITECTURE FOR MASTER DATA SERVICES

The business leadership and IT architecture teams worked together to gain an in-depth understanding of the overall requirements for their client-centric data services and classify them into different categories such as basic data services, intermediary data service, and business services (service categories was discussed in Chapter 7).

The first exercise taken in the detail design was to work with various business teams to identify master data elements that needed to be accessed by them using reusable data services.

The following criteria can be used to identify master data elements.

- Core data of an enterprise that is critical and shared across the organization (golden copy)
- Representative of business entities (customer, product, etc.) rather than trans-action (e.g., order processing)
- Non-transactional
- Include certain reference data (e.g., industry codes)
- Support need for standardized vocabulary for every data element
- Conforms to business-specified data validation rules

In this large global financial services group with several business divisions, stake-holders agreed to implement master data services using a federated approach. While the customer demographic profile was hosted using a central enterprise data

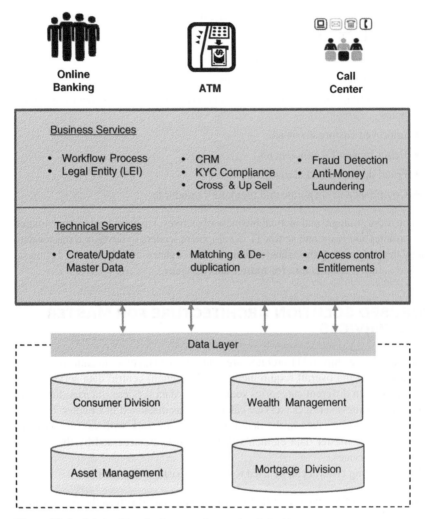

Figure 10.4   Solution blueprint for master data services in banking

service layer including elements required to identify a customer uniquely (first name, last name, date of birth, tax identifier or SSN, address). These handful of elements were required to be stored in the Demographic ODS, a central repository storing client information to help banks comply with regulations like KYC and anti-money laundering. However, other customer demographic elements that can be interpreted differently by the loan division versus investment banking division can be handled by localized services. The organization felt that these elements were necessary to be published over centrally governed master data services but they did not require storage in a centralized master data management hub.

Unique Identifier of Customer

The organization's relationship with a customer usually started as a prospect, when the FA listed them as a potential prospective customer lead. After the FA succeeded in selling a financial product or service to the potential client, an account was opened in the name of the client(s) and the prospect became treated as a client.

Earlier prospects and customer were traditionally not housed together physically in the same data repository. With the business and regulatory need for a unique customer ID under newly introduced KYC regulations in the banking sector, it was decided to store the customer ID physically in a database. This identifier was required for auditing purposes as well as to improve MDM service performance purposes. All customer-related queries and data access using data services were subsequently associated with a unique identifier. For these reasons, this ID would act as the unique identifier for customer (party) but not their structures or relationships.

The master data services used the following attributes for identifying and matching duplicate clients across financial institutions: name, data of birth, SSN/tax identifier or passport no/country, home phone, and legal address.

To publish comprehensive master data services, the organization also stored a few other cross-reference details on the customer's demographic profile and contact information to support a 360-degree view of a customer (Figure 10.5).

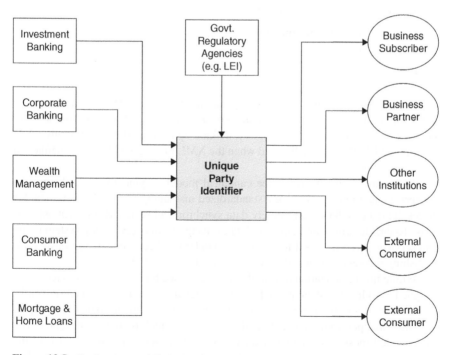

Figure 10.5   DaaS supports a 360-degree view of a customer with party identifier

ENTERPRISE AND CANONICAL MODEL FOR MASTER DATA MANAGEMENT IMPLEMENTATION

The initial effort by the enterprise modeling team was to identify some of the major types of master data to be published using data services across the organization. These were represented in the following entities of the logical data model developed for the customer master data services implementation (Figure 10.9). The following are a few customer demographic profile data elements that were in scope for initial implementation:

- Name
- DOB
- SSN
- Gender
- Marital status
- Address/Phone/Email
- Employment detail
- Investment objectives/Goals
- Risk Tolerance
- Dependent/Beneficiary detail
- Source of wealth information
- Net worth
- Portfolio balance

The entities shown are the enterprise logical data model (ELDM) for the customer, demographic, and contact location/address data subject areas. The data definitions are recorded on the enterprise data glossary, defined by the data stewards initially while creating the ELDM and finally used when the XML messaging blocks get defined in the canonical model.

As discussed in Chapter 5, the canonical model is typically derived from the enterprise data model to provide a standardized messaging format that is critical for successful data exchange and timely data synchronization across different applications. To enable proper and efficient data exchange from every legacy system to the data services layer, the need for common, standardized components responsible for publishing messages to the enterprise service bus is essential.

Within this organization too, all the messages used for master data services were designed to follow the standardized canonical message format and related standards. Therefore, entities and attributes in the master data management logical data model were then mapped to the reusable XML messaging block by the organization. The implemented messages for master data services followed standards defined in the enterprise canonical message format. This helped in making the exchange of data using enterprise data services across different systems seamless, timely, and efficient.

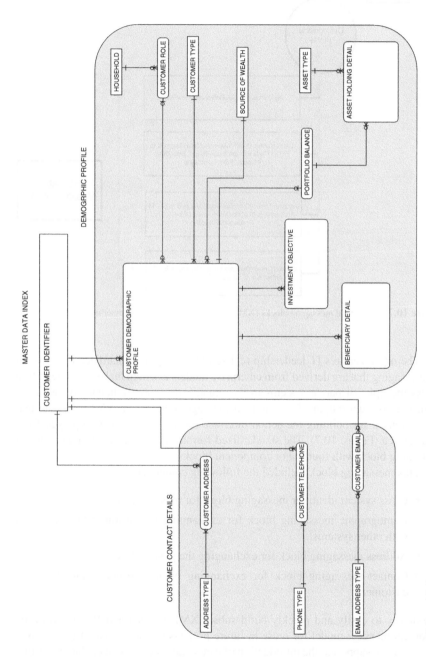

Figure 10.6 ELDM for customer (demographics) subject area

203

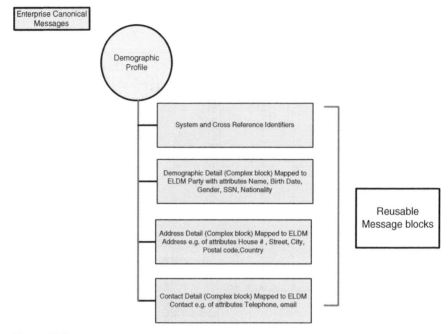

Figure 10.7 Canonical messaging blocks (XML) for data exchange of customer master data

The organization's IT leadership realized that using a standardized data format for messaging that are derived from enterprise models can help make data integration across multiple, disparate systems in the organization more efficient. As we have seen, the eventual output of a canonical message model is an XML message that can be reused for building the actual interface (or WSDL Schema) deployed for a data service (Figure 10.7). The standardized format was represented in a canonical messaging block with four major component blocks.

This messaging block included the following components:

- Cross system identifier messaging block for master data index.
- Demographic messaging block for exchanging the customer profile details with other systems.
- Address messaging block for exchanging the postal address.
- Contact messaging block for exchanging phone, fax and email details of customer.

The ability to easily and quickly build subset XML schema and WSDL from the canonical message model for reuse in future projects became apparent to IT stakeholders. They supported the introduction of canonical models as an enabler of virtual data integration. The organization quickly planned to use the canonical XML model for widespread reuse across the enterprise. During the implementation of XML

	CRM	Account Opening	Portfolio Minder	Net Flow	FA Desktop	myFi Web Portal	Risk Compliance
Customer Data	X				X	X	X
Account Data		X	X	X	X		X
Financial Products			X		X		X
Transactions			X	X	X	X	X
Positions	X	X	X	X		X	X
Common Reference Data (e.g. Branch, Industry codes)	X	X	X	X	X	X	X

Figure 10.8 Mapping XML message schemas to existing financial applications in the organization

messages for customer master data (demographic and address), the team designed the canonical message format as a core component for the company. Because the canonical message reused the ELDM data format and the definitions stored in the shared business vocabulary and definitions, it became easier to build XML messaging components that were reusable across the enterprise. Since the model had the correct vocabulary relationships added, users in different divisions could access the required data service components using the shared business vocabulary without misinterpreting the underlying usage.

The final results of this exercise were a set of WSDL XML schemas that contained specifications for the XML message requirement of various data services along with mappings on how the message maps to truth system sources and their data models (Figure 10.8).

While developing data services, the organization also developed an easy-to-use web portal interface that allows anyone to search and navigate the ECM schema (directly or through the application vocabulary familiar to them), find the components within the model that meet their message requirements, and generate a run-time optimized XML Schema. Valid message payloads were also tested to ensure performance and SLA for the data services.

The organization generated their own customer master data identifier and did not require the use of any vendor MDM tool for identity resolution and matching. This identifier was used for cross-reference purposes and linking master data existing in the matching legacy data stores. The unique identifier was useful while dynamically assembling a comprehensive unified view of master data elements to publish to users in real time. The only shared master data element centrally stored in the master data index were the identifying attributes used to identify a customer uniquely within the United States by the financial organization.

- Customer Full Name
- SSN or Tax Identifier Number

- Birth Date
- Legal Entity Identifier (discussed earlier)

Technical Architecture

The key technical requirements identified for data distribution were the following:

- Persistence of customer identifier was required for uniquely identifying a customer over its lifecycle.
- Cross-linking customer identifiers with other applications to ensure identity recognition and compliance to AML, KYC provisions introduced as part of U.S. regulations.
- Rules-based data synchronization from/to impacted legacy systems (e.g., account opening application).
- Reconciliation of data changes would be done in the demographic ODS and not in the MDS layer.
- Relationship/household aggregation grouping was requested to help the global wealth management business division gain a complete end-to-end understanding of their relationship with existing and prospective clients in the same relationship/household..
- Security and visibility (entitlements).

To meet these requirements the following major technology components were used for deployment of MDM implementation using data services (Figure 10.9).

- Message Server: This server supports real-time or near real-time messaging and data synchronization requirements with various upstream and downstream systems consuming the output from published data services.
- Enterprise Service Bus (ESB): The ESB was used to leverage messaging infrastructure to distribute periodic master data updates to downstream application consuming master data.
- Database Server: This server supports hosting the thin master data index with the minimum required data elements required for uniquely identifying a customer across the organization.
- Web servers to support publishing reusable master data services.
- An ETL server to support batch data load processing.
- Test management server for testing change management and quality assurance prior to deployment.
- Production server for final deployment of the MDS across the entire organization.

However, the organization also leveraged a leading data quality tool (already existing in the organization for supporting other applications) for address corrections and

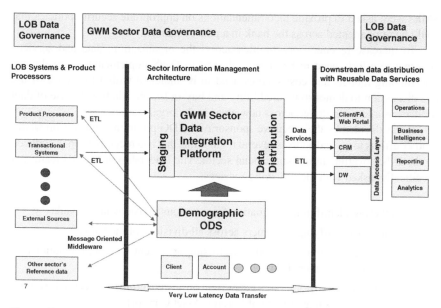

Figure 10.9 Overview of data integration environment in the global bank

validation of other master data elements using sophisticated algorithms to determine if the master records loaded from SOT systems had any errors or required to be matched with real world addresses.

Data Governance

The bank's governance program was sponsored by the risk management division. However, given the size and global nature of its operations, the financial institution appointed an executive function and set up DG as a separate business function for the entire global organization.

The enterprise DG council included key functional stakeholders to ensure IT was aligned with the business. Some of the stakeholders in the council included the chief financial officer, chief risk officer, chief information officer, chief information security officer, etc. Efforts were also made to ensure representation in the council at both the global and divisional levels. Thus, the European and Asia-Pacific banking operations had a formal representative in the DG council. Every month, DG council meetings were organized by the chief data officer on behalf of the DG program's executive sponsor.

Over the course of the initial stages, several key areas of data and services governance required inputs from SMEs. The DG council appointed sub-committees specifically to address these areas. For example, to address the issues related to access and security controls for published data services, a special sub-committee comprising enterprise information management (EIM), web services, and IT-security

SMEs were asked to provide recommendations on appropriate security policies that could be implemented across the bank in a phased manner.

To increase revenue opportunities across the organization, data and services governance efforts need to be closely aligned to DaaS-implementation roadmaps. The funding models and cost savings need to be included within the scope of the DG discussion to demonstrate credibility and buy-in for the additional reuse of data services as a revenue driver across new areas in the organization.

It was decided by the executive sponsor of the DG program that his team would fund IT efforts to try and address several regulations that had recently been introduced by the U.S. government in the financial sector. The leadership of the DG team was specifically tasked with the following services:

- Gathering identifying information from various divisions in the bank.
- Uniquely identifying customers across all divisions of the bank.
- Verifying a customer as authentic to support recent banking regulations on know your customer (KYC).
- Ensuring that a customer was not present on any government-specified criminal or terrorist lists (e.g., Office of Foreign Asset Control).
- Monitoring customers of the bank regularly for suspicious behavior, especially to comply with AML.
- Supporting risk and compliance reporting needs.

The sponsors set up a data services governance sub-team comprised of business, MDM, and data services SMEs from different divisions of the financial institution. The job of this task force was to provide detailed recommendations on the data services implementation approach and related architecture activities over the program's lifecycle. A series of activities were made part of a repeatable process for monitoring data services. These steps were to be enforced by the data services governance sub-team consistently across all the divisions, as a key part of overall governance efforts.

SUMMARY

This chapter explained how a business organization can leverage the DaaS-framework information to exchange master data with data consumers and downstream applications. The DaaS approach to implement MDM virtually through MDS is expected to lower the costs and to drastically improve service-level quality.

MDS can provide a virtual view of the organization's golden master data record after pulling input from multiple legacy applications across the enterprise. This is in contrast to the complex physical cleansing and merging of data that is involved while consolidating data from across multiple source systems into a full-blown MDM hub.

This chapter also provided a high-level overview of the major categories of MDS and discussed the critical role of identifying reliable data sources (SoT) for the success of MDS implementation.

Finally, a case study from the banking and financial services sector was presented on how to build MDS for illustrative purposes. The case study is based largely on my own real-life implementation experiences in several SOA-based MDM implementations in the financial services industry.

Chapter 11

Big Data and Analytical Services

TOPICS COVERED IN THIS CHAPTER

- This chapter covers big data and their potential in analytics space, mainly to enable readers to gain new insights that were previously hidden, and to use information that was not previously leveraged from big data and analytics.

- It provides a detailed solution blueprint for designing and developing big data analytical services that can be reused across the enterprise by using common design components and standards.

- How big data and analytics area users can leverage data services to access data needed for advanced analytics and make decisions in real time is also explained.

- There are several case studies presented from organizations that have successfully implemented big data and mobile-based analytics services, leveraging the Data as a Service (DaaS) framework.

"Without big data analytics, companies are blind and deaf, wandering out onto the Web like deer on a freeway."

—Geoffrey Moore, Technology Visionary and Author

$\mathbf{A}$s many of us have witnessed, the rapid explosion of data in all its forms has turned into a deluge of remarkable proportions. A major portion of the data generated over recent decades has been from the world of unstructured data—everything from social media posts, mobile phone texts, and tweets to credit card transactions and sensor-generated data. In addition to this, the advent of Cloud computing has introduced the delivery of computer services via the Internet, with a large amount of data stored in remote data centers.

Data as a Service: A Framework for Providing Reusable Enterprise Data Services, First Edition. Pushpak Sarkar. © 2015 the IEEE Computer Society. Published 2015 by John Wiley & Sons, Inc.

With the growing convergence of Cloud, Analytics, Mobile and Social Media (CAMS), the role of big data will grow further to become a strategic enabler for businesses. Another big reason that has unlocked the value of different forms of valuable data is the recently acquired capability of being able to quickly transform any form of structured or unstructured data into a data format that can be consolidated for predictive analysis by organizations. Consequently, several industry experts have predicted the growth of real-time services to support big DaaS.

Big DaaS refers to the capability of delivering business insights gained from large data sets using statistical modeling and analytic tools by a data provider for organizations to gain a competitive advantage. This capability will not only provide on-demand information availability to customers but provide discovery and predictive analysis and reporting capabilities, through the use of reusable data services.

Promise of Analyzing Big Data

Several leading Internet and technology companies have recently moved their demands from data analysis to a higher plane along three dimensions—volume, velocity, and the variety of data. Many of these innovation leaders (e.g., Google, Amazon, Facebook) are on the front lines of harnessing the deluge of information that they collect online, analyzing it, and providing the data to customers as a service. However, in most situations, the efforts around big data in businesses so far have focused upon ways to consolidate and store vast quantities of data for predictive analysis. This process can be time-consuming and businesses often get the results too late to make timely decisions. Over the next few years, businesses will expect IT departments to help them act faster on such analytical predictions. Data services can help by providing outputs in real time or near real time so businesses can respond faster.

Much of the effort around big data thus far has focused upon how to consume and understand vast quantities of information. Yet the reason for performing all of these analyses is not to develop understanding alone but to help create better actions and better outputs for data customers. Big data platforms need to also make sense of data in real time, which is fast enough for their organizations to respond to certain user requests before it is too late. Organizations can leverage the DaaS framework to provide these sub-second "sense and respond" capabilities within their big data platforms.

Classification of Big Data

Big data can be broadly classified into the following categories by origin:

Social media-generated data	Machine-generated data
Clickstream data	Oil-sensor readings
Facebook posts	Utility-meter readings
Twitter feeds	RFID readings
Blog feeds	GPS

Detail-transaction data	**Biometric data**
Insurance claims	Facial recognition
Telephone call details	Finger printing
Billing detail	
Human-generated data	
Voicemail	
Email transcripts	

Experian, the globally renowned information services provider, is a prime example of an organization that has successfully transformed portions of their business to a Data as a Service (DaaS) based subscription model. This organization is in a position to predict people's income level through analysis of a huge database of credit histories that they have already been built based on anonymous tax data collected from the U.S. Internal Revenue Service (IRS). They have recently launched a service called Income Insights to provide this income-related DaaS to clients for a fee. The move to a DaaS-centric model would not have been possible without an underlying big data platform as a technology enabler. However, Experian has successfully identified an opportunity to monetize its considerable data assets with its innovative application of DaaS and analytical capabilities from big data.

BIG DATA

Big data is a term that is used to describe processing data that have the following characteristics:

- Extremely large volume
- Being captured at a high velocity/dynamism
- Comprise a variety of structured and unstructured data (e.g., web site logs, email, SMS, video, Twitter, social media).

The big data platform (e.g., Hadoop) offers a new, innovative approach that addresses shortcomings faced by traditional relational-database management systems (RDBMSs). It offers several new capabilities and its flexibility frees the user from predetermining how he or she intends to use the data and supports a rapid, iterative approach. For querying different forms of data across multiple platforms and obtaining hidden insights that were not previously available, the big data platform has an architecture that is more flexible, scalable, and fault tolerant.

In the past, organizations have mostly neglected the management of unstructured data due to some inherent limitations in handling these data forms. In fact, most organizations were blissfully ignoring their unstructured data altogether, continuing to use only less than a quarter of their total data assets (structured data only) to drive their businesses.

However, there have been some significant breakthroughs that have made the use of unstructured data become more widely adopted. One of these notable breakthroughs was an innovative "datafication" project by Google in 2004 to digitize text from books from academic libraries worldwide. Datafication has provided the ability to make any text data indexable, allowing users to search for specific words, letters, or paragraphs within the digital edition of a book (Cukier, 2014).

The ability of companies to "datafy" unstructured text data is a significant advance in the field of data management, as business organizations can now utilize all forms of data—structured, unstructured, and semi-structured—to support their analytical needs. In fact, a large number of organizations have now begun to realize the huge potential opportunity (and challenge) of processing massive amounts of data, identifying patterns, analyzing the data, and making predictions.

Big Data Explained

Big data is all about seeing and understanding relations within and among pieces of data that until recently, we struggled to grasp fully. There is an inherent messiness in processing large amounts of data and this requires immense computing power that was not available in conventional, so-called relational-database technologies.

Big-data platforms have made solving this problem more feasible by providing organizations with the ability to collect, process, and interpret massive amounts of information. Businesses see it as a way of gaining competitive intelligence based on the analysis of weak market signals.

The immense promise of big data solutions can potentially change the face of many global-scale problems, making them one of the twenty-first century's leading technological drivers.

BIG DATA ANALYTICS

In the traditional world of data management (i.e., before the advent of big data), business intelligence (BI) solutions have largely been dependent on the analysis of historical data stored in enterprise data warehouses and departmental data marts by end users. However, the current model of having an enterprise data warehouse with departmental data marts (hub and spoke) used for BI is being enhanced with additional computing power. Now, IT professionals can pull huge amounts of raw data dynamically from a diverse range of data sources (e.g., structured, semi-structured, and unstructured data sources) and often in huge volumes. After processing these expanded forms of data on a unified big data platform, this on-demand information needs to be published to customers for real-time analytics and visualization. This is a new and exciting area of the data industry landscape and is commonly referred to as big data analytics. Some of the biggest potential areas of application so far have been in the financial services industry, the public sector, in health care, and in retail (Figure 11.1).

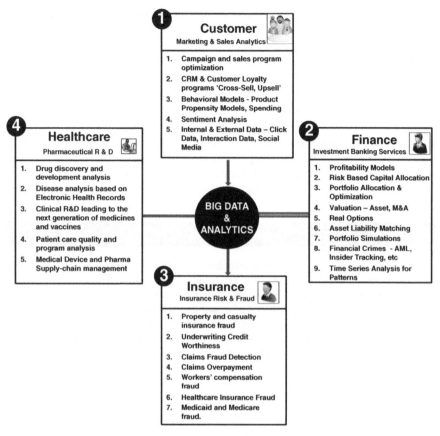

Figure 11.1 Real-life applications of big data and analytics

The strategic goal of big data analytics in a typical business organization is to harness the power of a huge amount of data to drive better business insights and predictions. Business leaders and analytical users can factor in predictions from big data analytics systems and this can help in making faster decisions to outdo their competition. Later on in this chapter, several organizations are discussed that are already in a position to leverage the huge amount of data that they have painstakingly gathered commercially. For example, clickstream analytics is being used extensively by leading retailers (e.g., Walmart, Target) to analyze sales and pricing behavior of customers and to tailor product selections in their stores or to determine discounts. Similarly, package shipping company United Parcel Service (UPS) mines traffic and weather patterns to optimize its delivery routing and to make significant savings on fuel costs.

Technical features of a big data analytics solution include the following (Figure 11.2):

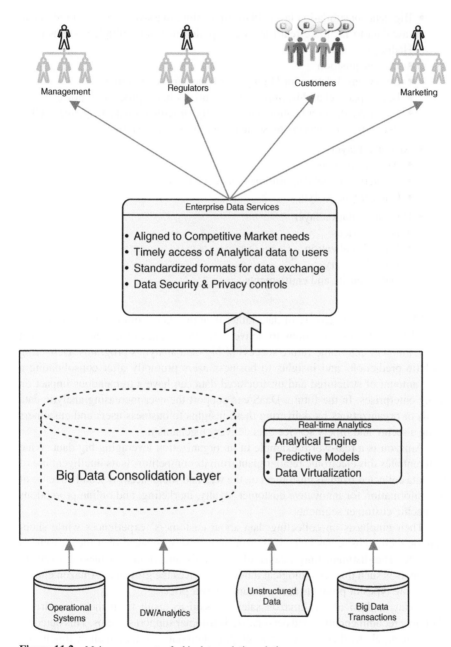

Figure 11.2   Major components of a big data analytics solution

- Big data consolidation layer: Platform to store massive amounts of redundant raw data to facilitate real-time views pulled in from multiple systems (e.g., Hadoop)
  - Data acquisition
  - Data Consolidation for High performance grid computing
  - Use of parallel architecture to exponentially boost processing power
  - Extensive data replication and specialty structured query language (SQL)-like tools for querying these huge data subsets in real time
- Analytical layer
  - Analytical engine
  - Predictive models/algorithms to detect patterns
  - Clickstream analytics
- Data presentation layer
  - Data services
  - Data virtualization
  - Data discovery
  - Data security and entitlements

The quality and velocity of data rather than the sheer volume of data is a more critical factor for organizations to deliver analytical data to their end users. Most likely, this will determine future success of big data analytics programs. Delivering analytic predictions and insights to business users promptly after consolidating a huge amount of structured and unstructured data can have a tremendous impact on many enterprises. In the future, DaaS can support the ever increasing analytic data needs of organizations by delivering these insights to business users and customers using a secure and timely service data delivery mechanism.

Amazon is a real-world example of an organization leveraging big data. What differentiates this electronic retailer giant from its competitors is its intelligent use of big data collected from its customers on the web and social networks, and its reuse of this information for innovative customer loyalty, marketing, and online promotions to specific customer segments.

Their emphasis on collecting data about customers' experiences while shopping on their website has helped Amazon stay closely engaged over the customer's lifecycle. The distinguishing feature of Amazon's underlying business delivery to customers is such that technological innovation drives the growth of Amazon.com to offer more types of products at significantly lower prices.

Today, a third of all Amazon sales are said to result from their data-driven shopping recommendation and personalized customer support systems. This outcome is driven largely by their success in leveraging their data services to allow timely and efficient access to their data. In Chapter 4, an Amazon case study was covered in greater detail.

The upcoming sections of this chapter look at different ways to use the DaaS framework and its components to support the exciting world of big data and analytics.

RELATIONSHIP BETWEEN DaaS AND BIG DATA ANALYTICS

There is a symbiotic relationship between DaaS and big data analytics. The successful deployment of any data analytics solution relies hugely on customers getting insights gleaned from big data earlier than their competitors. With the advent of big data, analytical solutions have started to include newer types of data sources—structured, semi-structured, and unstructured. This can make enterprise data services (EDS) with a shared virtual layer to access all these different data sources even more significant for data consumers. This is because the success of a big data analytics user is critically dependent on the utility of the underlying data at their disposal.

By analyzing the huge wealth of in-house databases and big data (text files, clickstream data, large volume transaction data, etc.), companies can predict data outcomes regarding the personal behavior of consumers and can offer them to clients using a subscription-based DaaS model.

While many companies have traditionally collected a wealth of data to support their primary operations, in the age of big data, some of these companies have identified secondary uses of the same data in commercial ways. Alternatively, they may choose to license this data to smaller big data analytics firms that can run innovative analyses for other innovative uses of the data on inexpensive Cloud platforms.

An example of this involves MasterCard, who collected a considerable amount of data on its credit card holders. It has recently chosen to license and sell some of this data through one of its subsidiaries. This division aggregates and analyzes billions of transactions from MasterCard credit card holders. It sells this information to marketing firms, who can predict business and consumer trends from the underlying data, and it sells these as specialized products to consumers using the DaaS model to an online firm that can earn revenues from selling highly sophisticated analyses based on licensed data. In this case, the firm used big data analytic capabilities on the wealth of purchased data to offer their customers cheap tickets over the Internet using data services and to reach out to potential customers. The firm also earned additional revenues from the data.

Social media and clickstream analysis will also play a big role in enabling big data analytics to become more and more popular. We have observed the market trends over the last few years and social platforms will embrace retail in a large way, with many advertising dollars spent over these channels, especially on consumer products. An emerging field known as sentiment analysis is becoming more relevant for helping marketing research, often as an outcome of the growth in promotions over social networking sites. For instance, eBay recently acquired an online shopping price research firm (Decide.com) for an improved price prediction capability. The new analytic tool helps their sellers price their merchandise on eBay and sell items faster.

Even traditional companies have started to use big data analytics platforms in a very innovative manner as an ancillary to their primary business operations. Take, for example, a reputable U.S. life insurance firm whose agents use inputs received from the social media platforms to identify suitable customers by screening their posts, blogs, and tweets. If the company identifies them as likely customers, their agents approach the prospective customers to ask them to consider purchasing life insurance policies and annuities appropriate to their individual profiles, including their health history, smoking status, lifestyle, etc.

Another pioneer in this area is the international shipping company United Parcel Service (UPS). Having fitted its fleets of UPS delivery vans with GPS, sensors, and wireless capabilities, it always knows the whereabouts of all its vans as they deliver freight. Consequently, in case of any route delays due to adverse road or weather conditions, it can promptly advise its drivers to change their route, thus saving the company millions of dollars in fuel costs. There is also a recent case of a European car producer leveraging inputs from past usage data and analytical capabilities to reshape its relationship with a parts supplier (Cukier, 2014).

Case Study: Airline Travel Site Leveraging DaaS

A recent example of a company that has successfully transformed portions of their business to a service-enabled subscription model is Kayak, a well-known airline travel-booking site, based in the United States. It consolidates booking information from a list of travel sites and airlines to help everyday travelers find the best prices for flights, rental cars, hotels, and cruises. The firm is able to help customers decide when the ideal time is for them to book a cheap flight or vacation. This has made the process of booking online travel far less painful for the average online consumer.

Kayak recently introduced its price-forecasting software. It includes an innovative feature to predict price trends; that is, price drops and increases over the near future. The firm is able to provide this to customers on their website as a service based on the rich collection of flight-related data at their disposal. Forecasting is based on Kayak's sophisticated algorithms that conduct detailed analyses of comparable prices for similar flights over the previous year. Unlike its competitors, Kayak's data also utilizes the billion-plus search queries from its users.

To the user, the price-predictor functions on the Kayak website appear very simple (Figure 11.3). When a user is booking a flight, they simply provide details on the flight they are interested in and click the price trend button. Kayak provides the following data to the user:

- Fare trends for the dates selected.
- A recommendation on whether you should buy now or not.
- A predictive list of when flights might be cheaper.

However, although this application appears intuitive and simple, it is quite complex to support behind the scenes. Travelers typically make over a billion requests on Kayak's websites and mobile apps for travel-related information each year. Their systems analyze these queries to forecast whether the price for a given destination and dates is likely to go up or down over the next seven days. Kayak's data scientists develop these flight-price trend forecasts using algorithms and mathematical models.

The company also monitors and measures the accuracy of their predictions to the customer on a daily basis. This monitoring is done by keeping track of a certain number

Price trend & tip details

 Price my rise within 7 days

82% Confidence: Our model has been 82% accurate on forecasting whether these fares will rise stay within $20 of the current price over the next 7 days. The forecast is based on anlaysis of historical price changes and is not a guarantee of future results.

tip explanation

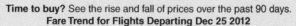

Time to buy? See the rise and fall of prices over the past 90 days.
Fare Trend for Flights Departing Dec 25 2012

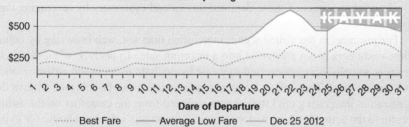

Date Price Was Found

Flexible travel dates? Find the cheapest departure date.
Fares for Other Departing Dates in Dec 2012

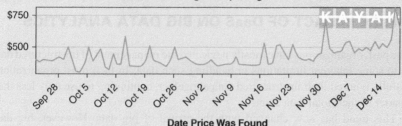

Dare of Departure

········ Best Fare ———— Average Low Fare ——— Dec 25 2012

Figure 11.3   Kayak's price trend predictor

of flights throughout the next seven days (or between the search and departure date, whichever is shortest) and the predictions they originally issued to the customer. Kayak then sends information to the customer verifying whether they turned out to be right or wrong. However, the company website warns customers in advance: "Predictions based on past history can never be perfect, so we can't guarantee they'll be correct, which is why we also let you know the confidence of the statistical analysis."

To summarize, Kayak has been able to support this complex and innovative solution by successfully building three major strengths:

- Utilizing the rich collection of big data at Kayak's disposal.
- Sophisticated analytics backed up by predictive algorithms designed by their data scientists.

- The innovative use of data services to reach out to online customers with attractive vacation offers and cheap airfares over the Internet.

In 2013, Kayak was acquired by Priceline for a record US$1.8 billion. Analysts concluded that Kayak was able to claim such a hefty premium from Priceline for one simple reason. It allowed Priceline to earn additional revenues from its innovative use of big data analytics and data services to reach the right selection of customers online.

FUTURE IMPACT OF DaaS ON BIG DATA ANALYTICS

In the past, organizations have mostly neglected the management of unstructured data due to some inherent limitations in handling such data. In fact, most organizations blissfully ignored their unstructured data altogether, continuing to use only less than a quarter of their total data assets.

This trend has now changed with the arrival of big data. However, big data platforms need to tie raw, unstructured data successfully to the structured (relational) data stored in legacy systems and data warehouses to provide a comprehensive picture to users. Only after this data synthesis can they derive competitive intelligence and provide prompt access of these data insights to end customers by leveraging data services.

For instance, in the airline sector, more often than not, web browsing by online airline customers is not converted into a ticketing sale. To analyze when the click-stream is actually being converted to a sale by analytic users in the airline is often what matters most. This critical business requirement cannot be achieved without the organization integrating clickstream data gathered from the customer on the airline website to the actual booking history stored in the airline's datawarehouse (or to the bookings completed in the airline reservation system). Only after these two streams of data are combined will the airline's marketing and analytic teams be able to predict the airline customers' behavior in a meaningful way.

To capture quantifiable information for relevant data analysis, end users need to be clear on what they want to analyze, and whether they have the right kinds of processes and tools to conduct the analysis. Many of the bottlenecks for big data success can be eliminated by adopting best practices in enterprise information management (EIM) and data governance (DG). For example, the ability to load data onto big data and analytical platforms using canonical models, move data across the ecosystem using standardized data services, incorporate business rules, and apply algorithms to validate that usability and latency of the published data meet with the end user service level agreement (SLA) requirement.

This view is supported by a recent study conducted on 129 companies by the MIT Center for Digital Business. The study concluded that companies that "adopt data driven practices, and use big data to guide decision making" would have output and productivity levels that were 5 to 6 percent higher than their counterparts who had not invested in these technologies (Brynjolfsson, 2011).

In addition to this, for the success of big data programs in the eyes of business users, it is critical to have timely and effective means through which to gain access to insights from big data, social networking, and web interactions. The leadership in many trendsetter companies (across multiple industry sectors) is hoping to improve its respective company's analytic capabilities by not only expecting to filter information insights from its raw, unstructured data successfully, but also to make results easy to access by users via enterprise data services (Zikopoulos, 2013).

Organizations supporting big data will most likely have to continue with similar advances to address ways to exchange unstructured data using specialized data services with related architectural solutions. For a holistic approach to data management, organizations need to use a semantic model that can be used to govern both structured and unstructured data activities. Under this approach, semantic information for both structured and unstructured data is managed by a single team. Models are developed, deployed, and monitored over time—just as they are during database design. Content tags and indexes can be defined by these models and can be used to create a semantic-based layer on top of existing technologies. In addition to this, ontologies (the hierarchy of concepts within an information domain) can be used to reference these systems to one another by defining conditions under which different metadata relationships are valid. End consumers of information are then assured that they have received a comprehensive representation of all relevant information, and that they are not blindsided by missing key topics, dependent activities, or influential events.

DaaS can be utilized as an effective data distribution mechanism in which data files (including unstructured files, text, images, and videos) are made available to customers as and when requested by them over a network of their choice—mobile devices, the Internet, or the Cloud.

Use of data services can also help address data quality issues in the big data environment in a significant manner. Often, the world of big data is a messy one of large-scale data ingestion, load-balancing, clustering, and massively parallel processing. Consequently, datasets are often loaded "as is" in big data applications without proper understanding of the critical data elements and their underlying relationships. This can result in poor data quality, which can affect the capability of business analytical tools used to provide insights from big data.

Executing this goal of providing analytical insights from different forms of data can be a challenge to most big data implementations without deciding on a well thought out reference architecture. The solution requires developing state-of-the-art capabilities around the following technology components: data discovery, predictive models/algorithms, quality data, infrastructure, big data integration platforms, and data distribution with data services.

EXTENDING DaaS REFERENCE ARCHITECTURE FOR BIG DATA AND CLOUD SERVICES

The primary goal of big data analytics is to provide analytical insights and business intelligence from a wide range of data—streaming in from structured, unstructured

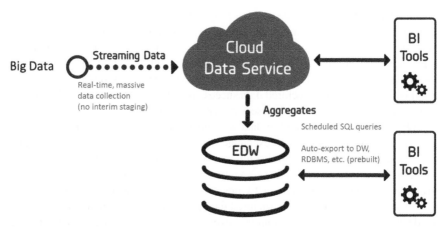

Figure 11.4   Integrating big data and Cloud services with enterprise data warehouse (*Diagram courtesy of Treasure Data*)

and semi-structured data formats. This process can also involve large volumes of big transaction data, e.g., transaction details of a bank or credit card with customers or sensor data collected from automobiles or oil rigs that arrive in a fast pace.

Handling these large volumes of streaming data collected from field sensors, e.g., can involve a lot of internal housekeeping such as ranging database administration, server maintenance, and underlying infrastructure. Oil drilling companies, auto manufacturers, or credit card issuing banks may find these disruptive to their core operations.

Engaging a managed service from a Cloud-based data provider can enable an enterprise to focus on their business, not the complicated problem of integration between data (or events) collection, aggregation, and management. The data provider typically provides end-to-end data-related capabilities, underlying infrastructure, and support for a flat monthly or yearly subscription rate.

Therefore, the Daas provider can supply these companies with their requested data in near real time over the web or via mobile apps. Users in these customer organizations can then analyze requested data in a matter of minutes (Figure 11.4).

Many industry observers are now realizing that the impact of big data operations can be enhanced substantially by aligning them with their internal enterprise data warehouses. This alignment can be instrumental in supporting business intelligence needs of users across the organization in an in-depth manner. This is because combining big data analytics services with other EIM components (reference models and metadata) can empower the customer with information that lends more meaning, in comparison to results filtered originally after analyzing big data. Having additional context (or metadata) on underlying data can also help clear up any doubts from senior business leaders, as they can make major decisions in a matter of seconds.

Companies pursuing big data initiatives should make additional efforts to align their big data platforms (often on Hadoop) with data repositories already existing in their organization. By aligning these systems, organizations can realize immediate benefits with greater sharing of enterprise data; linking data from various sources, e.g, consolidating master data in a hub and then providing results to users in the form of composite views; and publishing data to the right subscribers by using the DaaS framework.

Given the volume, velocity, and variety of data involved in a typical big data environment, it can be a challenge to support analytics needs of big data implementations without enhancing a few specialized components for advanced data analytics patterns to the DaaS reference architecture. Moreover, the complexity of this sophisticated data analysis capability is likely to increase further in the future with the ongoing convergence of structured and unstructured data sourced from CAMS data feeds across many industries. Let us look at an example to illustrate this convergence.

Consider a leading airline is using a big data platform (on Hadoop) to improve its call center performance. It can use Hadoop—a platform that stores, processes, and analyzes large volumes of unstructured data—to route customer calls more efficiently to the customer service center. However, if the company is more ambitious, then it can use big data analytics more productively, namely to boost customer service by analyzing their traffic on social media sites. If there is a customer who is facing some airline-related problems or even posting adverse remarks on social media about current flight delays he or she is facing, the airline company can identify its clients, by matching their social media profile against client and address information in the MDM system. Then they can reach out to the impacted customers using data services and proactively address their flight-related problems in real time. This example illustrates how DaaS can easily extend state-of-the-art capabilities around several specialized technology components to support on-demand services for organizations using big data analytics solutions in a real-time CAMS-oriented environment.

Data analytics services in DaaS reference architecture encompasses sophisticated data mining, statistical tools, neural networks, etc., to process huge volumes of big data. It also leverages several inbuilt data mining capabilities such as pattern matching, data association, data clustering, and data anomaly detection. Data analytics services can then combine these results with traditional DaaS service components to publish integrated results to the customer.

In some situations, the data analytics layer also needs to encompass the use of sophisticated data visualization to support business users involved in sophisticated data analysis. While most traditional users are likely to use DaaS services to support their query and analysis capabilities, some users responsible for predictive BI and real-time decision making are likely to benefit with data visualization capabilities.

Data visualization can help them filter through massive sets of consumer data with the help of dashboards, interactive bar/pie charts, and line or scatter charts. These visualization services also have to be combined with data federation capabilities and use of in-memory data to provide real-time or near real-time analysis and reporting services.

Including the data analytics layer within the overall DaaS reference architecture was discussed in Chapter 2. However, some of the specialized analytics components are not needed by every DaaS user as they may need advanced skills in statistics, data mining, etc. For example, specialized data mining or statistics-algorithms are

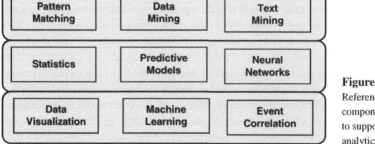

Figure 11.5
Reference architecture components required to support big data analytics

necessary to support only a smaller segment of power users interested in analyzing big data. Consequently, these specialized functions have not been included within the overall DaaS reference architecture. Some of the specialized functions that are essential for supporting a big data analytics environment are shown in Figure 11.5.

Case Study: Singapore Health Agency Leveraging DaaS

The Environmental Agency of the Singapore government has become a trendsetter by choosing to capitalize on their vast internal health and sanitation data, gathering resources from local communities to benefit their citizens with timely real-time alerts to stay away from dengue outbreaks. They provide innovative data services that use sophisticated data mining and statistical algorithms to predict dengue outbreaks across clusters of the island nation and alert subscribers through their mobile devices based on these projections.

This initiative has prevented further outbreaks of dengue in Singapore since early 2014. Consumers in Singapore who subscribe to the publicly offered application can get live alerts on their mobile device if they are close to a dengue-ridden locality. This innovative mobile application is presented to the user graphically with an effective data visualization tool. Figure 11.6 illustrates some cluster locations on respective maps.

As per the agency's definition, each dengue cluster map illustrates the extent of NEA's current vector control intervention. Put simply, you can look at a dengue cluster as a locality with active transmission of the disease where intervention is targeted operationally. It is formed when two or more cases have onset within 14 days and are located within 150 meters of each other (based on residential and workplace addresses as well as movement history). The clusters are categorized according to their current status.

The mobile DaaS application warns citizens of active dengue clusters in various Singapore localities with real-time updates. A list of preventive actions also accompanies each alert level. There are three alert levels.

Definition	Alert Level
High-risk area with 10 or more cases	**Red**
High-risk area with less than 10 cases	**Yellow**
No new cases, under surveillance for the next 21 days	**Green**

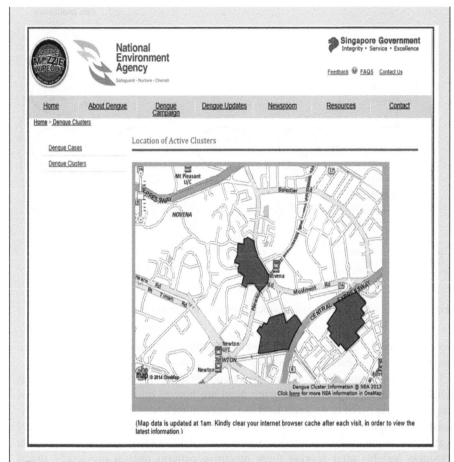

Figure 11.6   Real-time mobile DaaS application with data visualization

The user can zoom in on active dengue clusters by clicking on the highlighted dots on the map, revealing the exact location of a cluster and number of dengue cases contained within the cluster. Alternatively, they can search for dengue clusters by typing into the search bar provided to them.

Real-Time Analytical Services for Big Data with Stream Computing

As discussed, the foundation to a big data platform is its data processing engine termed Hadoop. The Hadoop engine can handle extremely high volumes of data in batch mode, irrespective of the structure that the data is ingested. The data is stored in

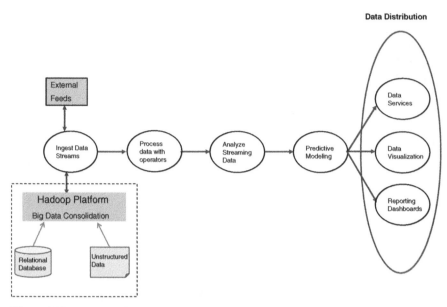

Figure 11.7 Lifecycle of real-time analytical processing of big data using stream computing

its distributed file system (called a Hadoop distributed file system). HDFS can store anything from completely unstructured to fully relational data.

However, in spite of many strengths seen in Hadoop systems, one of the biggest challenges facing organizations using them are how to quickly derive value from any significant event or data received and stored in their multiple clusters. Typically, analytical engines running off the big data platforms will not only need traditional capability to run analytical queries from historic data, but they also need to provide business insights after scoring these repetitive patterns against previously stored predictive models.

Stream computing enables high-throughput and analysis in real time because of its architecture that lets data flow in parallel instances (nodes) instead of following a sequential (standard assembly line) approach used for analysis by batch computing. This can enable businesses to provide intelligence to decision makers in real time, who can then perform their actions also in real time (Figure 11.7).

A stream receives a continuous sequence of data elements from a data source. After data is ingested, the stream computing system uses operators that process data from the stream. Based on pre-defined rules, the operator processes the data and can send it to an output stream or feed it to a split operator.

Streams do not process data sequentially, i.e., one set (called tuples) at a time. It analyzes large sets of datasets in real-time to gain insight across multiple streams. These packages of data can also get aggregated across different streams or join with relational databases.

Just to put things into perspective, let us look an example from the financial services sector. FICO scores can be a good example of how predictive analytics and data mining are applied on data gathered from endless sources to compute accurate credit scores that can be obtained promptly by bank lenders via a data service.

Banks, mortgage lenders, and credit card companies use credit (or FICO) scores to evaluate the potential risk of lending money to a potential consumer. Credit scores are determined after taking into account numerous factors of an individual's financial history that can determine the risk of him or her defaulting on future payments. Some of these factors could include:

- Length of credit history
- Payment history (included details on past bankruptcies, late payments, fore-closures, etc.)
- Debt burden
- Recent credit inquiries

To provide real time access and delivery of big data results (like the FICO score for checking creditworthiness), all information updates need to be packaged as an XML message and sent to various big data analytics service users or automated agents. For complex query result datasets, the solution can include new technology capabilities such as data virtualization tools. As summarized earlier with the DaaS approach, data does not require being copied and moved from pre-existing sources under this solution. Instead, a virtual or logical data view is created in real time under this approach after abstracting all the necessary data from underlying legacy data sources currently supporting daily operations.

Data virtualization technology can also improve the speed of the customer's accessibility in viewing big data by abstracting disparate data sources (databases, applications, unstructured and semi-structured data, files, websites, etc.) into a single, logical data access layer. The abstracted layer provided by the virtualization platform will provide big data clients attempting to target a single data access layer with a unified format or structure rather than making clients go through multiple tools or different platforms (Figure 11.8).

From a technology perspective, data virtualization enhanced with high-computing parallel platforms can handle high data throughputs to provide an inte-grated development environment (IDE). Streaming technology and virtualization can help development teams to define and implement appropriate virtual views to these integrated platforms. They need to merge the high performance strengths of big data with the data integrity and standards enforced on the traditional BI platform.

Several companies are going even further by leveraging private or public Cloud computing to extend integration a step further. A DaaS solution for big data requires a data provider to provide customer organizations with a platform that enables them with virtualized access to large amounts of unstructured and semi-structured data (hosted on the Cloud platform). There are several innovative cloud-based DaaS vendors who have successfully adopted this model (refer to the case study in this chapter on big DaaS in the automotive industry).

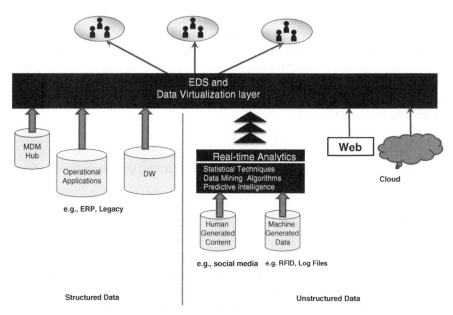

Figure 11.8 Use of data virtualization in big data analytics environment

This is an evolving field and there is no dearth of possibilities to having more advanced capabilities in the future when building analytical services used to support big data.

FOSTERING AN ENTERPRISE DATA MINDSET

Big data and analytics have created much publicity in the last few years because of their immense promise. This is, unfortunately, an outcome of a lofty vision sold to business leaders that could make big data a victim of Silicon Valley's notorious hype cycle. In short, the vision sold to them broadly tells them to consolidate all the available information within the enterprise, regardless of the data model or source, and then to mine it for analytical insights. Leaders are assured that by spotting emerging trends and opportunities, and anticipating crises based on their ability to access data from a range of data sources—unstructured as well as structured data—companies can outbid any competition. As mentioned, the promise of big data analytics is immense, but it still sounds too good to be true.

It is true that big data technologies (e.g., Hadoop) provides massive computing power at lower costs. It provides high performance, high availability grid systems with multiple nodes to consolidate data sourced from a large range of data sources. The Hadoop file storage can also store data in both structured and unstructured data formats, including various files, sharepoint folders, the Cloud, email attachments, spreadsheets, social media, or downloads across the enterprise. However, companies that are successful in this area need to integrate these new technologies with existing technology assets such as data warehouses, databases, or mainframe based legacy systems. However, this integration with the legacy data stores and externally hosted platforms (e.g., Cloud) does not come without a cost or risk. Organizations have to be prepared to confront inconsistent data structures, mismatched procedures, data quality, and integration challenges that must be brought into alignment before a big data analytics platform can be successfully deployed. It also requires dedicated data scientists (and enterprise data administrators) to develop, deploy, and manage sophisticated algorithms to impact the breadth and depth of managerial decision-making processes.

That said, organizations that allow users to leverage both their structured and unstructured data together in a real-time, managed environment with DaaS can gain a great competitive advantage by communicating hidden opportunities in real time to help business leaders address their data-driven needs. In most big data analytic environments, new forms of data are stored separately in a large storage environment with a dedicated platform (e.g., Hadoop) while the analytics and reporting are done using an analytical engine on top of the new storage. However, as the organization matures, it should ensure that the new big data platform becomes integrated with the current data warehouse environment (Sathi, 2013).

In a typical organization using big data, it is commonplace to see large volumes of data sourced from many data formats and files. Before diving into how businesses can better harness big data, enterprise data architects need to consider all the different types of data and how these data can benefit the company. Organizations with a higher maturity level in EIM should allow users to leverage both their structured and unstructured data together in a cohesive manner. Without tying the information gathered from new data sources to the older systems, there could be a concern regarding credibility of results due to the lack of data integrity, standards, and consistency. An example of this lack of data integrity is seen across big data analytics programs that do not validate quality of the incoming customer records against a list of allowable data values stored in a master data management (MDM) hub or reference table prior to data load. As discussed in Chapter 8, this gap can be addressed effectively by using master data services to validate incoming customer files with the MDM record system storing unique customer identifier records.

There are several other areas where big data analytic systems can benefit by applying EIM principles to focus on measures that improve the underlying integrity of data. Big data programs need to include data standards and related IT architecture components as part of their daily governance mechanism to improve their day-to-day processing of data. Some of these EIM components include having a canonical model along with a shared business vocabulary and taxonomy for usage of consistent definitions for reference data at the enterprise level. All of these components should be kept up to date and should be supported by leadership through active DG processes.

The use of a metadata repository to store the shared business glossary and taxonomy to ensure that there are consistent definitions of major data terms should also be a key priority. The metadata repository can be used to classify, manage, and organize sensitive data elements at the enterprise level. To enforce security policies in the big data environment, organizations can also invoke data services utilizing the business glossary to tag sensitive data or issue alerts to the big data security team.

Unfortunately, the majority of IT organizations have been slow to react to demands of unstructured data, text mining, and searching. In most cases, however, they have made huge efforts to respond to demands from stakeholders, provide insights, and analytical findings from their big data platforms without providing the end user with the capability to access data flexibly. Some of this inability has been due to a lack of sophisticated technology. Adopting the DaaS service delivery model can, however, be a great bridge for IT organizations to make their big data platforms more accessible, user friendly, and valuable in the eyes of their business leadership.

Addressing Big Data Privacy Concerns

Data privacy is a big concern in any big data implementation. This is because, unlike other areas in IT, big data implementations typically deal with a variety of data types: structured data, unstructured text files, social media, radio-frequency identification (RFID), or sensor-generated data. This diverse range of stored data makes enforcing standards particularly challenging for organizations implementing big data to protect the privacy of their customers. Social media firms in particular can collect rich datasets from their loyal user base to make predictions on consumer behavior. However, without an adequate review of privacy measures, the risk can outweigh the benefits of applying big data without adequate safeguards.

At minimum, an organization dealing with big data needs to have a comprehensive information security (IS) framework with up-to-date IS policies. They also need experienced security administrators in the organization to monitor effectiveness of all their security measures as well as to perform periodic checks to track some of the privileged users (e.g., database administrators, help desk personnel, and call center agents) who have access to sensitive data (Soares, 2013).

Using a metadata repository to support big data needs by utilizing a business glossary to tag sensitive data and their definitions can also be very helpful in preventing confidential data from falling into the wrong hands (Figure 11.9). Tagging sensitive elements that should not be published by the DaaS can also prove a very useful privacy monitoring and alert notification mechanism. The metadata repository can be used to classify, manage, and organize the security threshold of different stored data elements. Depending on the type of data (structured, unstructured text files, social media, RFID, or sensor-generated data), there can be security and privacy rules laid out for each business category. The sensitivity threshold for each type of data will be driven by the security team. Data services can be used to issue security alerts when a breach takes place; that is, whenever any data elements tagged as sensitive or whenever confidential data within the glossary become accessible to unauthorized users.

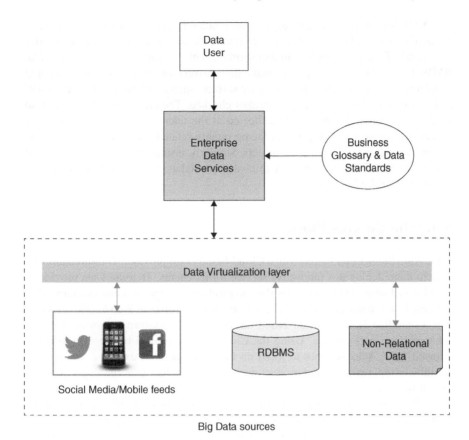

Figure 11.9 Leveraging the metadata repository for ensuring big data privacy

CASE STUDY: BIG DaaS IN THE AUTOMOTIVE INDUSTRY

As this case study illustrates, DaaS can play a major role in the field of big data and telematics—the technology used in vehicles which can track the performance of a car and its key such as monitoring engine speed, battery condition, or check fuel consumption—by storing and analyzing field sensor data collected from cars.

In 2013, a leading car audio and car navigation products manufacturer (for confidentiality reasons requested by this manufacturer, let us call them XYZ Auto Services) started its mobile telematics center, a cloud infrastructure for premier automobile manufacturers, to provide cloud-based navigation services, as well as advanced traffic updates to their drivers. The system did this by analyzing an enormous amount of data collected through car electronics and smart phones in real time. This often involved analyzing a diverse range of data including sensor data, logs, and other big data collected at the telematics center.

XYZ Auto Services essentially provides data services to its subscribers to make car driving safe and comfortable. For example, the real-time data service they offer to several of their automobile manufacturer clients (usually premium brands like BMW, Lexus, Mercedes, etc.) can make their drivers aware of potential car-related problems or failures, before they actually surface, such as while driving your BMW and being alerted to soon get your brakes checked. The car manufacturer can also leverage the vast amount of data collected at the telematics command center for modifying automotive components facing quality-related changes as well as issue prompter product recalls to the car owners. Similarly, insurers (like Progressive) could potentially use this auto data to help customers reduce their insurance premiums, based on their driving behavior.

How the Service Works

XYZ Auto Services partnered with a Cloud-based DaaS provider, Treasuredata.com, to help them deploy this innovative service for its clients. Treasure Data provides a cloud-based solution that includes data acquisition, storage, and analysis capability delivered as a managed service. The service utilizes Amazon Web Services (AWS) and a modified Hadoop stack, based on Treasure Data's own columnar database for maximum performance. Using the Cloud service offered by the data provider allowed XYZ Auto Services to focus on their core areas of expertise -automobile manufacturing, research, and product development—rather than running a complex IT infrastructure.

XYZ Auto Services have established a comprehensive mobile data command center for supporting telematics services. The center acts as a focal point for supplying actionable messages to DaaS subscribers, based on data from sensors placed in automobiles to its customers (e.g., automobile manufacturers, rental companies, and automobile insurance).

Data is collected from sensors provided in the car by the auto manufacturer. The collected data is then aggregated and analyzed by XYZ Auto Services in the data collection module within the mobile telematics center (Figure 11.10). Analytical results are then used to monitor the performance of individual vehicles (or auto components) or vehicles of a particular brand (BMW, Mercedes, Lexus, etc.). This data is also made available as a paid-subscription service by XYZ Auto Services to other related businesses such as car manufacturers, dealers, automobile repair shops, and rental car companies.

There are several other potential revenue-generating opportunities that the DaaS customers can exploit from the collected car sensor data. For example, the data provider can offer customers a mobile app with data services to alert them in case a hazardous event is likely to occur. For example, the driver can receive a notification on the road that their car has a limited amount of petrol in the tank left, or that they are using too much acceleration on a mountainous terrain.

The command center can also issue automated data analytic-driven corrective steps to drivers using real-time messages. For example, "when this error condition occurs, take this action." However, to design the workflow for automated action for

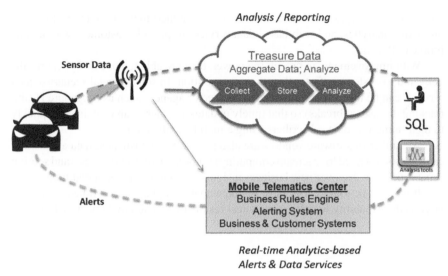

Figure 11.10   Data collection from automobile sensors to support big DaaS*(Diagram courtesy of Treasure Data)*

the driver to dynamically make corrections is tricky, especially diagnosing the correct error conditions is vital before suggesting a corrective plan to drivers. Manufacturers will need to define their own set of business algorithms and automation rules to address specific error-conditions. These rules are also likely to get refined over time through an ongoing, iterative process as more incidents from the field sensors get reported to the mobile telematics center.

The mobile telematics center can also track a driver's skills and driving behavior from sensor data collected over a period of time. Insurance organizations can then purchase this data from the vendor regularly as a service to fine-tune their underwriting and customize insurance rates. Using the data collected on the driver's behavior, the insurance firm can do the following:

- Determine the risk-profile of insurance applicants.
- Classify applicants as safe, inexperienced, or unsafe drivers.
- Price the insurance premiums of customers based on classification.

Overall, the various data services provided by the mobile telematics center (and the underlying big data analysis platform) has been a powerful differentiator for this car navigation products manufacturer. It has also presented them with several opportunities for monetizing their data by providing it to multiple industries.

SUMMARY

By innovatively employing data analytics technology, many pioneering organizations have already enhanced their data delivery models to become bigger, better, and faster. This chapter provided examples of a few companies such as Treasure Data, Amazon,

Experian, and Kayak who have innovatively combined their strengths in big data, predictive analytics, and web-based data services to provide customers with unique product offerings.

With improvements in processing power, they are able to have analytical results delivered to customers faster than their competition. In some special scenarios, data services can be hosted centrally by a public sector agency (such as Singapore Health tracking disease outbreaks) so that timely updates and alerts can be delivered quickly to their numerous data subscribers using a mobile application.

A number of software vendors are also providing sophisticated data acquisition capabilities (referred to as stream computing) for predictive data synthesis and scoring capabilities—to discover new business insights and opportunities in real time.

It will not be long before most big data analytics platforms will be expected to possess the capability to deliver analytical results to decision makers in real time.

Part Four

Ensuring Organizational Success

Chapter 12

DaaS Governance Framework

TOPICS COVERED IN THIS CHAPTER

- This chapter provides details on how an organization can establish a governance program for DaaS.
- It suggests various governance policies and controls for tracking and monitoring overall user experience while using a reusable data service:
- An overview of data governance and stewardship roles within the organization are then provided.
- Also discussed is the emerging role of the chief data officer (CDO) across organizations to align data initiatives with an organization's business strategy.

"We are what we repeatedly do. Excellence, therefore, is not an act, but a habit."

—Aristotle

Internet Technology (IT) is probably the most challenging program for any organization and its leadership to control over time, as it is affected by changes in the business environment. Governance is often heavily influenced by an organization's underlying culture. For many organizations, this involves successfully relinquishing local control of enterprise data by individual departments for the "greater good."

Any governance effort by an organization is associated with the exercise of authority, control, and shared decision making over the management of its data assets. However, governance is often the most challenging aspect of a Data as a Service (DaaS) program in any large organization due to the high degree of coordination required to gain consensus among the multiple stakeholders on major governance issues. This chapter discusses in detail how a data provider can establish a formal governance program that can be sustained over the lifecycle of a DaaS program.

Data as a Service: A Framework for Providing Reusable Enterprise Data Services,
First Edition. Pushpak Sarkar.
© 2015 the IEEE Computer Society. Published 2015 by John Wiley & Sons, Inc.

ROLE OF DATA GOVERNANCE

For a data provider to really succeed against competitors in the long run, it needs to offer service that is par excellence and create customers with complete confidence in its end-to-end capabilities as a service provider. The provider can realize this objective if it can consistently deliver the highest levels of service delivery while ensuring that its published data content is fit for business use. Only by gaining wider acceptance across organizations can it expect to develop and grow in the competitive marketplace

The significance of data governance in the DaaS context can be better understood with an analogy. Let us compare a data service to a utility service in another sector. As an example, perhaps there is a media entertainment company in which the service provider can be assured of customer loyalty, only if they provide entertainment that is rated higher by viewer households against their competitors. In addition to this, the media company also needs to meet all the local and national standards for communication (e.g., FCC, censorship board) to comply as a service provider. Information integrity plays a similar role for many IT providers who provide DaaS. (The term information integrity refers to end-to-end data quality within an organization.) In the context of enterprise information management, information integrity and quality refers to all the processes, procedures, and tools that ensure information is delivered via the EDS environment. Just as we know that good programming (or content) is a must-have for media providers, so too is the case with data provided by a DaaS organization to consumers. The information fed to DAAS subscribers has to be consistent, timely, and accurate. It also has to meet all the SLA specified by business stakeholder with regards to quality and fitness for use. A key component of information integrity is information quality, which is discussed in Chapter.

To successfully publish a set of data services, organizations need to view underlying data as a valuable asset that are owned by various parts of the business. Anyone launching a DaaS program has to be aware that data governance of these reusable assets are a critical success factor (if not the single most important factor) to the growth and sustainability of data services across the organization in the long run. At some point, there has to be a realization that some individual (or team) in the organization must take official responsibility as the owner of this corporate data asset. This is a core reason for data governance to be formally introduced in the organization with full support among senior executives.

In most IT organizations, pressures to meet business deadlines on key IT program initiatives (e.g., ERP and CRM) typically lead business executives to focus on immediate priorities and tactical business objectives. Consequently, many IT organizations have no budget for strategic quality initiatives and ignore the risks of implementing various data controls put in place by the centralized teams responsible for data administration. Fortunately, after decades of apathy and negligence with data issues, there has been a growing realization in most companies to address data governance and related data quality issues. Companies are realizing they are more vulnerable to risk providing bad data to consumers, especially in the context of recent trends where organizations are often required to provide access to more data to the consumer. The introduction of stringent government regulations has also made people aware of the need to have proper data controls.

Data privacy issues (or a lack thereof) can also cost organizations greatly as governments worldwide are penalizing consumer banks and health insurers heavily for breach of any confidentiality. These are a few reasons that have made IT leadership place governance as a higher priority, particularly when jointly introducing data governance and data ownership programs. The focus on data governance has to be on implementing a framework for setting up effective policies and controls to limit the adverse impact of poor data quality controls. Governance of EDS is a vital component of the overall data governance strategy.

DaaS governance primarily aims to formulate policies that leverage, optimize, and secure data services as an enterprise asset. In my view, for any data provider to be successful, it is critical that the content of published data services is of good quality. The major content (or product) offered by a data provider is their data assets. Consequently, the organization has to ensure the quality of published data that are intended for public consumption. This quality can only be maintained by actively governing underlying quality processes as well as data sources generating the data. Various policies and controls to track and monitor overall user experience while using a reusable enterprise data service (EDS) are discussed later on in this chapter.

However, this often makes governance one of the most challenging aspects of a DaaS program. There are multiple, subjective factors involved, and consequently, heavy coordination is required among different IT teams to successfully effect changes recommended by the business during the lifecycle of a DaaS program.

Therefore, most large organizations should set up a centralized DaaS governance team to look after different aspects of information access, distribution, and delivery. The following best practices ensure that an organization has addressed DaaS governance:

- Obtain executive sponsorship for the DaaS program.
- Identify the key stakeholders and data stewards for various divisions and subject areas in the organization.
- Improve reliability and trustworthiness of the published data services.
- Standardize core data assets across the organization to reduce maintenance and operational efforts.
- Align the interests of business/IT stakeholders with DaaS objectives, the mission, and goals.
- Define a common vocabulary for all key business terms and the hierarchy among them.
- Protect sensitive data from unauthorized access.

From a high-level perspective, the IT governance of a DaaS program can be decomposed into four major areas of coverage (Figure 12.1). These include data governance, people governance, process governance, and technology governance. The following sections discuss each of these areas in greater detail.

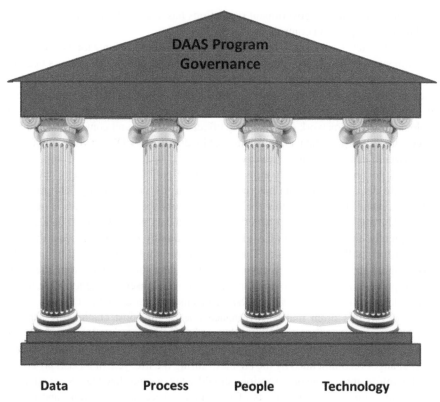

Data   **Process**   **People**   **Technology**

Figure 12.1   Critical pillars for IT governance to support a DaaS program

DATA GOVERNANCE

Data governance is defined as, "the exercise of authority, control, and shared decision making by an organization over the management of its data assets" (DAMA, 2009). For a data provider to succeed against its competitors, it needs to offer services that inspire customers with complete confidence in its capabilities. This objective can be realized by the organization if it can consistently publish data content that is relevant for business use. Only by gaining wider acceptance among subscribers can a data provider expect to develop and grow in the competitive marketplace.

Having a formal data governance program clearly demarcates the roles and responsibilities among various stakeholders. It also facilitates collaboration among data stewards. In addition, having a data governance steering committee that meets at regular intervals can provide a suitable forum through which to drive greater collaboration among data stewards, business, and IT leaders. They can also collectively discuss and resolve data quality-related issues faced by the organization at these meetings (Figure 12.2).

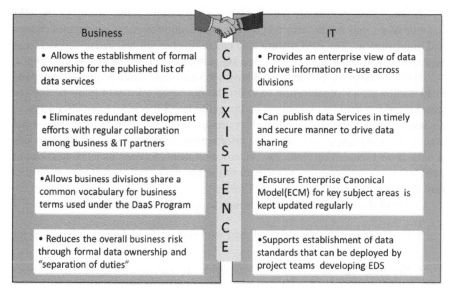

Business	COEXISTENCE	IT
• Allows the establishment of formal ownership for the published list of data services		• Provides an enterprise view of data to drive information re-use across divisions
• Eliminates redundant development efforts with regular collaboration among business & IT partners		•Can publish data Services in timely and secure manner to drive data sharing
•Allows business divisions share a common vocabulary for business terms used under the DaaS Program		•Ensures Enterprise Canonical Model(ECM) for key subject areas is kept updated regularly
• Reduces the overall business risk through formal data ownership and "separation of duties"		•Supports establishment of data standards that can be deployed by project teams developing EDS

Figure 12.2   Why do we need governance?

In the context of enterprise information management (EIM), data quality refers to all of the processes, procedures, and tools that ensure information delivered via the EDS environment is of a high quality. Just as we know that good programming (or content) is a must-have for media providers, this is also the case for data provided by a DaaS organization to its consumers. The information feed has to be consistent, timely, and accurate. It also has to meet all the SLAs specified by business stakeholders in regard to quality and fitness for use.

For any DaaS service provider, the quality of published data is the primary strategic asset that distinguishes them in the eyes of their service consumers. Therefore, it should be viewed as a key differentiator that must be exploited to drive market share by the data provider.

EIM As an Enabler for Data Governance

The key to successful adoption of DAAS is management buy-in and support for measures that clearly require relinquishing local control of shared data. Often, this is easier said than done, and thus formal data governance processes are usually required to effectively manage enterprise data through all phases of its project lifecycle.

It is recommended that most large organizations implementing DAAS set up a centralized EIM team to look after different aspects of data design, distribution, and delivery. As part of EIM, formal policies need to be established mandating all divisions to reuse data from EDS and not from individual data sources. However, having this completely accepted by project teams can be difficult, unless there is clear authority invested in the EIM governance team.

Another issue commonly found in large organizations is that setting up the EIM function alone may not be sufficient for the organization to effect meaningful change and improvement. The EIM mantra also has to receive full and active support from business stakeholders in addressing data standardization and data quality challenges.

While some of the previous areas may not necessitate a full-fledged EIM department within the IT organization to assist the business, a focused point person (or team) should at least be maintained on the entire DaaS lifecycle. Even after services are implemented in an organization, there are several business events that can compel management to change their enterprise information architecture and existing services at very short notice. Therefore, the organization needs to keep its EIM practices in a proactive state, responding to changes in the business environment very swiftly to stay ahead of its competitors (Figure 12.3).

Some of the major benefits EIM brings to a DAAS implementation include:

- Provides an enterprise view of data with standardized data models and metadata.
- Supports data integration across multiple applications, often on different platforms.
- Transforms abstract data structures into useful blocks for reuse to reduce data replication
- Enables the management and enterprise-wide governance of data.
- Consolidates data assets into a common data asset inventory.
- Facilitates sustainable cost-effective management of all types of data assets.

	EIM Component	Definition of Component
1	Analytics	BI procedures and techniques for exploration and analysis of data to discover and identify new and meaningful information and trends.
2	Data Governance	The exercise of authority, control, and shared decision making (planning, monitoring, and enforcement) over the management of data assets.
3	Data Modeling	A representation of the data describing real-world objects and the relationships between the objects, independent of any associated process. A data model includes the set of diagrams for each view along with the metadata defining each object in the model.
4	Data Quality	The degree to which data is accurate, complete, timely, and consistent with all requirements and business rules, as well as relevant for a given use.
5	Enterprise Data Architecture	Part of the complete enterprise architecture, including (1) an enterprise data model, and (2) the IVC analysis that identifies linkages and alignment of the data model with enterprise views of business functions and processes, organizations, applications, and enterprise goals.
6	Master Data Management	Processes that ensure reference data are kept up to date and coordinated across an enterprise. The organization, management, and distribution of corporate adjudicated data with widespread use in the organization.
7	Metadata	Literally, "data about data," metadata defines and describes the characteristics of other data, used to improve both business and technical understanding of data and related processes.
8	Reference Data	Any data used to categorize other data, or for relating data to information beyond the enterprise's boundaries.
9	Data Standards	A model or example established by authority, custom, or general consent, used in measurement and comparison of quality, value, quantity, or extent.
10	Data Services	Reusable messaging facility for supplying major categories of enterprise data to consumers on demand across an enterprise.

Adapted from the Data Management Body of Knowledge (DMBOK) (DAMA, 2009).

Figure 12.3 Major components of enterprise information management (EIM)

Data Asset Inventory (DAI)

DaaS service providers need to monitor their data assets regularly to ensure that all changes are formally documented. As a best practice, it is also suggested that they maintain a complete inventory of their data assets.

However, building this inventory is easier said than done, as one often finds that companies have little documentation of their existing application portfolio. Even when they have some documentation or a service catalog, there are few staff members from the original design team still working in the organization to help the current EIM architects. Use of sophisticated data-profiling tools can help in a detailed assessment of the existing IT landscape. Chapter 6 explained the detailed activities that are part of collecting this data asset inventory (DAI) in the discussion on metadata and data profiling.

After gathering all the information from the organization's application landscape into the DAI, major data governance initiatives can be launched within the enterprise. In fact, the current-state DAI can be beneficial to the organization in many other ways. The following are some major benefits of the data governance team maintaining a current and up-to-date DAI.

- The DAI serves as a useful resource for data owners and data stewards during data governance committee meetings, data strategy sessions, and other data governance activities.
- The DAI can be assessed by senior leadership for future-state roadmaps and planning opportunities to build new data services for DaaS consumers.
- The inventory creates a baseline for action on data governance by identifying all projects, including projected spending by the DaaS domain as part of funding requirements.
- The DAI enables the organization to carry out quick reviews and assessments of legacy data through data-profiling and metadata repository tools.
- The DAI assets can be accessed by the organization to identify decommissioning and simplification opportunities or priorities.

Data Policies and Standards

The mission statement should articulate the management's intentions on all aspects of data administration as well as specify fundamental rules of data usage. Data policies based on the mission statement should be laid out by the executive leadership and enforced by the data governance committee. Figure 12.4 is an example of a mission statement.

Data standards adopted by any part of the organization should be in alignment with data governance policies and procedures. These standards are usually enforced within an organization with pre-defined data controls or by enforcing existing checkpoints in the development lifecycle.

Mission Statement
for DaaS Governance

The goal of DaaS governance is to transform an organization's data into a strategic corporate asset by providing a consistent approach for structuring, describing, and governing data and information.

To ensure the achievement of this vision, the DaaS organization should adopt the following guiding principles of governance (or Mission Statement).

Data Will Be Managed As a Corporate Asset
Data are an asset of the enterprise, and not of any individual, business unit, division, or group within the whole. We will therefore maintain these resources with the appropriate information management standards as defined by the EIM stakeholders.

Advance Data Stewardship
We will all act as custodians of our enterprise data and must take responsibility for how we use, update, or enter data. Data and business stewards will have the responsibility for making data consistent with the standards defined for that data and for data quality by ensuring that the information that is created, acquired, and maintained is appropriate for its purpose, is of high quality, is up-to-date, and reliable.

Improve Data Quality
We will create a sustainable culture of managing data in a state of high quality such that information can be used as a strategic asset and as a competitive differentiator. To drive productivity, improve compliance, and reduce risk, data quality will address data completeness, accuracy, consistency, timeliness, and validity.

Ensure Compliance to Data Standards
We will ensure consistency in use of data by adhering to enterprise-approved data and service standards, and will strive to achieve a common vocabulary across boundaries, so that the data definitions are consistent and understandable to all users of that data.

Foster Data Transparency
We will ensure that data in the enterprise are accessible and available for re-use by any authorized persons, systems, and/or business processes. We will capture, record, manage, publish, and share information about our data in a reliable, timely, and secure manner.

Safeguard Data from Unauthorized Use
We will protect data from unauthorized use, disclosure, or loss. We will safeguard and protect our data according to approved security, privacy, and compliance guidelines and regulations established by state, federal, and international agencies.

Figure 12.4 Mission statement for DaaS governance

Organizations have to adhere to approved data standards and strive to achieve a common vocabulary across boundaries, so that data definitions are understandable to all users of that data. Every data area should have one owner assigned to it to ensure alignment with these principles and compliance with the published standards.

The following data-standard areas need to be governed as part of enterprise data services:

- Naming convention for XML schemas, message formats, entities, and attributes.
- Service-oriented architecture (SOA)-specific standards and messaging protocols to standardize service definitions.
- Common data standards for developing enterprise data models (EDMs) and a shared business glossary.
- Common standards for data access (SQL, JDBC, Views, etc.).
- Canonical XML schemas to help data exchange across the organization.
- Data privacy and security standards.

PEOPLE GOVERNANCE

Next, let us look at the "people-related factors" affecting governance in the DaaS environment.

Given the diversity of stakeholders involved during the planning and requirement-definition phase of a new EDS, it is important to establish a good communication forum among various DaaS stakeholders. Critical success factors include the quality of people involved in these planning and governance activities and the level of executive support received during this phase. In large organizations, the biggest cultural challenge facing governance is often determining which individuals are accountable for which decisions. Appointing a senior-level executive such as a chief data officer (CDO) as the sponsor of the enterprise-wide governance program can be an effective mechanism with which to address this challenge. It can also ensure that the program gets the necessary attention and support from the company's key data stewards representing all the different business divisions.

The DaaS program leadership should ensure that individual EDS development projects are in alignment with directions from the DaaS governance steering committee. The stewards also need to confirm the definitions of key terms being published as part of any new data service being launched.

To ensure that there is no ambiguity, formal data-stewardship roles need to be assigned for various data assets to the different business stewards or leaders responsible for individual business divisions. For example, in a pharmaceutical organization, the chief scientist (or head of R&D) is ultimately responsible for all the data in the clinical research subject area. They are also responsible for ensuring that a consistent set of business definitions on the key clinical terminology is stored in the metadata glossary. Similarly, the financial controller's office is ultimately responsible for all the data in the accounting subject area, and so on for other data domains.

For each subject area, it is also critical to select the right mix of people as data stewards to get involved in defining the information needs of the enterprise. The data stewards should meet regularly to determine priorities for every subject area. While the data-steward responsibility for a particular subject area is often a part-time responsibility, it is critical to emphasize that all the stewards need to feel a sense of ownership regarding the data governance program. This can be accomplished only when senior leadership in the highest levels of the organization make data governance a priority item, both in terms of words and actions.

The major responsibility for data/subject-area stewards is to determine priorities for their subject area and ensure their alignment with the enterprise data strategy. They should include representation from all major representatives on this data subject area. Thus, for customer subject areas, for example, the committee should typically have representation from business subject-matter experts (SMEs) on the following customer processes: customer relationship management (CRM), marketing and planning, sales analytics, customer support pre- and post-sales, as well as customer billing and collections.

Let us now look at the important tasks that need to be covered in this process:

- Evaluate the current state: Evaluate/review the DAI periodically to evaluate the current state of the organization as well as the baseline for future action.

- Define the enterprise metadata glossary: Provides a common view for the user with a shared business vocabulary agreed by data stewards and business SMEs across the organization.

- Assess data quality: Start by discovering the data across legacy data stores and profiling the data residing in those stores.

- Complete EDMs by subject area.

- Capture metadata: Documents application and data facts for repeatable and consistent access.

- Document data roadmap: Provides a comprehensive plan to implement the source of truth (SoT) and support reporting and analytics. This needs to be broken down by individual subject-area needs, as the roadmap for individual areas could be vastly different depending on organizational challenges, and priority could vary across subject areas.

- Recommend data integration and related technology solutions: Approach for data integration and storage. This needs to be provided for every subject area, as the user needs and business processes for individual areas can be vastly different. The technology evaluation may require upfront consideration of business requirements to support integration needs related to specific reporting and analytics, big data, or other challenges related to accessing timely data services faced by users in that subject area.

This set of steps should be made part of a repeatable process that are enforced consistently across all the data subject areas as a key part of day-to-day governance efforts.

Chief Data Officer (CDO)

The role of data management in most companies is being fundamentally transformed. Business leadership now sees the role of data management as far more critical than it was previously viewed. Data are perceived more as a company-wide asset because companies now leverage data more extensively in newer areas such as big data analytics and social networking.

Consequently, most organizations feel the need to have someone representing data-specific concerns at the executive table. Several leading industry analysts predict the emergence of the CDO in the near future (Griffin, 2008). This section briefly highlights how the CDO office works with other parts of the organization.

The emergence of the CDO at the C-level role has created considerable excitement in large organizations. CDOs are now being appointed across industries as diverse as financial services, insurance, healthcare, and government agencies.

A CDO is a corporate officer responsible for enterprise-wide governance and utilization of data as an asset for various types of services: statistical data processing and analysis, big data, customer relationships, etc. The CDO should be a high-level executive who possesses a combination of business knowledge, technical skills, and people skills, and who guides the data strategy.

Every organization needs to consider several key areas when they appoint a CDO for their organization:

- What motivates an organization to appoint a Chief Data Officer?
- Who does the CDO report to?
- What experience does it take to become a CDO?
- Do CDOs have their own staff and budget?
- How do functional responsibilities vary from industry to industry?
- What are the differences between the CIO and CDO roles?
- What are some of the pitfalls and unrealistic expectations for CDOs?
- What issues are on the horizon for Chief Data Officers?

The CDO should be invested with authority and oversight across different areas of the business and IT departments. Besides focusing on DaaS revenue opportunities, data acquisition, service-delivery strategy, and customer data policies, the CDO should be responsible for explaining the strategic value of data and their important role as a business asset to key stakeholders, executives, customers, and employees.

Business and Data Stewards

Business stewards and IT have to work in harmony. A formal governance program ensures that IT understands what the business prioritizes and measures as good quality data. Business leaders, in turn, understand the impact that quality data can have on the bottom line and project delivery.

To launch a data governance or related data-quality improvement initiative successfully, it is important that business organizations responsible for day-to-day operational processes be encouraged to own the responsibility for the governance of their data assets. While implementing data governance is a collective responsibility of IT leadership and their business partners, it needs to be recognized that data are ultimately owned by the business. Therefore, the leadership responsibility on data governance issues should ultimately reside with the data's business owner.

IT and data administrators can help business partners to implement data governance policies and control, but they cannot be expected to own these business processes. Thus, for finance-related areas, the governance efforts should be led from an ownership perspective by the chief financial officer (CFO) or his delegated representative. Similarly, for customer subject areas, business leaders who run the sales and marketing, the CRM leaders, should be asked to provide directions on major data governance issues.

Apart from the goal of ensuring data quality, there are other key organizational goals from a successful data-stewardship engagement. These include:

- Fostering communication and collaboration across the organization.
- Acting as an enabler for feedback and quality improvements.
- Increasing consistency and confidence in decision making.

The major responsibilities of business stewards include:

- Establishing a review and approval process for data definitions, domain-value specifications, and business rule specifications.
- Resolution of conflicting data definitions among multiple stakeholders of that information.
- Establishing information-related policies, standards, and guidelines for compliance across the enterprise.
- Establishing appropriate measures and SLAs to monitor performance improvements in the realm of data- and service-quality efforts.
- Establishing consistent data access because data visibility policies need to be enforced for all data services. There need to be adequate data security controls for all company data.
- The business data stewards should also try to keep information open to all employees. For some areas, access does need to be restricted, as the need to keep confidential information safe and secure should be given top priority.

PROCESS GOVERNANCE

Process governance activities need to be empowered by high-level executives to drive the necessary changes within existing operations supported by the data provider organization. Figure 12.5 illustrates a high-level process for governance of enterprise data.

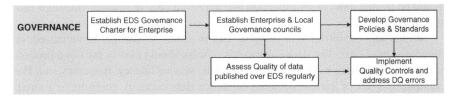

Figure 12.5   High-level process for governance of enterprise data

The initial phases focus on establishing core governance processes and technical capabilities that will act as the foundation for all future development activities. Consistent delivery of governance capabilities provides:

- Flexibility in addressing changing business needs.
- The ability to implement a mix of capabilities that are deemed more critical to the organization.
- The ability to realize a return on investment in a planned and timely manner.
- The ability to align the delivery of capabilities with related data-management project releases.

Establish a Data Governance Roadmap

The majority of enterprise data assets are defined by looking at the data by subject area. As part of the overall data governance program, a data subject-area steering committee needs to be formed. This committee should comprise a diverse group of members representing all sections of the business and IT stakeholders. Broadly speaking, the data subject-area steering committee are made the data owners (as well as made accountable) for running many of the EDS foundational components that have been discussed. For instance, these sub-committees would be responsible for determining the most suitable approach for building and maintaining enterprise artifacts such as the EDM and enterprise data glossary as well as for identifying how existing applications could be enhanced to become a SoT. This could then be used for determining the appropriate master data strategy for each individual data subject area.

Change Management Process for Enterprise Data Services

A key step in governance is to define a repeatable change management process that can be implemented across various areas in the enterprise. While issues affecting different areas in the enterprise can vary, it is critical that the enterprise steering committee as a whole implements governance with consistent standards across these different areas. Variations can be tolerated in some genuine situations. However, they should be treated more as an exception and approved only in genuine situations that warrant it.

Within any organization, enterprise data is certain to change, be enhanced, or eliminated over time. The data governance process should clearly lay out a process to administer changes to the impacted data sets, service latency, frequency, etc. For example, if a set of currency-related reference data codes is going to be retired, then the EDS support team has to carefully assess the impact it could have on the transactional elements. The reference data codes may still need to be maintained to ensure referential integrity. In some instances, changes to the reference data can be even more complex, as was discussed in Chapter 9 when ICD-9 (diagnostic) codes were being replaced worldwide by a new set of ICD-10 (diagnostic) codes in the healthcare sector.

Consequently, data services impacted by underlying data changes need to be managed using a formal change-request process. Even after the services are implemented in an organization, several business events can compel management to change their enterprise architecture (EA) and existing services at very short notice. Consequently, the organization needs to keep its architecture in a flexible, proactive state, responding to changes in the business environment very swiftly, and thus staying ahead of its competitors.

Some of the common steps to manage changes to data services include:

- Creating a change request after receiving business justification from users.
- Evaluating the impact of the proposed change.
- Identifying the impact on other stakeholders.
- Deciding to accept or reject the proposed change.
- Communicating the decision prior to making a change to the master or reference data.
- Informing stakeholders that the requested change has been made.

Establish Enterprise and Local Data-governance Processes

For Data Governance programs to succeed, it is very important to emphasize that sponsorship for these change initiatives has to be received from the senior-level leadership of the company (e.g., the CFO or chief operating officer [COO]). A centralized subject-matter steering committee should be formed and monthly committee meetings are essential to ensure that these stakeholders are engaged throughout the company's data governance journey (English, 1999).

However, it is critical to realize that for changes arising out of a data governance recommendation to be successful and sustainable in the long term, there needs to be a buy-in for data governance changes at all levels (Figure 12.6).

One can compare governing data to governing a major international sport such as tennis. Here, the highest decision-making body, the International Tennis Federation

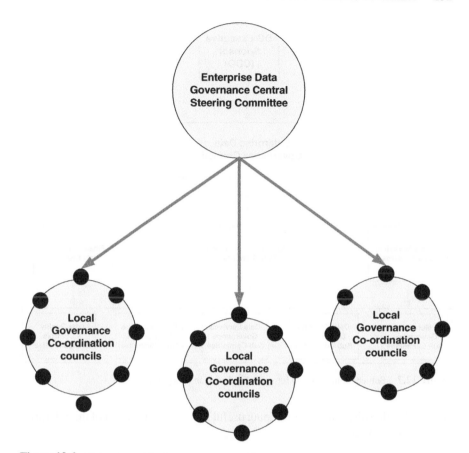

Figure 12.6   Enterprise and local governance committees

(ITF), is responsible for laying out the policies applicable at the global level (e.g., changing playing rules or determining some inter-continental commercial disputes). However, the ITF lets every country run their national federation autonomously (e.g., the USTA in the United States) and this same pattern follows within each country, where every district runs their federation independently. This works out well for all parties concerned, as administering the popular game of tennis (played in 200 plus countries across all continents) may have been too complex, if not unmanageable, had the ITF insisted on reviewing each policy at the national level.

Similarly, in large global corporations, the areas of improvement sought as part of the data governance program cannot be sustained in the end unless there is central coordination. It is, therefore, recommended that under the enterprise-level committee, multiple sub-committees be established that focus on resolving issues specific to each data subject area.

Similarly, for IT disciplines that need localized governance (e.g., governance of the canonical model or service components), specialized governance sub-committees are recommended, which can act as the custodians and owners of these areas, and

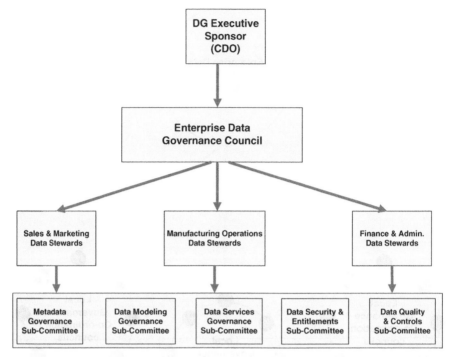

Figure 12.7   Sub-committees set up for specialized areas in data governance

provide detailed direction by developing useful standards for the rest of the enterprise going forward (Figure 12.7).

Data-Governance Executive Steering Committee Roles and Responsibilities

The Data Governance executive steering committee is responsible for making effective and efficient decisions related to resources, funding, goals, and business operations' needs across the enterprise. At the outset, an organization needs to define the charter for the data governance program. The steering committee's main role is to continuously improve its operations and add an expected value contribution to the organization based on the guidelines defined in the charter (Figure 12.7).

The enterprise-level data governance steering committee team members are typically led by the CDO or by the executive sponsor of the governance program. It also comprises a group of senior executives from across the enterprise, business, and IT department (although typically, the membership size of the core committee should not exceed seven members). Steering committee members can, however, invite other staff to its meetings, but these individuals do not have voting rights. Meetings should occur at least once a quarter but additional meetings may be suggested and voted on by members.

Responsibilities of the data governance executive steering committee team include:

- Sponsoring, approving, and championing strategic plans and policies.
- Arbitrating during conflicts.
- Communicating expectations and requirements to divisions and functional areas.
- Prioritizing business performance-improvement initiatives.
- Monitoring policies and tracking the progress of initiatives compared to a target plan.

The divisional governance councils and the subject area-based working committees need to have leadership representation primarily from a divisional or local team, with a minimum of one to two representatives from each department or division in every sub-committee. However, there should also be a minimum of one to two representatives in the sub-committee who represent the data governance council. This group meets more frequently (either weekly or bi-weekly).

Major responsibilities of the data governance council team include:

- Championing the adoption of an enterprise canonical model (ECM).
- Establishing data subject areas in alignment with the enterprise data strategy.
- Establishing metadata definitions for business terms within the subject area.
- Enforcing data policies, standards, and processes to promote reuse of enterprise assets.
- Certifying and governing the enterprise assets across data subject areas.
- Providing guidance to the chief technology officer (CTO) of the organization on the selection of appropriate EDS technology.
- Ensuring industry standards are maintained for data-exchange electronic messages (data-interoperability, reuse, etc.) while designing services.
- Evaluating data security threats posed following the introduction of any data services that require access by consumers, outside agencies, contractors, etc.

SERVICE GOVERNANCE

To cover the governance matters related to specialized technical areas such as data services, data standards, and information security, working committees should be set up with the oversight of the data governance council. The working committees are set up to address specific data/IT-specific challenges facing the organization.

Working committees include representatives from the specific areas being covered under the committee. For example, for data services, there should be representatives from EA, SOA, EIM, information risk management (IRM), and security organizations (possibly the Chief Information Security Officer or his delegate).

To ensure conformance to enacted governance policies, it is important to specify some steps to audit the implementation of data governance policies as well any related processes regularly. Apart from laying down policies, the data governance steering committee has to ensure that their directions are actually being implemented in day-to-day operations in a way that is effective and generates value for the organization. Enacting a set of effective data controls is a good mechanism for the data governance steering committee to ensure that their data governance recommendations and specific directions are actually being implemented in this way. Data controls are discussed in more detail in Chapter 8 in terms of data quality and standards.

As an organization matures and the number of enterprise data services increases, it is helpful to introduce a working committee specifically to govern the delivery of data services. It can be supported by a cross-functional governance council who represent different service-development teams across the organization. They monitor resources to make sure that the latest governance standards are being updated and governance activities are executed appropriately while issues are resolved in a timely manner.

EDS Governance Working Committee

The major responsibilities for the EDS governance committee should be defined jointly by an organization's DaaS program sponsor, IT, and business leadership. One of the major responsibilities of this service committee is to help in coordinating service specifications of various data objects and XML schema definitions across different business segment or projects (Figure 12.8).

The committee can also be used as a forum for jointly resolving any issues that affect enterprise-wide issues, e.g., service versioning or deciding on SLAs regarding the performance of the service in terms of response times as well as any potential throughput limitations.

Some of the initial priorities of the EDS governance team include:

- Providing input to leadership for DaaS roadmap development.
- Requirements and prioritization for new services to DaaS sponsors.
- Assessments and gap analysis of data services within the existing environment.
- Assisting in supporting data quality and master data management (MDM)/ reference data management (RDM) services.
- Assistance with organizational design and role definitions.
- Ongoing guidance and participation as a trusted advisor to the overall data governance program.

Service Governance Charter

One of the major objectives of the EDS governance team is to realize tangible cost savings from the reuse of data services across the enterprise. Along with this benefit,

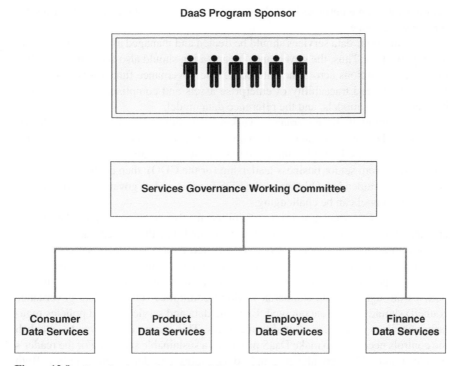

Figure 12.8   Co-ordination across individual data services development teams

greater operational efficiency is also a long-term outcome that is expected when following the DaaS paradigm. The EDS governance team requires an organizational charter to clearly define the scope and long-term objectives of the DaaS program. Since building enterprise-level services requires cross-functional discipline, having a formal charter ensures the timely resolution of issues and necessary tradeoffs among consuming application teams.

Data services meant for enterprise-level usage should be architected broadly, representing different parts of the organization, instead of just a specific application or service. Tradeoffs are frequently necessary among departmental stakeholders and the EDS design team. Thus, the EDS governance charter also has to define the stewards who represent a particular service and their ownership boundaries, as well as clearly specifying a fair-funding model for data services' future development and enhancement. Figure 12.8 illustrates the co-ordination required among different service teams to build an enterprise-wide service.

The EDS governance team should also monitor the deployment and reuse of services across the organization. Within any organization, ensuring a high degree of service reuse as well as maintaining a steady flow of enterprise-class service deployments is a critical yardstick to measure the success of service governance. In addition to this, having a lesser need for dialog among different web service development teams (to address team differences or error corrections) after the initial deployment of an enterprise-level data service is also a good indicator of successful service governance.

All enterprise data services should be treated and managed as corporate assets in the organization. Thus, the governance organization should also act as the custodian of service definitions across the enterprise. The governance function is responsible for the end-to-end traceability of enterprise assets and compliance with standards, business process models, and the reference data model.

It is helpful if the governance working committee is led by a senior leader such as a CDO in the organization, who will own the process as well as monitor available resources. If an EDS initiative within any organization has good backing or sponsorship from senior business leadership (or the CDO), then centralized funding is always recommended. Otherwise, the EDS funding and its governance efforts from a centralized pool can be challenging.

The Data Governance steering committee also has to ensure that the latest governance standards and policies are being updated and that governance issues are resolved in a timely manner. It should be assisted by a cross-functional governance council who represent different service-development teams across the organization.

The importance of introducing suitable data governance and data quality-related policies through the data standards working committee (under a data governance council) should also be encouraged. Enacting data and service related policies regularly reinforces awareness of quality measures. This can go a long way to establish the controls necessary to make DaaS programs a sustainable success. For the reader's benefit, Figure 12.4 provides a sample data quality and data security policy. Both of these areas were originally included as part of the mission statement for DaaS governance.

Example: Data Governance Policy Statement

Principle 1: Advance Data Stewardship across the Enterprise

Statement

As custodians of enterprise data, the data stewards take responsibility for data quality of individual business domains (e.g., Customer, Product) by ensuring information created, acquired, and maintained is appropriate for its purpose, high-quality, up to date, and reliable.

Rationale

- Clear assignment of data ownership to stewards assigned responsibility of managing a particular business domain up to the standard.
- Stewardship to be promoted as a guiding principle that embodies consensus-driven collaboration to optimize domain success.

- Self-sustaining collaborative stewardship practices enable continuous, adaptive assessment, and proactive balancing of SWOT factors, using patentable processes as well as properly enabled and incented human resources that cannot be duplicated.

- Stewardship is commonplace and largely self-sustaining in relatively small, self-enabled cultures where adoption of technology is preceded by established human practices.

Implications if Principle is Followed

- Data stewards must be accountable for the provision and consumption of data services in a domain and comply with service level agreements (SLAs).

- Service metrics that are gathered to proactively monitor and respond to usage or accessibility concerns across the enterprise.

- Data steward develops, implements, and communicates record retention requirements to the business they support.

- Data steward coordinates and resolves stewardship issues and data definitions of data elements that cross multiple functional domains with subject matter experts (SME).

- Data stewards develop, implement, and manage data access policies for enterprise data services.

Maintain Data Roadmaps that Address Long-Term Data Requirements for the Relatively Distant Future (3 to 5 years)

- Unambiguous RACI assignments, leading to single owner as data steward for individual domains.

- Percent of business domain that have a data steward formally appointed.

- Do best practices on data stewardship policies and standards exist?

Metrics for Measuring the Effectiveness and Compliance to Data Steward Recommendations by IT and Operations Teams as Defined in the Associated Policies/Standards Metrics

---

Example: Data Security Policy Statement

Principle 2: Safeguard Data from Unauthorized Use

Policies

We will protect data from unauthorized use, disclosure, or loss. We will safeguard and protect our data according to approved security, privacy, and compliance guidelines and regulations established by group, state, and federal agencies.

Goals

- Support data security teams to maintain the hard-earned image and reputation of our organization.
- Ensure compliance with legislative requirements.
- Reduce the risk of potential liabilities which may arise.
- Ensure privacy concerns of our customers and associates are maintained.
- Store data based on the enterprise retention requirement.
- Store data based on the legal retention requirement.

Benefits (if Principle is followed)

- Reduce overall risk posture of the organization.
- Enforces the rule of least privileged.
- Controls CRUD activity restricting access to "single versions of the truth."
- Meets regulatory and compliance requirements.

Risks (if Principle is not followed)

- Customer data is left unprotected and subject to a data breach.
- The organization will fail external and internal audits.
- Company Brand is at risk.

Metrics

- Raw: Percent of databases that have had a security assessment.
- Raw: Do best practices data security policies and standards exist?
- Metrics for measuring the adherence and effectiveness of these are defined in the associated policies/standards.

TECHNOLOGY GOVERNANCE

Technology Vendor Strategy and Oversight

Effective vendor management and oversight is critical to the success of any IT organization. Typically, businesses spend billions of dollars annually with outside vendors who deliver IT services to internal teams or customers on their behalf. Not only does vendor management and oversight make good business sense—in certain cases, vendor-oversight practices may be required by law for accreditation purposes, or may be required due to contractual commitments toward customers. For example, certain regulations require organizations to demonstrate sufficient oversight in managing relationships that provide vendor support under some customer contracts.

The EDS-related costs to consider during vendor-evaluation discussions include:

- Vendor tools and licensing costs
- Development and infrastructure costs
- Core application data charges
- Primary and secondary replication costs
- IT resource costs

While implementing EDS, the stakeholders and governance team have to work closely with the enterprise architects to define the appropriate solution architecture for all enterprise data services and the related data-integration tools. The selection should be based on a detailed understanding of the company's business operations in a particular area. The high-level business functionality and expected requirements from business stakeholders should be documented before the vendor selection process is started. Having a formal methodology to rate/score different vendors based on their suitability to stakeholder requirements is an example of a governance-related IT control that is highly recommended.

Based on these technology architecture recommendations received from the IT vendor selection committee, the IT procurement organization should purchase the technology required to implement the EDS-related tools. In large organizations, it is quite common to find that the vendor tool that is suitable for one specific area (say PIM technology for product domains) is unsuitable for another business domain. Depending on the overall priority of a particular area of business operations, it is possible that business stakeholders may decide to invest more in an area that they feel is more critical.

For example, a retailer may decide to invest heavily in a customer MDM-solution to cross-sell/upsell products, while a healthcare insurer may prefer to give a higher weight to the patient index or electronic medical records. These decisions are also likely to change over time, as realities in the marketplace can change the priorities of the organization's decision makers rather abruptly. Lastly, the technology governance standards for data providers should also include security recommendations for executive leadership. For example, these recommendations can include providing guidance to the governance council in the following areas:

- Technologies used to manage data-security and access mechanisms.
- Remote access procedures for customers, vendors, and contractors.
- Data-encryption technologies and evolving standards.
- Evaluating the tools/techniques for data transmission over the Internet, mobile devices, and the Cloud.

Information-security working sub-committees need to educate senior leadership appointed for governance about security threats and effectiveness of data services proposed for supporting external customers. They also have to perform security audits and report the effectiveness of their data-security setup on a regular basis.

Similarly, to ensure appropriate industry-specific standards are maintained on data-interoperability, data exchange, and reuse, there have to be SMEs on these areas guiding leadership on service-related governance issues.

Similarly, data governance working sub-committees have to work with the technology infrastructure organization to define the minimum acceptable standards for system performance, access requirements, downtime windows, etc. Efforts should also be made to reach SLAs with each of the IT technology teams as part of data governance efforts.

Standard tool selection and communication policies also need to be determined across the enterprise. However, it is critical that these tools are chosen by enterprise architects and enterprise system planners after keeping the long-term objectives and IT roadmap of the organization in mind.

Case Study: Governance Program at a U.S. Insurance Firm Introducing Data Services

A large U.S.-based insurer sponsored a data governance program as part of a major revamp to introduce enterprise-level data services.

The insurance firm set up a data governance organization that was comprised of multiple stakeholders. They included:

- A data governance executive sponsor
- An enterprise data governance council
- Business stewards representing individual divisions
- Data stewards addressing EIM and data governance issues
- A technology SME working group to address technology- and vendor-governance issues.

The enterprise data governance council included key functional stakeholders from sales, marketing, the agency, and finance, along with EIM representatives to ensure IT was aligned with the overall business. Some of the council stakeholders included the CFO, VP of sales and marketing, the chief information officer, and chief information security officer.

Efforts were also made to ensure representation in the council at both the enterprise and divisional levels. Consequently, each division had a formal representative in the data governance council. The data governance council meetings were organized every month by the EIM team on behalf of the executive sponsor of the data governance program.

Over the course of the initial stages, several key areas of data and service governance required inputs from SMEs. The data governance council appointed sub-committees specifically to address these areas (Figure 12.6). For example, to address issues related to access and security controls for published data services, a special sub-committee comprised of EIM, data services, and IT security SMEs was asked to provide recommendations on appropriate security policies that could be implemented across the firm in a phased manner.

After the initial list of data services was published, the funding models and cost savings were revisited by the data governance team and the sponsor to demonstrate credibility and buy-in for additional reuse of data services across new areas in the organization.

SUMMARY

This chapter covered a broad and varied range of topics, all focusing on how an organization can effectively govern its data services. It examined several best practices in service governance regarding how to coordinate the release of and changes to published services to consumers over their lifecycle. It also emphasized the role of EIM, data quality, data security, and related governance processes to ensure that information delivered via services meets the quality requirements of data consumers both within and outside the organization.

Since some of these areas are very subjective in nature, it is important to emphasize there is no one way of setting up governance processes in any organization. Therefore, it is critical to understand the concepts discussed in this chapter and yet adapt these governance processes to an organization's specific demands.

Appointing a CDO to head the data governance program can also be helpful in most organizations. Having effective and seasoned data governance leaders can help to attain buy-in and support from business leadership on new data initiatives and can aid in achieving firm-wide collaboration. In the DaaS context, these efforts to improve data quality should be combined with improving overall service quality to subscribers and generating revenues from its portfolio of enterprise-level data services.

Chapter 13

Securing the DaaS Environment

TOPICS COVERED IN THIS CHAPTER

- This chapter explains why data security and privacy-related issues have become such critical considerations for any organization interested in publishing data services.
- It examines some of the major data security considerations that are critical for implementing a DaaS framework in real life. A suggested multi-layered approach for securing the DaaS Environment is also discussed.
- Key features of a comprehensive information risk management program that can mitigate risks to the DaaS program are also shown.
- Finally, this chapter provides a practical list of data security and privacy measures that can be deployed by any organization planning to set up DaaS operations.

In many respects, data security at most organizations can be compared to a continuously evolving battle between data providers and cyber criminals. The more a data provider takes measures to protect their data, the more hackers improve their ability to get in. Credit card information and personal identifiers such as SSN and health records are just too tempting. Organizations setting up DaaS operations need to realize that as data providers they are especially vulnerable. If a cyber criminal wants to obtain customers sensitive data published by a data provider badly enough, they probably will. The best thing to do for a data provider is to be ready to take proactive measures to protect their data assets. When a data breach happens, an organization can implement damage control as quickly as possible. This chapter discusses some of the data security and privacy related measures that a data provider can employ to secure their DaaS organization.

With increasing occurrences of cyber attacks and data security breaches, securing the data environment has become critical for any organization interested in

Data as a Service: A Framework for Providing Reusable Enterprise Data Services,
First Edition. Pushpak Sarkar.
© 2015 the IEEE Computer Society. Published 2015 by John Wiley & Sons, Inc.

implementing a DaaS framework. While introducing data services offers significant benefits to both organizations and customers in terms of faster access to data (resulting in productivity gains), it also poses several security and privacy-related challenges to a data provider. Using mobile, web, and online social-networking services introduce additional threats of cyber attacks and data breaches to organizations.

IMPACT OF DATA BREACH ON DaaS OPERATIONS

A data breach is a security-related incident in which sensitive, protected, or confidential data is usually copied, stolen, used, or sold to unauthorized individuals. Banks, retailers, and credit-card institutions regularly report huge losses from data breaches involving confidential data of their consumers. For a commercial organization running a DaaS operation, such incidents not only result in explicit losses arising out of fraud and legal costs but also result in implicit costs, such as the consumer's complete loss of trust in the vendor.

In the health sector, data breaches usually involve loss of confidential patient information including sensitive protected health information (PHI) and clinical results. This area of security, privacy, and confidentiality has therefore become a source of major concern to both customers as well as the organizations handling their sensitive or confidential data (e.g., health records or financial data). This is largely due to the serious legal and reputational risks faced by organizations who fail to protect private data.

Some underlying causes that can result in data breaches and security-related incidents include the following:

- Negligent data security practices.
- Inadequate internal controls and security audits, which can result in threat of insider attacks.
- Lack of suitable data entitlements (e.g., too many permissions).
- Data privacy violations with non-adherence to industry laws.
- Outdated technology, e.g., failure of most U.S. banks to encrypt credit cards with the latest encryption chip or organization failing to implement a proper firewall.

Given how critical the threats faced by most data providers, this chapter provides a high-level overview on the risks and security considerations impacting any organization interested in deploying DaaS.

Average Cost of a Data Breach

It is hard to quantify the cost of a data breach for any data provider in the long-term. However IBM and the Ponemon Institute have been providing a benchmark on this by annually conducting a cost of data breach study.

This world-wide research study included the costs incurred by companies that experienced the loss or theft of protected personal data across all the major industry sectors. Although findings differ from country to country, the study reveals some general trends that have significant implications, especially for data providers across the globe:

- The cost of a data breach is definitely on the rise. Most countries saw this rise both in the cost per stolen (or lost) record and in the average total cost of a breach.

- In the United States, the cost of a data breach rose from $5.4 million dollars to around $5.9 million dollars. The average cost for each lost or stolen record containing sensitive and confidential information increased from $188 to $201.

- Companies are far more likely to have a small data breach than a mega breach. While the likelihood of a data breach involving a minimum of 10,000 records is estimated at approximately 19 percent over a 24-month period, the chances of a data breach involving a 100,000 records is less than one percent.

- More customers terminated their relationship with the company that had a data breach. In fact, the loss of customers following a data breach also resulted in sizeable additional expenses to preserve the organization's brand and reputation.

- For most countries, malicious or criminal attacks have taken the top spot as the root cause of the data breaches experienced by participating companies.

- Research also reveals that having business continuity management and presence of certain organizational factors can help reduce the overall cost involved in the remediation of a breach, e.g., strong security posture or a formal incident response plan, appointment of a CISO.

To calculate the average cost of a data breach, the research team collected both direct and indirect expenses incurred by the impacted organization. Direct expenses include engaging forensic experts, outsourcing hotline support, and providing free credit monitoring subscriptions and discounts for future products and services. Indirect costs included in-house investigations and communication, as well as the projected customer loss resulting from diminished customer acquisition rates or turnover.

Source: Cost of Data Breach Study: A benchmark research independently conducted by Ponemon Institute LLC and sponsored by IBM, May 2014.

MAJOR SECURITY CONSIDERATIONS FOR DaaS

To implement security policies in an organization, it is important to understand the nature of the business that the DaaS is supporting and create a data security policy accordingly. For example, in any business organizations handling sensitive data (e.g., credit card data by retailers or patient data by hospitals), the degree of enforcement and rigidity could be more stringent compared to other businesses. Organizations should consider classifying all enterprise data based on a classification schema for confidential data. Information that is sensitive and confidential to the business should be treated as higher priority from a security perspective and handled more carefully by the DaaS service organization. As an example, since a personally identifiable information (PII) data element can be misused by cyber criminals to steal the identity of a DaaS consumer, there should be rigid policies to limit distribution and accessibility of PII.

At the business level, a security policy describes the rules on how information should be protected. However, they need to be enforced at a technical level by policy enforcement points. The data security policy should be created after consultations with IT security, legal, and business professionals to ensure the organization is complying with necessary regulations and standards in the industry.

A broad security framework in a DaaS environment comprises the following components:

Authentication: Authentication is the process of verifying the identity of a person and ensuring that they actually are who they say they are. The authentication process validates the true identity of the DaaS consumer by asking them to present some verifiable proof of the identity they claim before allowing them access to sensitive corporate data. The DaaS security layer has to confirm that the potential user requesting this data has the proper credentials and is not a cyber criminal trying to illegally use information. Inadequate authentication can lead to a possible security breach of data exchanged by the DaaS system (or hacker) over the computer/mobile network.

Authorization: There is an inherent vulnerability for DaaS service providers that sophisticated cyber criminals can masquerade to intercept sensitive information or alter data contents after getting unauthorized access to corporate systems. Granting authorization to access confidential data is critical since the consequences of private or confidential data falling in wrong hands can be extremely risky. A DaaS provider has to authorize the right privileges to a DaaS user for them to view enterprise data based on their security entitlements. The authorization process grants access to a user based on their identity, the type of access being requested, and the security policy of the applicable component.

Access and identity management: A data provider has to enable authorized individuals and their security privileges in a timely manner. Granting access to data services should require a thorough analysis of the DaaS consumer's needs and responsibilities before assigning them to a particular role. Granting access privileges enables the authorized users with access privileges and offers appropriate and timely views of data based on their security profile. Larger organizations usually prefer role-based access control, granting permission/privileges to role groups. Any individual who belongs to the role group automatically are granted privileges assigned to the group.

An individual user may need access to multiple applications based on their identity-specific roles. Some DaaS users also require additional access to data using blackberry and mobile devices. To support identity management, large organizations need a synchronization mechanism with an enterprise user directory to ease user password management. With an identity management system known as single sign-on capability, a user can sign on once and all the various authentication and identification procedures are taken care simultaneously.

Audit: A DaaS provider has to review user activity periodically to ensure that their activities are in compliance with security regulations policy and standards. The

DaaS Security team has to perform regular IT security audits for evaluating the effectiveness of their security setup. They also have to monitor compliance to privacy policies and regulations on a regular basis during the audits.

Process: It is recommended that a clearly documented workflow approval process to grant privileges be followed in the organization to document each user authorization request. Similarly for modifying existing access requests, a change management system should be used to track revised permissions, which are followed by assigned permissions based on the change request.

Administration: The implementation of data security for the data provider organization should be handled by a dedicated group of security administrators over the long term. Even after successful implementation of DaaS within an organization, there needs to be regular monitoring of confidential information being transmitted over the network via data services. Real-time monitoring can alert administrators of suspicious activities and inappropriate access. The underlying database security is often the responsibility of database administrators but their security activities also should be under the purview of the data governance team.

MULTILAYERED SECURITY FOR THE DaaS ENVIRONMENT

The major fallout for corporations and government agencies from not having sufficient entitlement and data visibility rules implemented is in making themselves vulnerable to unlawful users, hackers, etc. Business organizations need to establish, implement, and monitor reasonable administrative, physical, and technical information-security (IS) safeguards to protect corporate data transported by enterprise data services (EDS).

In the context of data protection in the DaaS environment, the security framework should be built like a fortress, with multiple layers of protection, with information as the core element that needs to be protected against attacks from unauthorized, external intruders and hackers to prevent data breaches in sensitive customer data (Figure 13.1).

Data providers must develop a strategy to protect their data assets and related infrastructure on multiple levels. This includes closing every opportunity for cyber criminals to exploit the vulnerabilities of a DaaS operation. The multilayered security framework to support a DaaS-based organization should include end-to-end security controls, i.e., both from a logical and physical control perspective (Figure 13.2).

Let us now briefly discuss each of these perspectives to examine their security issues.

Logical Security Controls

Logical security controls are steps taken by an organization that restrict data access capabilities only to authorized users. They also limit the access of authorized users only to those data assets to which they are entitled. Logical security controls can

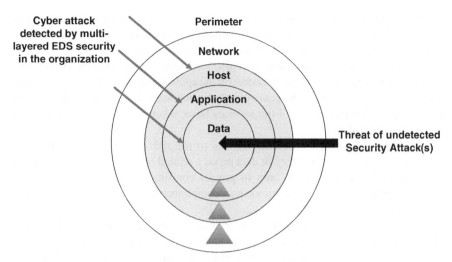

Figure 13.1   Multi-layered security framework for data services

exist within the application layer, data layer, or user interface layer. The number and types of logical security controls vary with each application, database, or with the customer-security layer. In contrast, physical controls include controls in the physical hardware, network, and other peripheral devices (Champlain, 2003).

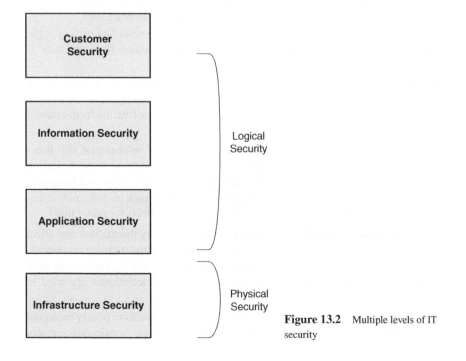

Figure 13.2   Multiple levels of IT security

Given this context, the major issues affecting security in an organization can be broken down into four major broad categories: application security, information security, customer (or end-user) security, infrastructure security.

For security to be sustainable over the long term, many security checks and validation procedures need to be embedded in the application- and information-related design processes. Application security includes the security validation that occurs during application processing of the services layer, whereas information security is related to the data layer.

Customer (or end user) security relates to the risk taken by an organization when there is a breach of security or data privacy related to a customer's confidential information. There are several laws to protect consumer privacy and to hold the business liable in case of an error or non-compliance by the organization during business processing.

Infrastructure security experts in an organization are responsible for protecting and safeguarding their infrastructure assets (including data assets) from unauthorized users. Network security operations have to ensure that data made available over a data service or via other forms in any organization are protected from unauthorized usage, access, storage, public disclosure, viewing, or any other illegal operations.

Physical Security Controls

Some of the risks to a DaaS organization can have more far-reaching implications on the entire organization. This often originates at any of the other physical layers within the security framework of the organization (see the following list).

As noted earlier, there are several impacts from security risks and privacy regulations on an organization planning to reach out to data consumers through DaaS.

- **Perimeter security**: This layer deals with external security threats that arrive at the enterprise boundary via the network. For example, companies use network anti-virus software and firewalls to protect corporate information from external threats.
- **Network security**: This deals with the protection of information that flows over the network. It authorizes access to network resources and authentication of the network users. It can also include intrusion-detection and intrusion-prevention systems. This layer may use technologies such as SSL, public key infrastructure (PKI), and virtual private networks (VPNs) for protection.
- **Host/platform security**: This layer deals with security threats that can affect individual devices in the organization and other IT infrastructure components (e.g., application servers, file systems, operating systems). Techniques such as authentication, authorization, and access-control techniques are used to prevent being taken over by a hostile agent.
- **Application security**: This layer deals with security threats to poorly protected applications that can end up compromising private data. Application security

standards and controls are used to protect the application layer from spyware, worms, etc.

- **Data security**: This layer provides techniques to protect the data used by an organization. Protection of data residing in local data stores, archived in files, and so on can be achieved through implementing authentication, access authorization, and control measures. This is highly dependent on the capabilities supported by the data store.

Techniques to Protect Data-in-Motion

This section discussed some popular approaches to implement message level security for data transmitted in the DaaS environment. The message payload (including the actual data content in the message) has to be made difficult to decipher for cyber criminals while data traverses the network.

The DaaS message payload can be secured by using sophisticated techniques like data encryption, hashing, and digital signatures. Currently, these are among the leading solutions to ensure secure electronic transmissions of data.

- Most modern encryption makes use of the science of cryptography using secret keys or codes. This science has been employed since the Roman Empire to ensure official secrets are not compromised when messages get relayed (or 2000 years ago that couriers do not fall in the hands of adversaries). In the context of DaaS, cryptography is used to secure electronic transmissions as well as ensure integrity and authenticity of data being transmitted. Modern cryptography is heavily based on mathematical theory and cryptographic algorithms that make password keys hard to break in practice by any adversary or rogue hacker. In the early 1970s, the National Institute of Standards and Technology (NIST) and IBM jointly introduced the data encryption standard (DES) as a U.S government-wide standard for encrypting unclassified, sensitive information being transported over networks. Since then, the use of DES became rather widespread among government agencies. It was also previously used at financial institutions and ATMs to help secure ATM transactions.

  In 2001, NIST selected a new standard called advanced encryption standard (AES) as a replacement for DES. AES is based on a symmetric-key algorithm, meaning the same key is used for both encrypting and decrypting data. Since the block size in AES has been raised from 56 bytes to 128 bytes, it is not vulnerable to brute force attacks. On May 26, 2002, AES became effective as the U.S. government standard. Even the National Security Agency (NSA) uses AES for exchanging top secret information.

- Hashing is yet another technique that can ensure message integrity by ensuring information passed over the data service has not been altered or no other information has been deleted during services transmission. This kind of message integrity can be seen with deployment of one-way hash functions. In simple layman terms, a one-way hash function is a mathematical formula that uses an electronic message as its input.

- Digital signatures and certificates are also an effective way to secure a message. This technique is similar to cashing checks at the local bank branch. When we sign checks, they get verified by the bank. The bank compares the signature on our check with the official copy of our signature in the bank's records. When an organization needs to implement public key encryption on a large scale, such as a secure web server, digital certificates become absolutely essential. Digital certificates are used to confirm to message recipients that the message they are receiving from (or to) the data device is authentic. The underlying message components are encrypted using the sender's private key resulting in a digital securitization. A digital certificate indicates to potential user applications that a web server is trusted by an independent source known as a certificate authority. The certificate authority acts as the middleman that both computers trust. It confirms that each computer is in fact who they say they are and then provides the public keys of each computer to the other. Authentication using digital certificate becomes critical in areas related to electronic payment as the chances of an online criminal misusing the identity of the naïve online user increases dramatically without safeguards.

IDENTITY AND ACCESS MANAGEMENT

Data services often require access to extensive information about a user, including address books, preferences, entitlements, and contact information. Since much of this information is subject to privacy and/or confidentiality requirements, controlling access to services is crucial.

Organizations are expected to continue to add data services for use by both internal users and customers. Helping users to decide how to manage access to their personal information has become an issue of broad concern (Gross, Acquisti, & Heinz, 2008; Taylor, 2008). Moreover, from a business perspective, it is critical to know which organizations and individual users are entitled to access data services, how they authenticate themselves, and when their identities need to be revoked or renewed.

The answer lies in using identity management systems to provide personal security and to protect the identity of the subscribers to DaaS. For internal users of data services, identity management is useful to control access to all digital assets, including devices, network equipment, servers, portals, content, applications, and/or products. In the case of external users, security is also needed to provide differentiated identities to support users in their different roles. The necessity for multiple identities has further increased with consumers using mobile, web, and online social networking services (Figure 13.3).

A consumer can choose to use a particular identity profile based on the context and usage of data in a specific situation. Thus, a person may choose to use partial identities for work, shopping, or financial transactions where they disclose only a

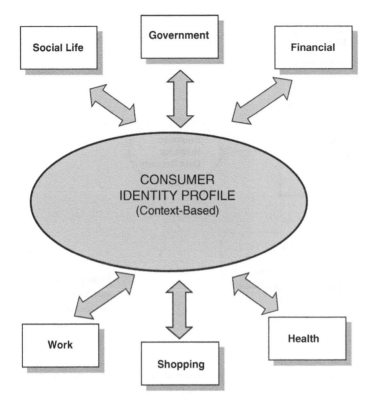

Figure 13.3   Multiple identity profiles for a consumer

subset of relevant attributes. For example, access to identity attributes related to purchases made by a doctor over the Christmas holidays should be limited to his partial identity as an online shopper, not to work-related attributes regarding how his patients perceive him online.

Given this plurality of usage, one individual can have a diverse set of customer-identity profile, which he or she may want to keep separate. From an identity-management perspective, the requirement is to support differentiated, partial identities linked to the same person. This need for differentiated identities needs the heavy use of identity management techniques to ensure customers are protected. It is also likely that identity management needs to be separated from application functionality, so that a single identity can have different role-based profiles to serve its different activities.

DATA ENTITLEMENTS TO SAFEGUARD PRIVACY

Indiscriminately sharing sensitive data outside the boundaries of an organization can make a data provider vulnerable to data breaches and denial of service attacks. These attacks allow sensitive data of customers falling in the wrong hands and subsequently resulting in large-scale data privacy violations.

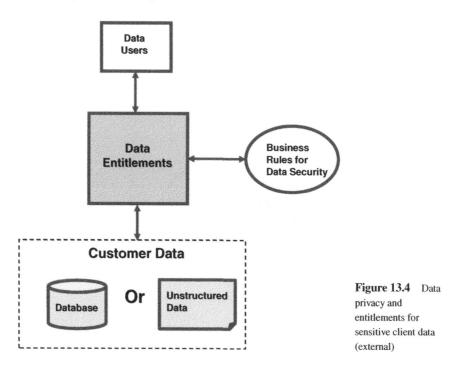

Figure 13.4   Data privacy and entitlements for sensitive client data (external)

To comply with data privacy laws, data providers should formally institute policies related to data access entitlements for individual subscribers. These policies should be introduced under the general oversight of the data governance council (described in Chapter 12). Policies should ensure that privacy and legal rules are complied with internally while sharing any sensitive data across the organization.

For example, if a bank is implementing data services, only internally authorized employees of the customer's branch or customer service centers should be able to access their published data. For sensitive PII information of customers (private information such as SSN, financial net worth, etc.), there must be even further restrictions placed on access. Entitlement policies and related business rules should clearly specify what types of data can be viewed by financial advisors (FA), branch employees, and customers (Figure 13.4).

Given that data visibility/entitlement rules can be sufficiently complex and subject to local government regulations in a specific country or industry, it is critical that organizations stay abreast of local regulations passed by law makers for their industry.

IMPACT OF INCREASED PRIVACY REGULATIONS ON DATA PROVIDERS

In recent years, governments in many countries have enacted strong privacy regulations for businesses to respect the privacy of their customer information. In order to meet this mandate, business organizations have to behave more responsibly as they collect personal information from consumers. The use of personal information collected by them should be limited to only those specific categories of use that meet legal provisions.

The definition of sensitive personal information varies across countries. Even within a country, there can be different privacy standards across industry sectors. For example, the interpretation of privacy in the context of a financial institution can be very different from a healthcare environment dealing with the sensitive health conditions of its consumers. Business organizations must limit the collection of sensitive personal information to that related to a legitimate business purpose. Privacy standards can also vary across organizations, but they usually include information regarding race, ethnic origin, political opinions, religious beliefs, trade union membership, physical or mental health, sexual life, committed or alleged committed offenses, court proceedings, financial information, government-issued identification numbers (such as social security numbers), and more.

As required by law in the United States and several other countries, business organizations can collect sensitive personal information only with the consent of the individual. Similarly, these organizations have to identify whether, in accordance with applicable law, an intended collection, use, or disclosure of personal information requires that a customer be provided with an opportunity to consent or opt out, and if so, to provide and honor those individual choices.

It is understood that security provisions such as those discussed earlier have to be respected by the entire organization. Global organizations with operations across several countries have to look at these provisions with care. The leadership in these organizations is responsible for identifying applicable local privacy laws and identifying personal information in its operations. It also has to develop policies, procedures, standards, and guidelines for mitigating security and privacy risks with a comprehensive approach to information risk management.

INFORMATION RISK MANAGEMENT

This section looks at the major security and privacy risks affecting organizations providing enterprise level data services and what the appropriate policies are to protect data in transit. This area is especially crucial for data providers as any data transported over public internet using messages are especially vulnerable to external intrusion by unauthorized cyber criminals or to sell confidential information internationally. Such data breaches would make the Data provider legally liable to their consumers. Any organization exposing confidential data of customers has to therefore assess their own internal risks and come up with appropriate procedures to safeguard the confidential data of their customers.

Data breaches occurring due to security vulnerabilities can be classified into the following major risk categories.

Operational Risk

Operation risk refers to the risk of data being compromised by an organization as a result of inadequate or failed internal processes and security controls. Often when these incidents are large spread, they can affect an organization critically, perhaps even resulting in complete closure. For example, several outsourced operations in offshore subsidiaries can be shut down completely if their client data is compromised or if data theft occurs in local operations.

Reputation Risk

Whenever there is a major event concerning breach of data security, the affected organization receives a lot of bad publicity and usually affects the company's performance negatively. This can impact the company's reputation and its overall brand in the long run. An example of this type of security risk is seen when an organization loses credit card details of a large number of their customers (e.g., U.S. retailer Target). Irrespective of who is to blame, this type of situation can result in a complete loss of the company's reputation among existing customers as well as affect a company's future prospects.

Compliance Risk

There have been numerous data privacy compliance regulations passed by government agencies around the world to protect the consumer. Compliance concerns usually arise from adverse effects faced by average consumers when an organization has failed to protect the confidentiality and privacy of their data privacy. The Sarbanes-Oxley Graham Leach Billey Act, U.S. Patriotic Act, and the Privacy of Health Information (PHI) act in the healthcare sector are a just few examples of regulations passed to address these concerns.

Third Party Information Risk

An organization is responsible for any adverse data privacy and security failures, even if these events are caused due to a failure created by a third party. Examples of third parties include outsourced operations run by a vendor, contractors, service providers, etc. Therefore, information security and risk factors arising from third parties should be treated by organizations carefully. Security procedures related to other third parties must be consistent with the applicable privacy notices, contracts, agreements, and laws. Information disclosures to third parties should ideally be limited to the minimum necessary for the intended purpose. Organizations should also allow the transfer of confidential information or allow access to these third parties only for legitimate business purposes.

Intellectual Property Risk

Due to vast differences in intellectual property rights across countries, incidences of large-scale violations of intellectual property by leading technology and pharmaceutical companies have occurred. Due to these risks, organizations should also take note of intellectual property risks for operations run by their external entities in other countries. Organizations should allow disclosure only when they are assured that information will be lawfully processed and protected based on local country's laws.

To eliminate the major categories of security risks previously listed, organizations need to define an information risk management (IRM) program to oversee data services by conducting periodic risk assessments and audits regularly. These risk assessments need to be primarily performed to determine the adequacy of security standards and controls required by the organization based on legal, regulatory; and internal corporate IT security policies.

This IRM function will be a joint responsibility of business units and the IT organization that runs various operations (e.g., data base administration, web services applications, system administration).

IMPORTANT DATA SECURITY AND PRIVACY REGULATIONS THAT IMPACT DaaS

Stronger government privacy regulations around the world are dictating the need for organizations to protect the confidentiality, security, and privacy needs of consumers (e.g., the Sarbanes–Oxley Act, the GLBA Act, and PHI). This has led to the growing need for organizations to protect their sensitive information by using corporate security policies.

In the United States, legislation on online privacy has moved slowly (relatively speaking) for reasons that range from complexity to an awareness of its sheer impact. Lawmakers often grapple with weighing the interests of consumers and companies in the battle for personal information.

Part of the difficulty in regulating online privacy and security is because the rate at which technological innovation happens makes it difficult to regulate it swiftly. For law enforcement, this makes it difficult to go after cybercrime when underlying technology changes so abruptly, making security-related steps easily obsolete.

Since DaaS often involves exposing sensitive consumer data to external parties, Appendix B lists some major international regulations and guidelines on security and privacy standards. Readers are encouraged to consider local privacy laws when deploying data services in individual countries.

Besides complying with these acts through technical security procedures (e.g., role-based access implemented in a policy server based on user entitlement roles), having data controls that are administered through the governance committee can further prevent chances of a security problem. Again, Appendix B lists a few major regulations impacting data privacy and security of data providers globally for readers' benefit.

Governance of Data Security and Privacy

As a trustee of all the data published by the DaaS organization, the data governance council is responsible for formulating the organization's security policies. It should also be responsible for the oversight of all security and confidentiality matters in respect to DaaS consumers. However, the day-to-day governance of security-related activities should be left to a sub-committee on data security appointed by the data governance council.

Major components to consider while setting up data security governance and control framework include:

- Establishing effective security and risk controls.
- Establishing IRM policies and guidelines.
- Performing regular data security audits.
- Keep customers and regulators informed if there are security attacks.

As mentioned, data security governance needs to be regularly reviewed and monitored by the security governance sub-committee. In the context of enforcing information-security and privacy regulations, organizations have to set appropriate policies for security and governance.

However, apart from introducing updated policies, they also need to institute adequate levels of control that are relevant to the implementation of their security and privacy policies, and ensure their effectiveness in day-to-day business operations. While every employee is responsible for compliance with privacy laws, as well as for promptly raising any concerns about possible violations of this policy, organizations should set up a security and privacy compliance office to address such issues formally at the corporate level. Employees or groups should be encouraged to report any incidents of non-compliance with company policy with details promptly reported to the data security office.

The governance council should also ensure that the organization ensures regulatory compliance to laws such as PHI, GLBA, SOX, etc. Organizations should also consider classifying the privacy of all enterprise data based on a confidential data sensitivity classification schema.

Case Study: Monitoring Sensitive Data Using the Metadata Glossary

Even after DaaS is implemented and running smoothly, information security administrators need to monitor the effectiveness of all their security measures within the organization. They need to perform IT security audits and track effectiveness of their IS security setup on a regular basis.

Using a metadata repository to tag confidential and sensitive data can be a very useful aid as a security monitoring and alert notification mechanism. The metadata repository can be used to classify, manage, and organize data elements based on well-defined criteria and security policies set by the organization. The business glossary can be used for the following purposes by a DaaS service organization.

- Identify sensitive or confidential data being published in a service that needs to be protected from unauthorized access. Sensitive data within the glossary needs to be tagged so it can be kept under strict controls and comply with privacy regulations by regulatory agencies. For example, any organization within United States cannot distribute PII information of consumers (e.g., SSN). Similarly, healthcare organizations cannot expose a patient's health condition in the public domain.

- Enforce data privacy policies based on a security classification level. The data security team has to strictly enforce compliance for identified data elements based on a well-defined security classification system. To enforce the various levels of security requirements in the DaaS environment, there has to be a security team to monitor compliance on a day-to-day basis.

- A special set of data services can be prepared to issue security alerts when a breach takes place to ensure that access to any data elements tagged as sensitive or confidential data within the glossary (e.g., PIH data) are not accessible by unauthorized users.

CHECKLIST TO PROTECT DATA PROVIDERS FROM DATA BREACHES

The close of this chapter provides a practical list of security measures that can be easily implemented by any organization interested in securing their DaaS operations. Following the steps outlined can also greatly minimize chances of large-scale damage to the reputation of a commercial data provider.

- **Retain customer data only for as long as necessary**: When data is no longer of business value, properly dispose of it. For example, remove hard drives from computers before disposing of them.

- **Minimize the customer data you collect**: Data providers should acquire and keep only data required for legitimate business purposes (e.g., marketing, billing, shipping).

- **Encrypt sensitive data:** Install encryption on all laptops, mobile devices, flash drives and backup tapes. Encryption makes it more difficult for unauthorized parties to read lost or stolen data.

- **Monitor traffic use regularly**: Data providers need to regularly monitor online traffic and create a central log of security-related information. They should also alert customers of any suspicious activity on their accounts. If a data provider suspects the possibility of a major data breach impacting multiple customers, they have to inform external regulators of the attack at the earliest.

- **Educate employees about their role in data security**: Leadership has to regularly train all employees regarding potential threats to the data provider in case customer data is compromised as well as the legal implications for not taking prompt corrective actions.

- **Appoint departmental security coordinators**: Organizations should designate some employees to serve as departmental security coordinators, overseeing day-to-day operations in a DaaS organization from a security perspective. This should also minimize the possibility of data becoming internally compromised or stolen by individual employees of the data provider. Security coordinators can be vigilant regarding sensitive activities within their departments. In case of suspicious employee activity, they can report to the central IS security team and senior leadership.

- **Conduct regular security audits**: Data providers need to conduct regular audits of their security measures, especially the infrastructure that can be vulnerable to attacks, e.g., connections commonly used as gateways for attacks and make appropriate adjustments.

- **Build measurable security intelligence around your data assets**: It is recommended that organizations maintain security-focused intelligence around all data assets, including their privacy sensitivity, trust rating, threat, prevalence, and inherited vulnerabilities. Having a high level of security intelligence also enhances the ability of a DaaS provider to report on any asset at audit time or during pre-compliance assessment and security intelligence gathering. It also enables them to take a proactive stance and act pre-emptively against attacks by data hackers.

- **Communicate with customers responsibly**: If a major data breach has taken place (e.g., Target), it is vital that data providers keep customers and regulators informed in a responsible manner. Lack of timely communication or misleading customer can result in irreparable damage to the organization. There is also a possibility of regulators imposing hefty penalties for compromising consumer data privacy (e.g., fines are regularly imposed in the healthcare sector in response to consumer privacy violations).

SUMMARY

With the cost of data breaches across industries reaching billions of dollars, pressure to maintain the security on organizations has become intense globally. Since organizations providing Daas are essentially data providers (or data brokers), any data breach involving sensitive, protected, or confidential data falling into the hands of unauthorized individuals can prove incredibly damaging. It can result in a consumer's complete loss of trust in online and mobile transactions with the data provider. Therefore, organizations providing DaaS have to ensure that while they provide easy access to enterprise data, they do so without compromising on security risks.

The need for having a well-formulated information risk management strategy is especially crucial for an organization introducing enterprise-wide data services for the first time. Typically, the risk mitigation strategy of an organization providing data services is also impacted by IT related factors such as the underlying infrastructure environment, current application development, future technology trends, risks of obsolescence, and so on.

Lastly, underlying business and technology scenarios affecting an organization can change over the course of time. Therefore, data security policies and governance matters need to be regularly reviewed and monitored by data governance and security councils. In the event of a data breach taking place, it is vital that data providers keep their customers and regulators informed in a responsible manner. Lack of transparency, i.e., delaying or misleading communication to customers in these situations, can result in irreparable damage to the data provider along with penalties from regulatory agencies.

Chapter 14

Taking DaaS from Concept to Reality

TOPICS COVERED IN THIS CHAPTER

- This chapter is essential reading for anyone interested in managing DaaS projects, as it discusses a realistic approach on how an organization can go about defining, establishing, and maintaining a DaaS initiative for its specific needs.

- It explains the steps to build a DaaS performance scorecard for monitoring the level of DaaS service performance. Monitoring DaaS service performance against service-level agreements (SLAs) ensures that the DaaS program continues to provide long-term business value to its stakeholders.

- The book concludes by providing best practices with respect to data as a service (DaaS) project management and delivery. The benefits of employing AGILE methodology for new data services development as an alternative to the traditional software development life cycle is discussed.

- Adopting these best practices and guidelines will ensure that the DaaS program continues to be useful and relevant to stakeholders over the long term.

"A journey of a thousand miles must begin with a single step."

—Lao Tzu

Data has always been considered by organizations as a necessary accessory to the core operations of running a business. In spite of this, for many years it was not considered an asset that could be monetized, in and of itself. However, a complete paradigm shift was witnessed with the advent of several on-demand IT services (e.g., Software as a Service). The latest popular wave of on-demand services is Data as a Service.

Data as a Service: A Framework for Providing Reusable Enterprise Data Services,
First Edition. Pushpak Sarkar.
© 2015 the IEEE Computer Society. Published 2015 by John Wiley & Sons, Inc.

In the last few years, it has been encouraging to see various industries adopt DaaS as part of their business model. The benefits of adopting DaaS have been seen by several organizations that monetized their data assets. As discussed, several data providers such as Experian, Acxiom, D&B, Treasure Data are all utilizing data as a source of profit. As commercial DaaS vendors, they already charge handsomely for providing clients with dossiers of personal data, demographics, credit histories, etc.

The growing acceptance of DaaS is not only restricted to commercial businesses, but is also seen within traditional organizations across industries. Many of these organizations are adopting only some parts of the DaaS framework, using it primarily as an information-delivery mechanism for effective sharing and reuse of enterprise data. However, adopting the DaaS delivery model can also help organizations improve customer satisfaction and save on internal costs significantly, as opposed to merely growing their revenues. Chapter 1 discussed how several public sector and international organizations (such as the UN Statistics Division and the World Bank) already leverage DaaS as a functional component to disseminate data across a widely dispersed global user base. Government agencies around the world such as the Environmental Agency of Singapore are leveraging data services innovatively to alert their citizens swiftly of deadly epidemics such as dengue outbreaks using mobile DaaS applications (see Chapter 11).

Several innovative online retailers are also reshaping their industry by enabling various aspects of DaaS and big data analytics in their business model. Amazon's unique ability to provide product recommendations to customers based on a wealth of data resources including storing a customer's past purchasing transactions, clickstream analysis, friends, and groups has provided them a unique competitive advantage over rivals (Cukier, 2014). Amazon's lead is now being followed by many other online businesses, notably online businesses such as Kayak and Netflix.

Even traditional retail organizations such as Target, Tesco, and Walmart have expanded the nature of their IT operations to big data. They have provided their decision makers with predictions based on big data correlations. For example, by tracking a pregnant consumer's purchases in the first three months of their pregnancy, Target can send relevant sale coupons to the expectant mother for the remaining period of her pregnancy. Such insights gleaned by organizations from their daily business operations using their big data analytics programs will become increasingly commonplace.

As the distinguished computer scientist and father of ubiquitous computing, late Professor Mark Weiser, stated in the early 1990s, "The most profound technologies are those that disappear. They weave themselves into the fabric of our everyday life until they are indistinguishable from it." Much like the telephone or electricity in the late twentieth century (and social networking or mobile phones nowadays), different forms of innovative technology have seeped into our surroundings, quietly and pervasively, often without our realizing it. Many technology-driven business changes also play an integral role in our everyday lives, while our society becomes increasingly connected digitally. DaaS is projected to become a quiet yet ubiquitous part of the networked lives of most consumers and organizations globally.

Getting Ready to Adopt DaaS into an Organization

In spite of its rapid adoption in many sectors, getting started with DaaS is a journey that is unique for every organization. It is unique because not all businesses encounter the same kinds of market pressures, industry competition,n or government regulations. Consequently, they usually do not face the same challenges while sharing data with their service consumers.

This section focuses on sharing a realistic approach to how an organization can go about defining, establishing, and maintaining a DaaS initiative for its own unique needs. Given the complexity involved in each of these areas, having an initial assessment of the current state of data management maturity can be very helpful for setting up a DaaS roadmap for an organization (Figure 14.1).

The business-driven roadmap for DaaS can act as a glue to hold all activities together and align the enterprise's direction with data-integration efforts on individual project initiatives.

Identify Core Business Capabilities

At the outset, any organization needs to identify the core set of business processes that need to expose data as a reusable service. These are usually a small and stable set of company processes that the organization needs to pay close attention to in order to stay ahead of its competitors (e.g., supply chain services). The business needs to look at their existing capabilities and collectively assess if they want to continue to retain these capabilities, or alternatively, if they want to look at developing new capabilities to respond to future market opportunities and challenges. While developing this strategic roadmap, most companies wish to evolve and grow further in areas in which

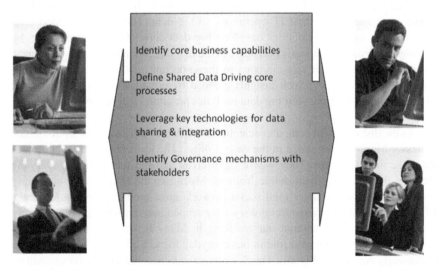

Identify core business capabilities

Define Shared Data Driving core processes

Leverage key technologies for data sharing & integration

Identify Governance mechanisms with stakeholders

Figure 14.1   Initial assessment and planning for setting up a DaaS framework

they already have a core competency. For example, when Amazon launched its new foray into the tablet market with the Kindle fire, it was banking on its capabilities of online book selling, e-book readers, and the Cloud infrastructure.

Define Shared Data

The enterprise also needs to identify data that are critical at the enterprise level and that need to be shared across business divisions.

Defining relevant shared data is an essential aspect of any DaaS planning effort. It is required to accurately rationalize, consolidate, and analyze information from numerous data sources. Certain program initiatives such as building an enterprise data model, business glossary, and related governance controls/policies should be one of the first steps in the improvement process, as they establishes broad consensus and agreement between various divisions on the relationships and hierarchies between data entities and business terms. It can also help reduce the risk of non-compliance to government regulations (SOX, HIPAA, PHI, etc.).

Identify Key Strategies for Data Sharing and Integration

Part of achieving an effective foundation for DaaS deployment includes defining underlying technology integration components, the ways in which systems and capabilities should be built, and how they should interact with one another.

The use of appropriate project management-related control techniques is also necessary to help minimize the project scope and feature creep for individual data services. During the project definition phase, commercial data providers who are introducing any new set of data services for the first time should prepare a draft version of the proposed service blueprint.

As part of the overall blueprint, organizations should clearly identify all critical data services that will need to be built from scratch. They should also identify existing services that may require significant modification or enhancements. Adopting these best practices can help ensure that development efforts are in line with the overall vision of DaaS stakeholders and that programs are effectively managed.

Finally, it is important to emphasize that it is critical to develop a realistic timeline for the deployment of new services and realize that it's an ongoing process, not a time-limited project when embarking on a DaaS program.

DaaS Project Lifecycle

The key project lifecycle phases in a typical DaaS environment include the following:

- **Strategize and plan:** The key activities of this phase include making a business case for introducing Enterprise-wide Data Services. Draft a charter to gain agreement on the DaaS vision from stakeholders and obtain funding for the project.

Scope the project and establish resources, budget, and governance systems. Integrate the project with strategic IT and business plans.

- **Architect solution:** Define the architecture, technology, and standards for the project: Create a canonical model based on business requirements. Finalize the most critical services that have to be developed and recommend how to implement the project. Define process details and performance metrics then communicate the plan.

- **Recommend solution:** Finalize solution requirements and service-design specifications for solution delivery. Evaluate vendor/service-provider options and then choose technologies and vendors/service providers. Conduct proof of concept (POC) to demonstrate the feasibility of the proposed solution. Negotiate service-level agreements (SLAs) and contracts.

- **Deploy data services:** Develop a realistic timeline for the program implementation. Deploy the solution and manage the implementation of data services, implementing a robust and scalable infrastructure to establish the DaaS framework for your environment. Revise in response to feedback, risks, and changing business requirements. Measure performance and also monitor use and compliance. Develop skills and define best practices for users. Refine data governance (DG) processes to address change-management issues in the future.

- **Post-implementation:** Maintain and support data services. Periodically monitor the level of DaaS service performance to mitigate risks after the data services are implemented and the program evolves over the long-run. Look for new growth and improvement opportunities, and realize that it's an ongoing process, not a time-limited project.

SERVICE PERFORMANCE MEASUREMENT USING THE BALANCED SCORECARD

Using the balanced scorecard approach, businesses can help address multiple business priorities across the organization to improve their performance against key performance indicators.

Historically, performance measurement systems for most businesses have been financial in nature. However, in many business situations, financial indicators do not tell the entire story. Comparing two companies with similar financial situations but in completely different market environments could be disastrous.

Robert S. Kaplan and David Norton, who invented the balanced scorecard concept, saw the necessity for a framework to obtain and implement feedback on the effectiveness of any company's strategies within the organization. They coined the term "balanced scorecard" in a series of articles for the *Harvard Business Review* in the mid 1990s. Instead of focusing solely on a company's financial goals, this tool requires decision makers to consider the impact of strategic decisions on staff, customers, and on the organization's function (Kaplan, 1996). More specifically, the balanced-scorecard model offers a way for a corporation to gain a wider perspective on its strategic decisions by considering impacts on finances, customers, internal processes, and employee learning. The analysis takes into account financial and non-financial measures, internal improvements, past outcomes, and ongoing requirements as indications of future performance.

To measure success in organizational performance, you must view the organization from the following perspectives: customer perspective, financial perspective, internal business-process perspective, as well as learning and growth perspective.

These four perspectives should contain measures that have a unity of purpose directed toward achieving an integrated business strategy for the organization. Every measure selected should be part of a link in cause-and-effect relationships, ending in financial objectives that ultimately affect the growth of the organization.

A well-defined scorecard should contain a good mix of outcome measures (or long-term targets) along with performance drivers to track progress in the short term. Usually, outcome measures are generic in nature (e.g., employee productivity, user satisfaction) and are *lagging indicators*. In contrast, performance drivers are usually company-specific measures that reveal the effectiveness of company strategy.

A word of caution here. In spite of capturing multiple perspectives, the balanced scorecard must retain a strong emphasis on financial outcomes if the tool is to be accepted by senior management. In fact, according to Kaplan and Norton, when they proposed the balanced-scorecard methodology, they noted that if a company's improved operational performance fails to be converted into an overall improved financial performance, the managers responsible for the balanced scorecard should rethink the company's strategy or its implementation plans (Kaplan, 1996).

The balanced scorecard approach can be used by IT departments for measuring the overall performance of information management (IM) in the enterprise as well as the effective utilization of data services published by any organization.

Typically, the IT department can use the balanced scorecard approach to assess the impact of the organization's business strategy (e.g., entering a new business line or product category) on the existing DaaS portfolio of data services. It can further determine how the IT organization can align itself to support the customer organization's overall objectives on what kind of data services they want. The introduction of a metrics-driven dashboard to measure actual performance against stated objectives can go a long way toward increasing the credibility of enterprise-driven IM initiatives (such as DaaS) in the eyes of external subscribers to these data services.

Organizations can also utilize this scorecard for data quality measurement. This can go a long way in establishing credibility and tracking the progress of large, multi-year DaaS programs. IT leaders developing a balanced scorecard specifically for their EDS projects should take the following steps to develop measurable goals in each of the model's four areas:

- **Financial contribution**: Determine the overall business value of EDS after weighing the overall cost of the project against the benefits it will deliver. Both short-term and long-term investment costs need to be evaluated against projected value and benefits.

- **Customer focus**: Consider the impact of DaaS projects on the customers requiring information and the expected benefits to the customers over the lifecycle of the organization. The overall quality of customer experience for subscribers of a data service needs to be given a high priority.

- **Operational excellence**: Define the core internal processes of the IT department that determine operational excellence of service delivery in terms of timelines, accessibility, and scalability aspects of a data service.

- **Organization maturity**: Determine whether the organization is ready to meet future technology challenges (Sarkar, 2003). This topic is discussed further later on in this chapter.

From the customer's perspective for an EDS, the following measures are performance drivers for the DaaS Performance scorecard:

- System availability of DaaS applications.
- Response time of user requests.
- Timely delivery of published data.

Similarly, the DaaS team should invest significantly in user training in order to boost overall department productivity. Top managers in IT cannot measure whether their overall strategy is effective without tracking both actual training days as a performance-driver measure as well as outcome measures in the form of employee productivity.

IMPLEMENTING THE PERFORMANCE SCORECARD TO IMPROVE DATA SERVICES

During the initial stage, the DaaS scorecard is a shared vision for a corporate IT strategy that the entire organization is trying to achieve. It is a shared strategic framework used for sharing best practices that facilitate synergies across the organization. Figure 14.2 depicts a sample scorecard for tracking DaaS improvements.

The shared vision for quality and performance improvement is only the starting point because organizations can *benefit* only when the corrective actions identified in the data service scorecard receive appropriate funding to be implemented by the IT organization.

The cause-and-effect relationships between various measures in the data service scorecard can also enable the organization to embark on a strategic learning process. To achieve long-term success, the data service scorecard must be integrated with other management systems/monitoring mechanisms in the IT organization. During the capital-budgeting process, IT managers can use the scorecard as a key mechanism for tracking progress on strategic data services initiatives. IT portfolio planning should also include corrective steps identified from the scorecard to ensure the alignment of future investments and discretionary spending plans with company-wide priorities.

Customer Focus	Operational Efficiency

Mission
 To be the preferred supplier of DaaS to help customers maximize business opportunities
 	
 Objectives
   – Develop trust and collaboration by sharing information with internal partners and external customers
   – Become the preferred supplier of data to internal and external data subscribers
   – Enhance customer/user satisfaction with quality of data services received
	Mission
	 To deliver high-quality and efficient operations of data services across the enterprise
	
	 Objectives
	   – Provide flawless DaaS operations
	   – Fulfillment of service levels/SLA
	   – Establish quality design and development processes that follow industry data standards
	   – Better management of IT resources and infrastructure
	   – Build reliable partnerships with data suppliers and vendors

Financial Contribution	Organization Maturity

Mission
 To obtain a measurable financial contribution from investment in data services
 	
 Objectives
   – Reduce IT department expenses by reuse of shared data services
   – Achieve cost savings by reuse of deployed data services on new and existing IT projects
   – Maximize business revenue by providing "data as a service" to external/third parties
	Mission
	 To develop opportunities to position DaaS to answer future growth opportunities
	
	 Objectives
	   – Identify and ensure growth in strategic technology/skills
	   – Build employee skills and expertise on DaaS-related areas with regular training and education programs
	   – Improve employee satisfaction and productivity

Figure 14.2   Example of balanced scorecard for driving data service quality improvements

EMBARKING ON THE DaaS JOURNEY WITH A VISION

As this book near its end, do be reminded that implementing DaaS (or even some of the individual EDS components) and that taking this journey from concept to reality in your organization can initially be arduous. For a few organizations, the journey is similar to Christopher Columbus and his attempted journey to reach India. Of course, it is yet another matter that he reached the shores of America, and that fame and fortune followed him thereafter. While these kinds of unforeseen events can happen to a few organizations, for most organizations taking the DaaS journey from concept to reality is a challenging process that may often veer off course. This is why developing a DaaS vision and roadmap is so essential. The DaaS roadmap can also include key functions and work deliverables to plan the architecture that matches the organization's current processes, capabilities, and maturity level.

However, not all organizations will have matured completely along this roadmap or at the same pace. Many organizations can face challenges that may be influenced by external business factors. In these situations, sometimes it is wise for the organization not to be subservient to business needs.

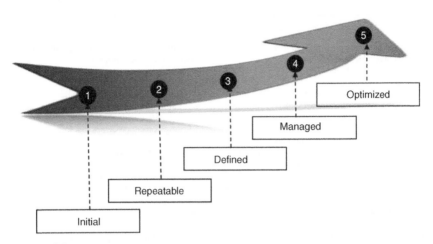

Figure 14.3 Data maturity curve for data providers

The roadmap needs to assess where an organization is currently on the overall data maturity curve and then define what steps are needed to create a streamlined path to an actively controlled, data-driven enterprise that leverages its data as a strategic asset. The underlying philosophy behind data maturity levels is how much governance and how many process-related controls need to be put in place by any data provider. There are four maturity levels for organizations as they encounter the challenges of managing data and their related service components.

Figure 14.3 shows the maturity levels that can be seen evolving in organizations implementing DaaS with growing organizational maturity. These maturity levels are largely adapted from the capability and maturity model (SEI-CMU, 1994).

Maturity Level 1: Initial

These organizations are in the initial stage of maturity and have no awareness or understanding of the pit that they have already fallen into without realizing it while developing data services to support divisional applications in a siloed manner. The chaos seen across the organization in this state is visible and stressful to whoever works in such a DaaS environment (as many of us have seen firsthand). It goes without saying therefore that this chaotic approach has several failings: It is disruptive to both the key business stakeholders and the IT operations supporting data. The organizational leadership soon realizes that it is expensive to maintain DaaS like this over a period of time and might then initiate efforts to improve its maturity toward the next level.

Maturity Level 2: Repeatable

These organizations have already employed a few software (SW) engineering capabilities reactively to solve IM problems in specific departments or functional areas.

Maturity Level 2 introduces a few of these processes in a repeatable manner across several projects in the organization. Few resources with skilled people are made available to initiate this change within the organization to reuse these processes. However, during the initial days, the project resources that are committed are often either not adequate or individuals work part time on DaaS projects. There is also no compliance expectation in the newly defined quality processes at the project level. The focus is mainly on fighting fires as and when they surface to the leadership.

Maturity Level 3: Defined

These companies view enterprise data as a key asset and differentiator for the company's business. They often have defined processes and technologies in place to gain insight into their data and to make decisions that are more intelligent. They consider DaaS to be a core infrastructure component of their business landscape. These companies use EDS as a competitive weapon, not just as something to be governed and managed. Most of these managed processes are also planned and executed in accordance with the policy defined by the enterprise data governance council. Adequate resources with skilled people are made available to make this change within the organization over the lifecycle. However, major portions of the organization cannot opt out.

Maturity Level 4: Managed

These companies recognize the opportunity in employing greater levels of information governance and implementing DaaS systems with expanded sets of user bases. They proactively engage with data subscribers before it hurts the company. Most managed processes are controlled with proven statistical and other quantitative process-control techniques. The impact of this type of a managed environment and work culture can be compelling, often helping to lower the total cost of operation (TCO), lower the risks and regulatory costs, streamline the IT infrastructure, create greater visibility of the enterprise data, and implement proper data management policies. The DaaS and IT support organization form partnerships with the business team leadership to identify new applications for reusable data services in the future.

Maturity Level 5: Optimized

The organization has seen significant benefits from DaaS and its impact on the bottom line is significant and dramatic. Process performance is continuously improved by the leadership in these companies through innovative and incremental technology advances. Most of the managed processes defined in the organization earlier are now optimized to keep them ready for any future changes in the industry. The leadership in these organizations will design new categories of data services where the possibility of error is nearly zero. This is because they would not consider having any new types of services without having EIM standards in place.

Typically the preparation for a business transformation or radical infrastructure changes that are required to initiate a DaaS program need continuous architecture reviews or development efforts. These will be effective when IT efforts made are aligned to current processes, capabilities, and maturity level of the business organization.

USING AGILE PRINCIPLES FOR NEW DATA SERVICES DEVELOPMENT

The waterfall method of software development with a software development life cycle (SDLC) is still quite popular in large organizations. However, the AGILE methodology has grown increasingly popular for iterative SW development as an alternative to the traditional SDLC. This is largely because of the assumption (some term this as a limitation) in the waterfall methodology, which is to complete full documentation at the end of every phase. Without sign-off and approval, projects following waterfall methodology cannot progress to the next phase. In contrast to this, most users working on new technology services or projects often are not clear what they want, until they see the service working. This makes it vital that business and IT teams become close partners from the early development phase on any new service.

In contrast to the waterfall approach, AGILE processes can allow for changing requirements throughout the development cycle and this makes them ideally suited for projects with rapidly changing or volatile requirements such as web projects or new SW product development. AGILE is a conceptual framework that promotes foreseen interactions throughout the development cycle. The methodology includes a group of SW development methods based on iterative and incremental development, where requirements and solutions evolve through collaboration between self-organizing, cross-functional teams. Let us now briefly discuss how an organization can adopt an AGILE approach to DaaS deployment.

A major trend seen in the data services industry is the increased need felt by business organizations to react faster to changes in the marketplace. In the early days, before services became popular, companies built large monolithic applications to support specific needs of the organization. However, with time, the SW landscape became increasingly complex. Most people realized that to integrate these applications in tandem with other legacy areas was time consuming, expensive, and often had risky impacts on business operations. Business events such as company mergers and acquisitions are becoming commonplace, which compels management to change their plans at very short notice. Moreover, as frequently observed in complex, real-life IT project environments, many detailed project requirements are modified by the client as they see data services develop (Larman, 2004).

Therefore, the DaaS organization has to keep its architecture flexible and be in a changeable state at any time. This can be better addressed if an organization follows a methodology such as AGILE as opposed to the traditional waterfall methodology. The AGILE methodology has proven to be very effective in driving collaboration between SW developers, business analysts, and end customers, resulting in early product delivery. The processes that are most commonly considered in AGILE include lean development, extreme programming (XP), and SCRUM.

Consequently, data provider organizations will continue to shift toward a more iterative, AGILE-driven development model to focus on enhancing business changes for the customer's competitive advantage. This may mean developing and delivering data services modules in an iterative mode with smaller intervals and at shorter frequencies. Following the AGILE approach can also help in identifying gaps quicker and lowering overall delivery risk by releasing the DaaS product in smaller increments.

QA Best Practices for Managing Data Service Projects

Quality assurance and testing is a critical aspect for DaaS because of its impact at the enterprise-level. The cost of failure can be especially hard for a commercial data provider deploying data services that are likely to be reused by different clients on multiple projects. Even organizations deploying data services on projects internally have to rigorously test their critical data service components. This heavy emphasis on QA/Testing is similar to any other complex, enterprise-level IT development project.

Testing efforts can be broadly categorized into the following group of activities:

- Unit testing: This refers to testing an individual data service component.
- Load testing: This refers to testing a component under a specified load in a given timeframe.
- System testing: This refers to the end-to-end testing of the service as a part of an integrated system to verify that it meets its requirements.
- User acceptance testing (UAT): This form of testing ensures that the operational results of a DaaS component are consistent with the user's original expectations (usually specified in their functional requirements specification).

Thorough integration and testing efforts ensure that the different services developed independently, perform well together in a real-life DaaS environment. These efforts should also be complemented with a full regression test (preferably in a blackbox environment) to generate confidence among users before actually deploying the new data services.

Under AGILE, the business people and developers must meet together daily or a few times a week to identify issues and adapt or make changes in direction. This is in contrast to the waterfall model, where IT and business people do not often not validate each other's work until the system testing and user acceptance testing (UAT) phases. More detail on the AGILE methodology is beyond the scope of this book but readers are encouraged to use the suggested reading listed on this topic at end of the book, because the AGILE methodology (and related components such as SCRUM) are highly recommended for organizations interested in rolling out data services on a large scale. AGILE can be leveraged to drive DaaS development efforts, as the methodology is well suited for parallel, iterative developments.

Major Drivers for Adopting a DaaS Framework

Business

- Make data available to consumers easier and faster
- Generate revenues by selling data based on pricing structure
- Enable global accessibility of data
- Ensure compliance to industry standards on sensitive data
- Facilitate data interoperability/sharing with major partners

Enterprise

- Provide a consistent enterprise view of data across an organization
- Use a common and shared business vocabulary for usage
- Reduce maintenance costs through reuse and less rework
- Prevent investments in redundant systems
- Ease of administration and compatibility among diverse platforms

---

SUSTAINING DaaS IN AN ORGANIZATION: HOW TO KEEP THE PROGRAM GOING

Once the quality scorecard measurement system is in place and tangible performance improvements are gradually realized, it is very important for the DaaS program team to periodically monitor overall service quality of data services it publishes. It is always recommended to start small in the initial phase while setting up the DaaS quality and performance measurement system. However, once the EDS scorecard-measurement effort has resulted in data being compiled, analyzed, categorized, and flagged for known defect anomalies, the case can effectively be made to increase size and funding for a fully developed data quality program.

While implementing the scorecard in the organization, the strategic feedback and learning process is a critical factor in determining the success of IT quality and performance-improvement initiatives. Ultimately, strategic feedback/learning mechanism help the organization to adapt the DaaS IM strategy to emerging conditions in the business environment (Figure 14.4).

Performance-measurement objectives captured formally in the scorecard should be communicated throughout the IT department in order to maximize employee commitment. In addition, the individual objectives of IT employees should be linked to the EDS scorecard for maximum effectiveness because individuals in different parts of the organization cannot often understand how their individual pieces fit together. Understanding the correlation between two or more measures enhances

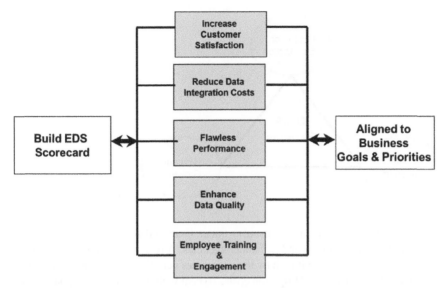

Figure 14.4   Role of feedback/learning process in data services scorecard initiatives

cross-functional system thinking for individual managers across divisions, and can lead to further performance improvements (Sarkar, 2003).

In addition, it may be beneficial to conduct regular, periodic reviews for leadership to assess and understand the DaaS program's positive and negative aspects. While positive areas can be used to reinforce and encourage others to use DaaS components, the negative aspects and risks encountered (e.g., data security breach) need to be addressed promptly. There needs to be a proactive approach taken by DaaS program leadership in preventing any major risks to the organization as they distribute data to service subscribers and external agencies.

Managing Risks to a DaaS Program

Any organization interested in deploying Data Services has to regularly assess their own internal risks and vulnerability while publishing data as a service. Any security incident resulting from data being exploited by cybercriminals and hackers can have serious consequences for the organization if it exposes sensitive or confidential data of their customers (e.g., PII data like SSN, Name). Therefore, it is recommended that organizations adopt a comprehensive mechanism toward managing information risks at the enterprise level. In recent years, many of these risks completely damage an organization's image and goodwill as exposure of sensitive client data can harm customers in a very significant manner. The data breach at Target mentioned earlier severely impacted not only its revenues but also its brand and trust among millions of its loyal customers

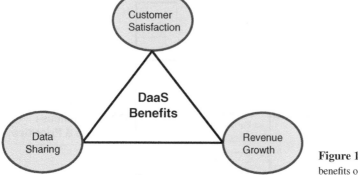

Figure 14.5   Key benefits of adopting DaaS

Additionally, organizations are also under increased regulatory pressures and oversight from government and consumer agencies. Any non-compliance, deliberate or otherwise, are being dealt with by these agencies very firmly resulting in damaged reputation, loss of trust, and litigation costs. To deal with these risks, most businesses across industries are increasingly being driven to set up a comprehensive risks and security framework to manage the complex process of identifying, assessing, measuring, managing, and mitigating the various risk factors seen when implementing DAAS and related technology.

In addition, having a lessons-learned document from immediate project failures is highly recommended while the pain of the negative experiences is still fresh. As many of us are aware, those who fail to learn from the mistakes of their predecessors are destined to repeat them.

DaaS and Its Value Proposition

Adopting the DaaS framework make businesses *more agile* by becoming less impacted by dependencies on technology or data platforms. While technology decisions will not become irrelevant, they will not slow down business organizations from making key decisions due to technology or platform constraints. This will make the question as to which service to offer more relevant compared to what technology is required to implement that service. Figure 14.5 reflects some of the key benefits of a DaaS program.

- **Customer satisfaction**: With its focus on reusable and flexible architecture, the DaaS framework offers a foundational data access layer for querying data in real time across the enterprise. DaaS can become a strategic enabler for sharing data with customers about company products that they are interested in purchasing or in browsing online or on social media sites. This is likely to increase customer satisfaction in the long run.

- **Revenue growth**: By improvising on-demand data services to potential clients, DaaS can be leveraged even further by organizations through mining customer, social media, and online conversations over a big data platform. By predicting the monetizing intent of consumers to buy company products through sophisticated predictive algorithms and data analytics tools, DaaS can help drive revenues for some organizations.

- **Information sharing**: Establish and maintain data flow to a federated or virtual data layer that is accessible through a standardized set of data services. The underlying canonical model and exchange format is agreed upon by the data stewards as the enterprise standard for data exchange. By ensuring that common data and XML standards are used, DaaS enables easier data integration between applications on different platforms.

Moreover, building an infrastructure based on the DaaS framework can provide an organization with an alternate approach that is likely less costly, but also introduces less risk to IT stakeholders.

The majority of business organizations offer DaaS to consumers as a complimentary or public service for information distribution (again, reflect on the examples of the environmental agency in Singapore battling epidemics or the UN Data division disseminating statistical data globally). On the other hand, there are several business organizations that have already identified data assets they can rent to consumers for commercial advantage as data providers. More companies are anticipated to follow this trend of monetizing data utilizing the DaaS framework.

IN CONCLUSION

The true value of data reuse is still not fully appreciated by most businesses today. The DaaS framework can be viewed as an innovative approach toward introducing reusable data services as a strategic enabler to a business. The DaaS-related concepts presented in this book will also allow organizations to utilize data as an enterprise asset that can be monetized with relative ease. These changes can drive some data provider businesses to increase revenues by publishing different types of data as a service to their consumers. This is in contrast to the older view of data and database systems as mere backend IT functions.

Throughout the book, how organizations can leverage data as a service has been demonstrated whether by adopting various architectures, best practices, or techniques. The demand for data providers to publish a catalog of data services to subscribers will increase exponentially as consumers come to expect on-demand data for day-to-day usage. With the recent preference seen among consumers toward social shopping and mobile computing, the adoption of the DaaS business model in a few industry sectors such as retail, healthcare, and finance will only continue to grow. As organizations engage customers more heavily in these sectors, DaaS is likely to become a core aspect of their business strategy.

With additional acceleration in the demand for big data analytics, IT divisions are being challenged by their leaders to obtain analytical insights collected from data sets that are available to them. They are expected to provide data driven insights to decision makers in a quick, timely, and efficient manner. DaaS can help a company gain a substantial market advantage over its competitors if it executes these activities better.

Defining reusable data services at the enterprise level with standard data formats and applications can also make it faster and more convenient to deploy new services. Standardized XML schema-based messages that utilize the canonical model, controlled vocabularies, and industry standards can make data exchange processes more efficient and secure (as trendsetter organizations such as Amazon, Google, and Kayak have visibly demonstrated).

A few setbacks should be expected during the initial steps of your DaaS journey, as with any other strategic-transformation initiative. However, organizations have to look beyond these roadblocks and remain on the journey (just as Columbus did) by employing patience. Visionary organizations need to consider DaaS as a vehicle to reorient themselves fundamentally to meet the growing demands of service-enabled organizations. Their IT divisions need to make data available to consumers securely, at a time and place of their choice. I hope that by reading this book, you will take the first step in your journey by welcoming DaaS into your organization.

Appendix A

Data Standards Initiatives and Resources

Most of the comments in this appendix are taken from the websites provided in the table.

Resource	Description	Source
National Institute on Standards and Technology, (formerly the Bureau of Standards) (NIST)	An agency of the Department of Commerce that creates many of the federal government's security standards, which are mandated for use in government agencies and often by their contractors.	www.nist.gov
Data Management Association Body of Knowledge (DMBOK)	Data Management Association (DAMA) Body of Knowledge comprises a comprehensive list of Data Management standards and guidelines.	www.dama.org
National Resource for Global Standards	A search engine that provides users with standards-related information from a wide range of developers, including organizations accredited by the American National Standards Institute (ANSI), other US private sector standards bodies, government agencies, and international organizations.	www.nssn.org

Data as a Service: A Framework for Providing Reusable Enterprise Data Services,
First Edition. Pushpak Sarkar.
© 2015 the IEEE Computer Society. Published 2015 by John Wiley & Sons, Inc.

Resource	Description	Source
Standards.gov	Maintained and operated by the National Institute of Standards and Technology (NIST), Standards.gov supports the requirements of the National Technology Transfer and Advancement Act (NTTAA), which became law in March 1996. The NTTAA directs federal agencies with respect to their use of private sector standards and conformity assessment practices. The objective is for federal agencies to adopt private sector standards, wherever possible, in lieu of creating proprietary, nonconsensus standards.	http://standards.gov/ standards_gov/v/ Standards/index.cfm
ISO/IEC/IEEE 42010:2011	ISO/IEC/IEEE 42010:2011 defines requirements on the description of system, software, and enterprise architectures. It aims to standardize the practice of architecture description by defining standard terms, presenting a conceptual foundation for expressing, communicating, and reviewing architectures as well as specifying requirements that apply to architecture descriptions, architecture frameworks, and architecture description languages.	www.IEEE.org
IEEE standard 1471-2000	IEEE standard 1471-2000 defines SOA as an Integration Architecture in which components are available through services. This standard has been superseded in 2011 by the ISO/IEC/IEEE 42010:2011.	www.IEEE.org
ISO 3166	The purpose of ISO 3166 is to define internationally recognized codes of letters and/or numbers that we can use when we refer to countries and subdivisions. However, it does not define the names of countries. This information comes from United Nations sources.	www.iso.org
ISO 4217	ISO 4217 is a standard published by the International Organization for Standardization, which delineates currency designators, country codes (alpha and numeric), and references to minor units in three tables.	www.iso.org
ISO 9362	1994 Banking—Banking telecommunication messages—Bank identifier codes.	www.iso.org

Resource	Description	Source
ISO 20022-1: 2004 and ISO 20022-2:2007 Financial services	Comprises specifications for Universal Financial Industry message schema.	www.iso.org
ISO 10383	2003 securities and related financial instruments—Codes for exchanges and market identification (MIC).	www.iso.org
ISO 15022:	1999 messages (Data Field Dictionary) (replaces ISO 7775) Securities—Scheme for messages (Data Field Dictionary)	www.iso.org
ISO 13616	2003 IBAN Registry—The International Bank Account Number (IBAN) is an internationally agreed system of identifying bank accounts across national borders to facilitate the communication and processing of cross border transactions with a reduced risk of transcription errors. It was originally adopted by the European Committee for Banking Standards (ECBS), and later as an international standard under ISO 13616:1997. The current standard is ISO 13616:2007, which indicates SWIFT as the formal registrar.	www.iso.org
ISO/IEC 11179-3:2013	ISO/IEC 11179-3:2013 specifies the structure of a metadata registry in the form of a conceptual data model. While the model diagrams are presented in UML notation, ISO/IEC 11179-3:2013 does not assume nor endorse any specific system environment, database management system, database design paradigm, system development methodology, data definition language, command language, system interface, user interface, computing platform, or any technology required for implementation. ISO/IEC 11179-3:2013 does not directly apply to the actual use of data in communications and information processing systems.	www.iso.org
Web Services Security (WS-Security)	Web Services Security is an extension to SOAP to apply security to Web services. It is a member of the Web service specifications and was published by OASIS. The protocol specifies how integrity and confidentiality can be enforced on messages and allows the communication of various security token formats, such as Security Assertion Markup Language (SAML), Kerberos, and X.509. Its main focus is the use of XML Signature and XML Encryption to provide end-to-end security.	https://www .oasis-open .org/

Resource	Description	Source
eXtensible Access Control Markup Language (XACML)	The XACML standard is specified by Organization for the Advancement of Structured Information Standards (OASIS). It defines a declarative access control policy language implemented in XML and a processing model describing how to evaluate access requests according to the rules defined in policies.	https://www.oasis-open.org/
Society for Worldwide Interbank Financial Telecommunication (SWIFT)	SWIFT is the Society for Worldwide Interbank Financial Telecommunication, a member-owned cooperative through which the financial world conducts its business operations with speed, certainty, and confidence. More than 10,500 banking organizations, securities institutions, and corporate customers in 215 countries trust SWIFT every day to exchange millions of standardized financial messages. SWIFT has become the industry standard for syntax in financial messages. Messages formatted to SWIFT standards can be read by, and processed by, many well-known financial processing systems, whether or not the message traveled over the SWIFT network. SWIFT cooperates with international organizations for defining standards for message format and content. • ISO 15022: 1999 messages (Data Field Dictionary) (replaces ISO 7775) Securities—Scheme for messages (Data Field Dictionary) • ISO 20022-1: 2004 and ISO 20022-2:2007 Financial services—UNIversal Financial Industry message scheme	www.swift.com
Legal Entity Identifier (LEI)	A unique ID associated with a single legal entity, LEIs allow for consistent identification of parties to financial transactions, facilitating a consistent and integrated view of exposures. The establishment of an LEI system is a foundational and critically important element towards the improved measurement and monitoring of systemic risk.	http://www.gfma.org/initiatives/legal-entity-identifier-(lei)/legal-entity-identifier-(lei)/

Resource	Description	Source
	A global, standardized LEI will enable organizations to more effectively measure and manage counterparty exposure, while providing substantial operational efficiencies and customer service improvements to the industry. Significant progress has been made on the FSB's global LEI initiative. The foundation of LEI reporting is underway: the LEI Regulatory Oversight Committee (ROC), established by the FSB, has endorsed 12 utilities to date to issue pre-LEIs that firms can utilize as work on the global system is finalized. There is a regulatory mandate for pre-LEI reporting in the United States through the Commodity Futures Trading Commission's (CFTC) swaps recordkeeping rules; the European Banking Authority (EBA) recently published its Recommendation on LEIs; the European Market Infrastructure Regulation (EMIR) deadline for pre-LEI reporting is February 12, 2014; and regulators around the world in places such as Canada, Australia, and Hong Kong have embraced the LEI concept.	
Association for Cooperative Operations Research and Development (ACORD)	The ACORD-based standards has gained significant acceptance and usage in the insurance sector for exchange of data across insurance companies, their agents, and third-parties in the last few years.	www.acord.org
Payment Card Industry Data Security Standard (PCI–DSS)	PCI DSS is a proprietary information security standard for organizations that handle branded credit cards from the major card brands including Visa, MasterCard, American Express, Discover, etc. The PCI Standards is now mandated by the card brands and run by the Payment Card Industry Security Standards Council. The standard was created to increase controls around cardholder data to reduce credit card fraud via its exposure.	https://www.pcisecuritystandards.org/index.php

Resource	Description	Source
United Nations Standard Products and Services Codes	This is an open standard to define a cross-industry classification of products and services for global use throughout the e-commerce market place efficiently and accurately.	www.unspsc.org
Web Service Description Language	WSDL is an XML-based language for describing web-services.	www.w3.org/TR/wsdl
Web Ontology Language (OWL)	A language designed for use by software applications that process the content of information instead of just presenting information to humans. There are three sublanguages currently available: OWL Lite, OWL DL, and OWL Full.	www.w3.org/TR/owl -features/
XML Schema Definition (XSD)	XSD specifies how to formally describe the element in a XML document in a standardized manner. This description can also be used to verify that each item of content in a XML document adheres to the description of the element in the syntax.	www.w3.org/XML/ Schema
Systematized Nomenclature of Medicine (SNOMED)	SNOMED is a clinical terminology used as a common vocabulary to facilitate communications between healthcare professionals in clear and unambiguous terms.	www.ihtsdo.org/our _standards
Accredited Standards Committee X12 (also known as ASC X12)	ASC X12 comprises of Electronic data interchange (EDI) and Context Inspired Component Architecture (CICA) standards along with XML schemas which drive business processes globally. ASC X12 standards encompass health care, insurance, transportation, supply chain, and other industries.	www.x12.org
Health Level Seven (HL7)	Health Level Seven (HL7) provides standards for interoperability that improve care delivery, optimize workflow, reduce ambiguity, and enhance knowledge transfer among healthcare organizations, including healthcare providers, government agencies, the vendor community, and patients. "Level Seven" refers to the seventh level of the International Organization for Standardization (ISO) seven-layer communications model for Open Systems Interconnection (OSI).	www.hl7.org

Resource	Description	Source
Health Information Technology Ontology Project (HITOP)	The Health Information Technology Community of Practice and its Health Information Technology Ontology Project (HITOP) is a federal group that will make recommendations for systematically improving healthcare while reducing healthcare costs and help achieve semantic interoperability through the use of ontology software in high priority health IT projects that will both save money and improve the quality of care.	http://colab.cim3.net/ cgi-bin/wiki.pl?He althInformationTec hnologyCommuni tyofPractice#nid 35Z7
Healthcare Information Technology Standards Panel (HITSP)	One of the Department of Health and Human Services (HHS) contracts charged with bringing U.S. standards developers and other stakeholders together to develop, prototype, and evaluate a harmonization process for achieving a widely accepted and useful set of health IT standards that will support interoperability among healthcare software applications.	www.ansi.org/standar ds_activities/standa rds_boards_panels/ hisb/hitsp.aspx?me nuid=3
National Cancer Institute Cancer Biomedical Informatics Grid (caBIG)	The Cancer Biomedical Informatics Grid, or caBIG, is a voluntary network or grid connecting individuals and institutions to enable the sharing of data and tools, creating a World Wide Web of cancer research. The goal is to speed the delivery of innovative approaches for the prevention and treatment of cancer. The infrastructure and tools created by caBIG also have broad utility outside the cancer community.	https://cabig.nci.nih .gov/
National Center for Health Statistics (NCHS) Public Health Data Standards Consortium	The NCHS Public Health Data Standards Consortium is a national nonprofit member-based partnership of federal, state, and local health agencies, national and local professional associations, and public and private sector organizations and individuals. It serves as health data collectors and data users who actively support the overall goals of developing, promoting, and implementing data standards for population health practice and research.	www.cdc.gov/nchs/ otheract/phdsc/ phdsc.htm

Resource	Description	Source
Office of the National Coordinator for Health Information Technology (ONC)	The Office of the National Coordinator for Health Information Technology provides leadership for the development and nationwide implementation of an interoperable health information technology infrastructure to improve the quality and efficiency of healthcare and the ability of consumers to manage their care and safety.	www.hhs.gov/healthit/
Public Health Information Network (PHIN)	The Public Health Information Network (PHIN) is CDC's vision for advancing fully capable and interoperable information systems in the many organizations that participate in public health. PHIN is a national initiative to implement a multi-organizational business and technical architecture for public health information systems.	www.cdc.gov/PHIN/

Appendix B

Data Privacy & Security Regulations

Listed here are only a few of the major data security and privacy regulations that could globally impact data providers and subscribers.

- **Health Insurance Portability and Accountability Act (HIPAA) 1996** places liability on the healthcare organizations who fail to protect the privacy of patient health information, including bills and health related financial information. The Administrative Simplification provisions in HIPAA requires the establishment of national standards for electronic health care transactions and national identifiers for data related to providers, health insurance plans, and employers.
- **Gramm-Leach-Bliley Financial Modernization Act of 1999 (GLBA)** mandates protection of personal financial information through several data protection measures. It is a landmark act in the area of consumer rights on data privacy dictating how financial institutions can preserve the security and confidentiality of personal and financial data of consumers.
- **Health Information Technology for Economic and Clinical Health Act (HITECH Act) 2009** addresses the privacy and security concerns associated with the electronic transmission of health information. Subtitle D of the HITECH Act requires HIPAA covered entities (providers, insurance, etc.) to report data breaches affecting 500 or more individuals to U.S. agencies and the media, in addition to notifying the affected individuals.
- **Sarbanes Oxley Act (SOX) 2002** requires executives of U.S. corporations to know who has access to what information and ensure that their organizations set up adequate security controls to ensure data confidentiality and integrity. As a result of the Sarbanes Oxley Act (SOX), top management must now individually certify the accuracy of financial information. In addition, penalties for fraudulent financial activity are much more severe.
- **USA Patriot Act (AML and KYC Provisions)** provide greater powers to authorities to regulate financial transactions and gathering of intelligence

Data as a Service: A Framework for Providing Reusable Enterprise Data Services,
First Edition. Pushpak Sarkar.
© 2015 the IEEE Computer Society. Published 2015 by John Wiley & Sons, Inc.

particularly on foreign individuals and entities to prohibit companies from engaging in a financial transaction with organizations and individuals terrorist engaged in specific crimes as well as anti-money laundering (AML). The act also introduced provisions to identify identity of customer with new Know Your Customer (KYC) provisions to strengthen the already existing provisions to make money laundering a federal crime. AML and KYC policies are also becoming used globally by financial institutions to monitor suspicious or illegal movement of money.

- **Code of Federal Regulations (CFR) Title 21 Part 11** defines rules for usage of electronic records and electronic signatures for the U.S. pharmaceutical industry. The Food and Drug Administration(FDA) has established these guidelines to ensure that any individual or organization governed by the FDA, that uses electronic recordkeeping and electronic signatures protect the integrity of data. Part 11 specifically requires drug makers, medical device manufacturers, biotech companies, and other FDA-regulated industries to implement controls, including audits, system validations, audit trails, electronic signatures, and documentation for software and systems involved in processing electronic data.

- **Health Level Seven (HL7)** is a non-profit organization involved in the development of international healthcare informatics and data interoperability standards. HL7 provides a series of standards and guidelines that provide functional specifications for an electronic health record (EHR) enabling hospitals, physician practices, insurance payers to exchange, share, and access medical information more effectively.

- **BASEL Accord (II and III)** is a comprehensive risk and regulatory control framework used in the financial and banking sector globally. It defines various requirements for operational and credit risks in banks and financial institutions. The regulations facilitate the review process by developing a set of disclosure requirements that can allow the market regulators and other related parties to gauge the capital adequacy of an institution. Banking institutions are required to create a formal policy on what will be disclosed as well as set up security controls around them along with the official validation of these disclosures. BASEL also supplements the current regulations and oversight of banks through sharing of information and facilitates assessment of the bank by external and regulatory means to ensure good corporate governance.

- **National Information Exchange Model (NIEM)** is a U.S. government-sponsored program and international community to provide government and industry with standards for information sharing in support of critical national needs such as fighting terrorism and reducing healthcare costs. NIEM provides XML-Schema based information exchange packages that utilize the controlled vocabularies of the NIEM community, developed under the NIEM process.

- **Australia Privacy Act 1988 for Healthcare information** stipulates a number of privacy rights to consumers. The rights are known as the Information Privacy Principles (IPPs). These principles apply to Australian Government and Australian Capital Territory agencies or private sector organizations contracted to these governments who provide a health service. The principles essentially govern when and how personal information can be collected by these government agencies and ensures that Australians have a right to know why such information about them is being acquired, and who will see the information.

- **EU Data Protection Directive of 1998** is a European Union directive which regulates the usage, identity, and processing of personal data within the European Union. It is an important component of EU privacy and human rights law. The Directive requires organizations to ensure personal data of all their consumers must be kept confidential. Individuals should also know what information is collected about them, how it will be used and by whom, who is entitled to change their personal data, and how it will be stored securely. On 25 January 2012, the European Commission unveiled a draft European General Data Protection Regulation that will supersede the Data Protection Directive.

- **Personal Information Protection Law of Japan (2003)** (PIPL) is a data protection law that regulates the collection and handling of personal information of consumers by business organizations. The law has provision to protect the privacy of customers by ensuring that their information is maintained accurately and up-to-date. It also restricts organization from distribution of private information of consumers to third parties, acquiring personal information in an unlawful manner.

- **Children's Online Privacy Protection (COPPA)** is a United States federal law enacted in 1998 to safeguard online privacy of personal information by persons or entities under U.S. jurisdiction from children under 13 years of age. It details what a website operator must include in a privacy policy, when and how to seek verifiable consent from a parent or guardian, and what responsibilities an operator has to protect children's privacy and safety online including restrictions when marketing to those under 13. In December 2012, the U.S. Federal Trade Commission extended the rules to mobile phones and tablets recognizing the growing use of these devices. The regulations also cover areas like voice recognition, location technology, and behavior-based online advertising.

- **California Senate Bill 1386** requires an agency, person, or business that conducts business in California using computerized "personal information" to disclose any breach of security (to any resident whose unencrypted data is believed to have been disclosed). The bill mandates various mechanisms and procedures with respect to many aspects of this scenario.

- **Homeland Security Information Sharing Act** prohibits public disclosure of certain information on nation's critical infrastructure by the concerned private sector entities.

- **Legal Entity Identifier (LEI)** is a global standard introduced recently by the G20 and managed by the Financial Stability Board (FSB). It will help enable organizations to more effectively measure and manage risk, while providing substantial operational efficiencies and customer service improvements to an industry. In the United States, the LEI Regulatory Oversight Committee (ROC), established by the FSB, has endorsed 12 utilities to date to issue pre-LEIs that firms can utilize as work on the global system is finalized.

- **Do Not Call Implementation Act of 2003** is a U.S. government regulation that includes opt-out requirements to protect customer's privacy for use by unauthorized organizations. The National Do Not Call Registry maintained by the Federal Trade Commission is intended to give U.S. consumers an opportunity to limit the telemarketing calls they receive.

- **Office of Foreign Assets Control (OFAC) and Specially Designated Nationals (SDN).** The Office of Foreign Assets Control enforces economic and trade sanctions based on U.S. foreign policy against doing business with certain foreign countries, terrorist, international drug traffickers, and those engaged in proliferation of weapons of mass destruction. The SDN is related to KYC to verify for U.S. organizations that their customers are not on the OFAC SDN list.

- **Homeland Security Act 2002 (HAS) and Information Analysis and Infrastructure Protection Title.**The Homeland Security Act of 2002 was enacted in the aftermath of the September 11 attacks and subsequent mailings of anthrax spores. The HSA is divided into 17 titles that establishes the Department of Homeland Security and other purposes. The Information Analysis And Infrastructure Protection Title is specifically used to access, receive, and analyze law enforcement information, intelligence information, and other information from federal, state, and local government agencies for further use toward the prevention of terrorist acts.

- **The Payment Card Industry Data Security Standard (PCI DSS)** is a proprietary information security standard for organizations globally that handle branded credit cards from major card brands including Visa, MasterCard, American Express, Discover, etc. The PCI Standards is now mandated by the card brands and run by the Payment Card Industry Security Standards Council. The standard was created to increase controls around cardholder data to reduce credit card fraud via its exposure.

Appendix C

Terms and Acronyms

List of common terms/acronyms used in the book.

ACL	Access Control List
AML	Anti-Money Laundering
B2B	Business to Business
B2C	Business to Consumer
BDAAS	Big Data as a Service
BDSC	Big Data Stream Computing
BI	Business Intelligence
BPM	Business Performance Management
BRE	Business Rules Engine
BRMS	Business Rules Management System
CAMS	Cloud, Analytics, Mobile and Social media
CDI	Customer Data Integration
CIF	Customer Information File
CRM	Customer Relationship Management
CRUD	Create, Read, Update, Delete operations
CMM	Capability Maturity Model
DNC	Do Not Call
DQ	Data Quality
DG	Data Governance
EA	Enterprise Architecture
ECM	Enterprise Canonical Model
EDI	Electronic Data Interchange
EDM	Enterprise Data Model
EDS	Enterprise Data Services
EDW	Enterprise Data Warehouse
EII	Enterprise Information Integration
EIM	Enterprise Information Management
EIA	Enterprise Information Architecture
ELDM	Enterprise Logical Data Model

Data as a Service: A Framework for Providing Reusable Enterprise Data Services,
First Edition. Pushpak Sarkar.
© 2015 the IEEE Computer Society. Published 2015 by John Wiley & Sons, Inc.

EHR	Electronic Health Records
ESB	Enterprise Service Bus
ETL	Extract, Transform, and Load
FDA	U.S. Food and Drug Administration
FDIC	Federal Deposit Insurance Corporation
GLBA	Gramm-Leach-Bliley Act
HDFS	Hadoop Distributed File System
HHS	U.S. Department of Health and Human Services
HIPAA	Health Insurance Profitability and Accountability Act
HL7	Health Level Seven
IAA XML	Insurance Application Architecture XML
IAAS	Infrastructure as a Service
ICD	International Classification of Diseases
IRM	Information Risk Management
ISO	International Standards Organization
IT	Information Technology
IM	Information Management
JDBC	Java Database Connectivity
JMS	Java Message Service
KYC	Know Your Customer
KPI	Key Performance Indicator
LOB	Line of Business
LEI	Legal Entity Identifier
MOM	Message-oriented Middleware
MDM	Master Data Management
MDS	Master Data Services
NPI	National Provider Identifier
OASIS	Organization for the Advancement of Structured Information Standards
ODBC	Open Database Connectivity
ODS	Operational Data Store
OFAC	Office of Foreign Asset Control
OIG	Office of Inspector General
OLTP	Online Transaction Processing
OTA	Open Travel Alliance standard
PAP	Policy Administration Point
PHI	Protected Health Information
PII	Personally Identifiable Information
PEP	Policy Enforcement Point
QA	Quality Assurance
RDBMS	Relational Database Management System
RDM	Reference Data Management
RDS	Reference Data Services
RBAC	Roles-Based Access Control
RFID	Radio Frequency Identification
RUP	Rational Unified Process
SAAS	Software as a Service
SDM	Service Delivery Model
SDN	Specially Designated Nationals
SEC	Security and Exchange Commission

SLA	Service Level Agreement
SOA	Service-Oriented Architecture
SOX	Sarbanes Oxley Act
SSN	Social Security Number
SQL	Structured Query Language
TIN	Tax Identification Number
UI	User Interface
W3C	Worldwide Web Consortium
WSDL	Web Services Description Language
XACML	eXtensible Access Control Markup Language
XML	eXtensible Markup Language
XSD	XML Schema Definition

Appendix D

Bibliography

1. BEAN J. *SOA and Web Services Interface Design*. Burlington, MA: Morgan Kaufman; 2010.

2. BERSON A, DUBOV L. *Master Data Management and Data Governance*. New York: McGraw-Hill/Osborne Media; 2010.

3. COHN, M. Succeeding with AGILE: Software Development Using SCRUM. Boston: Addison-Wesley; 2009.

4. CUKIER K, MAYER-SCHONBERGER V. *Big Data: A Revolution that Will Transform How We Live, Work and Think*. Boston: Houghton Mifflin Harcourt; 2014.

5. DAMA International. *Guide to the Data Management Body of Knowledge (DMBOK)*. Westfield, NJ: Technics Publications, LLC; 2010.

6. DREIBELBIS A, HECHLER E, MILMAN I, OBERHOFER M, VAN RUN P, AND WOLFSON W. *Enterprise Master Data Management*. Armonk, NY: IBM Press; 2008.

7. DRUCKER PF. *The Daily Drucker*. New York: Harper Business Press; 2004.

8. ENGLISH, L. *Improving Data Warehouse and Business Information Quality*. Hoboken, NJ: John Wiley & Sons; 1999.

9. GRIFFIN, J. "The Role of the Chief Data Officers." *DM Review* 18, no. 2, 28; 2008. http://www.information-management.com/issues/2007_44/10000690-1.html.

10. HUANGE K-T, LEE YW, AND WANG RY. *Quality Information & Knowledge*. New York: Prentice Hall; 1999.

11. IEEE Standards Association. Software and Systems Engineering Standards Committee. "1471-2000 – IEEE Recommended Practice for Architectural Description for Software-Intensive Systems." *IEEE Computer Society*. https://standards.ieee.org/findstds/standard/1471-2000.html.

12. KAPLAN RS, NORTON DP. *The Balanced Scorecard: Translating Strategy into Action*. Boston: Harvard Business Review Press; 1996.

13. KRAFZIG D, BANKE K, AND SLAMA D. *Enterprise SOA: Service-Oriented Architecture Best Practices*. New York: Prentice Hall; 2007.

14. LADLEY J. *Making Enterprise Information Management (EIM) Work for Business: A Guide to Understanding Information as an Asset*, Burlington, MA: Morgan Kaufman; 2010.

15. LARMAN C. *Agile and Iterative Development: A Manager's Guide*. Boston: Addison-Wesley; 2004.

Data as a Service: A Framework for Providing Reusable Enterprise Data Services,
First Edition. Pushpak Sarkar.
© 2015 the IEEE Computer Society. Published 2015 by John Wiley & Sons, Inc.

16. Loshin, D. *Master Data Management*. Burlington, MA: Morgan Kaufman; 2009.

17. Loshin, D. *Enterprise Knowledge Management: The Data Quality Approach*. Burlington, MA: Morgan Kaufman; 2001.

18. Moore GA. *Crossing the Chasm*. New York: Harper Business Press; 2002.

19. Paulk MC, Weber CV, Curtis B, Chrissis MB. *The Capability Maturity Model: Guidelines for Improving the Software Process,* SEI Carnegie Mellon University. Boston: Addison-Wesley; 1994.

20. Ross JW, Weill P, and Robertson DC. *Enterprise Architecture As Strategy: Creating a Foundation for Business Execution*, Boston: Harvard Business Review Press; 2006.

21. Sathi A. *Big Data Analytics: Disruptive Technologies for Changing the Game*. Boise, ID: MC Press Online (IBM); 2013.

22. Shih C. *The Facebook Era*. New York: Prentice Hall; 2009.

23. Soares S. *IBM Infosphere: A Platform for Big Data Governance and Process Data Governance*. Boise, ID: MC Press Online (IBM); 2013.

24. Twentyman, J. "Sentiment Analysis at Work: A Sentiment Analysis for the Data Rich." *IT in Europe* 1, no. 1, 1–19; 2011. http://cdn.ttgtmedia.com/rms/pdf/ITinEurope_DM-BI_May2011.pdf.

25. Wood J, Silver D. *Joint Application Development*. Hoboken, NJ: John Wiley & Sons; 1995.

26. Whitten JL, Bentley LD, and Dittman KC. *System Analysis & Design Methods*. New York: McGraw-Hill; 1997.

INTERNET RESOURCES AND FURTHER READING

Following are websites and reading materials providing useful information on the latest developments in DaaS, big data, and analytics. I recommend these resources to gain insight on these evolving topics.

1. Centers for Disease Control. 2012. ICD: Classification of Diseases, Functioning, and Disability. Available at http://www.cdc.gov/nchs/icd.htm.

2. Chisholm M. 2006. Master Data Versus Reference Data, Information Management. Available at http://www.information-management.com/issues/20060401/1051002-1.html.

3. Cohn, M. Succeeding with AGILE: Software Development Using SCRUM. Boston: Addison-Wesley; 2009.

4. DoD CIO. 2007. Department of Defense Net-Centric Services Strategy. Available at http://dodcio.defense.gov/Portals/0/documents/DoD_NetCentricServicesStrategy.pdf.

5. Dyche J. 2011. Data as a Service. Techtarget. Available at http://searchdatamanagement.techtarget.com/answer/Data as-a-service-explained-and-defined.

6. Gartner. 2014. Treasure Data Named Among Cool Vendors in Big Data. Available at http://www.gartner.com/technology/reprints.do?id=1-1TP5I62&ct=140502&st=sg&mkt_tok=3RkMMJWWfF9wsRonu6rJZKXonjHpfsX56ewoXKKxlMI%2F0ER3fOvrPUfGjI4ATMJgI%2BSLDwEYGJlv6SgFTbHBMbhp0LgJWxM%3D.

7. Gartner. 2014. Gartner Says Beware of the Data Lake Fallacy. Available at http://www.gartner.com/newsroom/id/2809117.

8. LADLEY J. 2010. Defining EIM and IAM: Defining the Terms. Available at http://www.b-eye-network.com/view/14512.

9. LARMAN C. *Agile and Iterative Development: A Manager's Guide.* Boston: Addison-Wesley; 2004.

10. IBM Corporation. 2013. Preserving Quality: Fundamentals of Reference Data Management. *IBM Software Group.* Available at http://public.dhe.ibm.com/common/ssi/ecm/im/en/imm14099usen/IMM14099USEN.PDF.

11. IBM. 2005. Transforming Data Management in the Financial Markets Industry. Available at http://www-935.ibm.com/services/us/imc/pdf/g510-6100-transforming-data management.pdf.

12. INMON B. 2014. Look at Big Data in Different Ways to Find Business Value. Available at http://ibmdatamag.com/2014/09/look-at-big-data-in-different-ways-to-find-business-value/?utm_source=IBM+Data+magazine+newsletter&utm_campaign=d7f65a9e7 b-September_30_2014&utm_medium=email&utm_term=0_dc6dac6039-d7f65a9e7b-61028745.

13. JANSEN B. 2013. Kayak Now Gives Advice to Buy or Wait on PlaneTickets. *USA Today.* Available at http://www.usatoday.com/story/travel/flights/2013/01/15/kayak-advice/1834225/.

14. KALAKOTA R. 2011. Analytics-as-a-Service: Understanding How Amazon.com is Changing the Rules. Available at http://practicalanalytics.wordpress.com/2011/08/13/analytics-as-a-service-understanding-how-amazon-com-is-changing-the-rules/.

15. DUBRAY JJ. 2007. Establishing a Service Governance Organization. InfoQ. Available at http://www.infoq.com/articles/soa-governance-organization.

16. PARDUCCI B, LOCKHART H, AND LEVINSON R. 2002. OASIS eXtensible Access Control Markup Language (XACML). OASIS. Available at https://www.oasis-open.org/committees/tc_home.php?wg_abbrev=xacml.

17. RAHUL S. July 2014. Big Data as A Service, Service Technology Magazine. Available at http://www.servicetechmag.com/I84/0514-1.

18. SARKAR P. 2003. Applying the Balanced Scorecard in the IT Organization. DM Journal. Available at http://www.information-management.com/issues/20031201/7762-1.html.

19. SODERLING P. 2010. Data as a Service: Pricing Models for the Future of Data. Available at http://blog.programmableweb.com/2010/08/26/data-as-a-service-pricing-models-for-the-future-of-data/.

20. SUN D, ZHANG G, ZHENG W, AND LI K. Key Technologies for Big Data Stream Computing, Tsinghua University. Available at http://www.cs.newpaltz.edu/~lik/publications/Dawei-Sun-Tsinghua-University.pdf.

21. TAYLOR P. 2012. Continuous Monitoring As a Big Data Alternative. Available at http://www.dbta.com/Articles/Editorial/Trends-and-Applications/A-Lighter-Load—

22. WEISER M. *"The Computer for the 21st Century."* *Scientific American Special Issue on Communications, Computers, and Networks,* September 1991.

23. WINTERMAN D. 2013. Tesco: How One supermarket Came to Dominate. *BBC News.* Available at http://www.bbc.com/news/magazine-23988795.

Index

Data as a Service: A Framework for Providing Reusable Enterprise Data Services,
First Edition. Pushpak Sarkar.
© 2015 the IEEE Computer Society. Published 2015 by John Wiley & Sons, Inc.

Printed and bound by CPI Group (UK) Ltd, Croydon, CR0 4YY

27/10/2024

14580471-0005